THE AWAKENING

THE AWAKENING

Written by
NEAL SHAFFER

Illustrated by
LUCA GENOVESE

Lettering by
MANFREDI TORALDO

Designed by
KEITH WOOD

Editorial Assistance by
RANDAL C. JARRELL

Edited by
JAMES LUCAS JONES
&
MICHELE FOSCHINI

Published by ONI PRESS, INC.

JOE NOZEMACK, publisher

JAMES LUCAS JONES, editor in chief

RANDAL C. JARRELL, managing editor

"Little Miss No Name" typeface designed by
Sara Pavan and developed by ManFont

ONI PRESS, INC.
6336 SE Milwaukie Avenue, PMB 30
Portland, OR 97202
USA

www.onipress.com

First edition: September 2004
ISBN 1-932664-00-9

1 3 5 7 9 10 8 6 4 2

PRINTED IN CANADA.

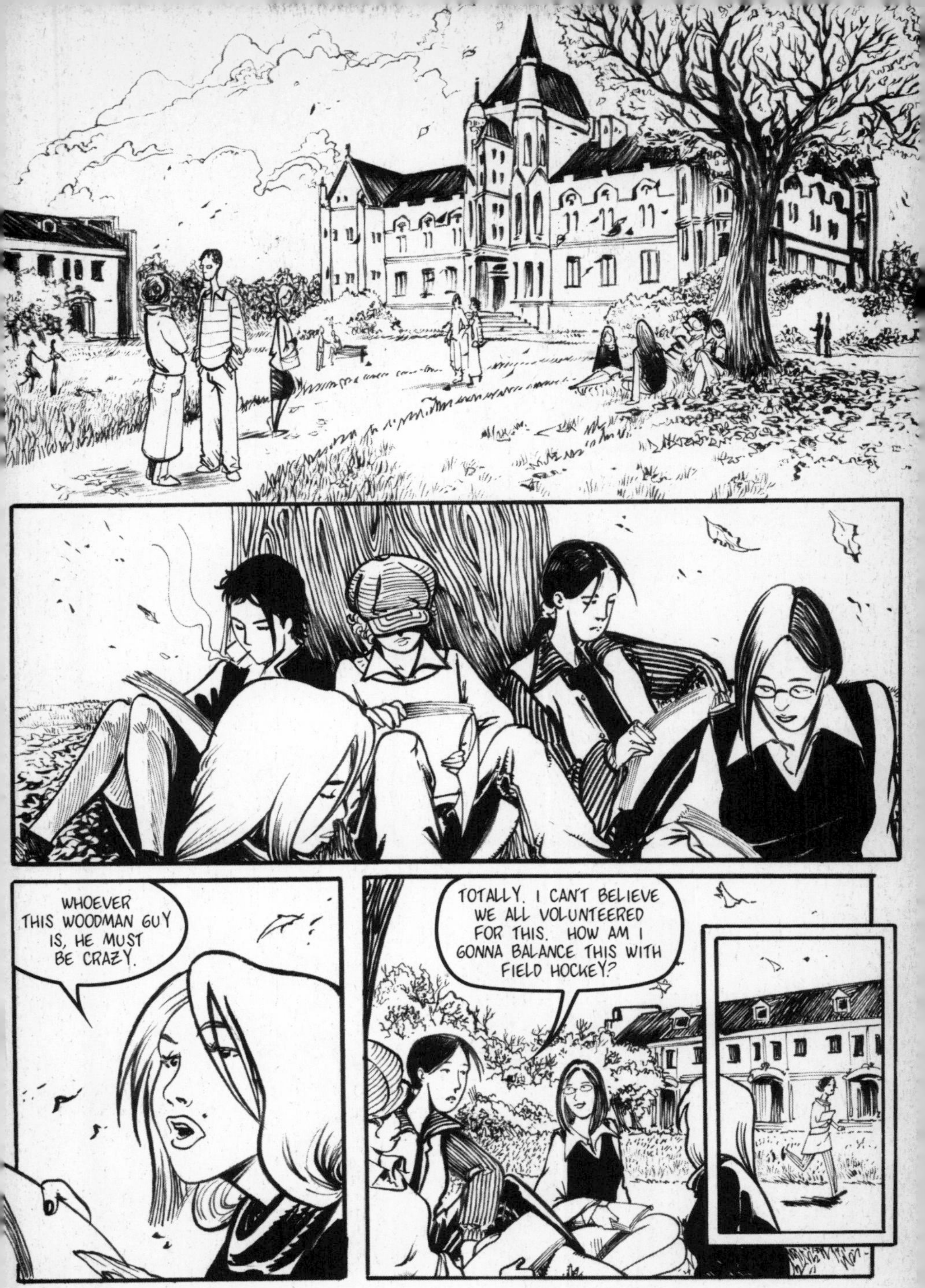
WHOEVER THIS WOODMAN GUY IS, HE MUST BE CRAZY.
TOTALLY. I CAN'T BELIEVE WE ALL VOLUNTEERED FOR THIS. HOW AM I GONNA BALANCE THIS WITH FIELD HOCKEY?

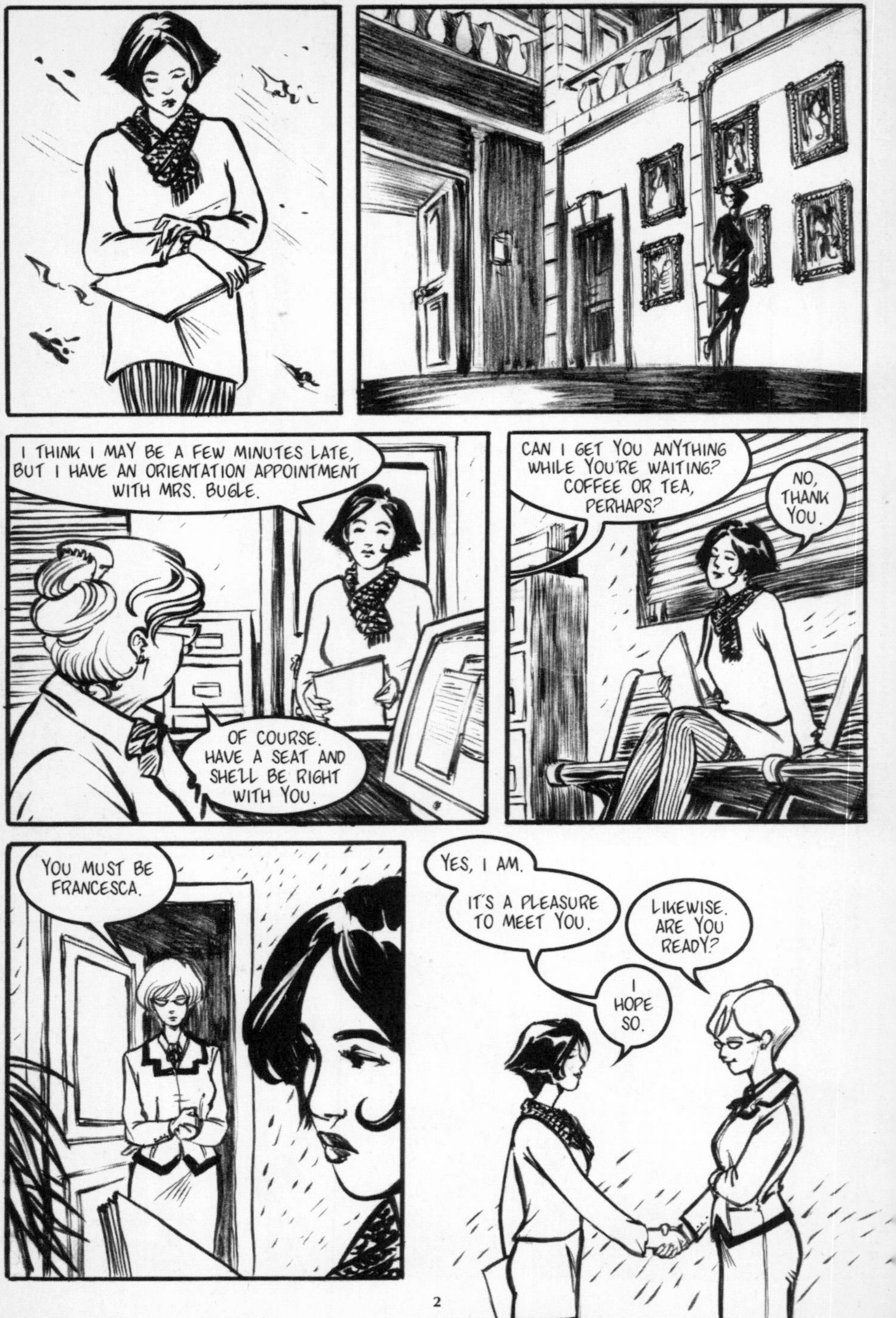

I THINK I MAY BE A FEW MINUTES LATE, BUT I HAVE AN ORIENTATION APPOINTMENT WITH MRS. BUGLE.
OF COURSE. HAVE A SEAT AND SHE'LL BE RIGHT WITH YOU.
CAN I GET YOU ANYTHING WHILE YOU'RE WAITING? COFFEE OR TEA, PERHAPS?
NO, THANK YOU.
YOU MUST BE FRANCESCA.
YES, I AM.
IT'S A PLEASURE TO MEET YOU.
LIKEWISE. ARE YOU READY?
I HOPE SO.

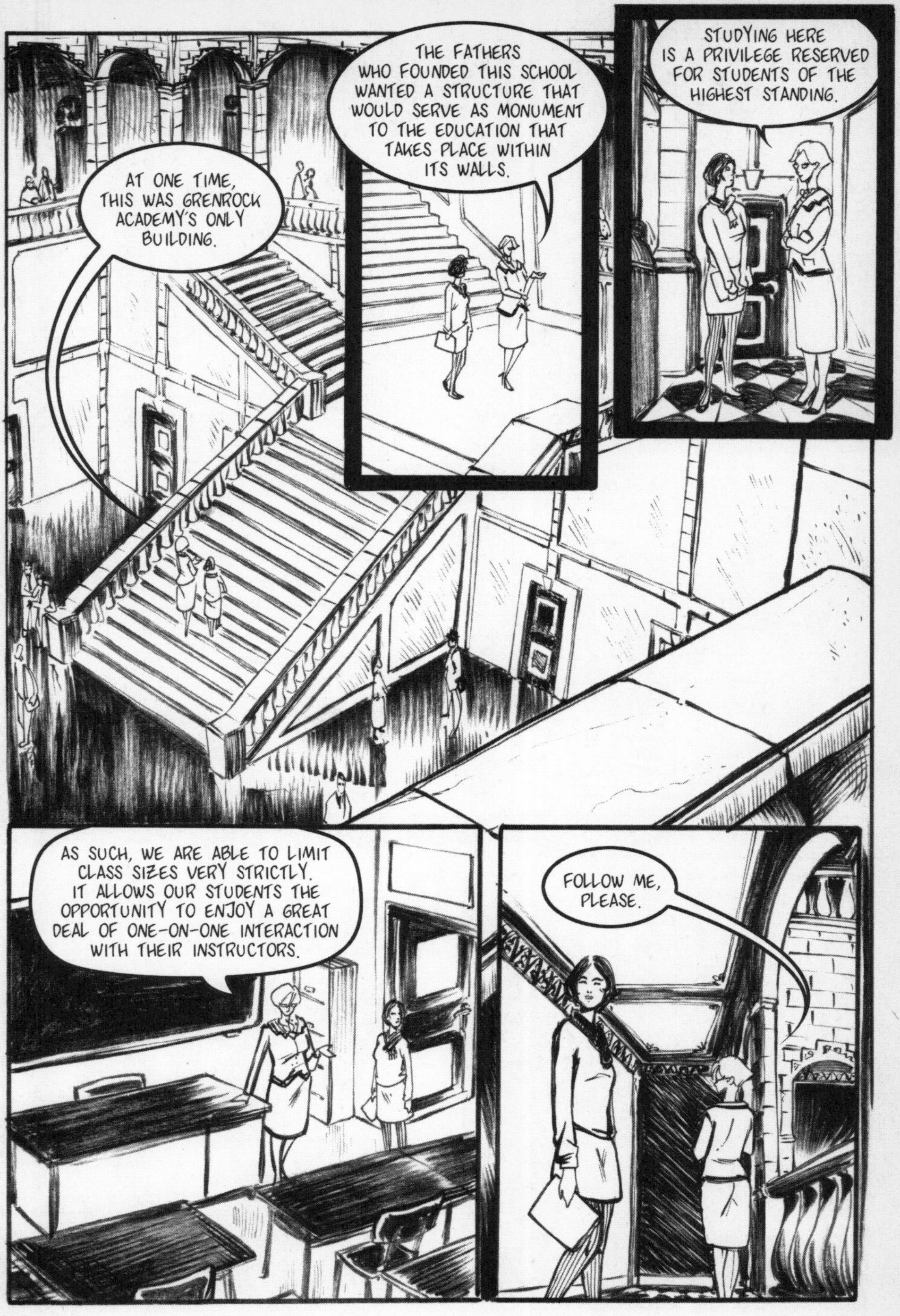
AT ONE TIME, THIS WAS GRENROCK ACADEMY'S ONLY BUILDING.
THE FATHERS WHO FOUNDED THIS SCHOOL WANTED A STRUCTURE THAT WOULD SERVE AS MONUMENT TO THE EDUCATION THAT TAKES PLACE WITHIN ITS WALLS.
STUDYING HERE IS A PRIVILEGE RESERVED FOR STUDENTS OF THE HIGHEST STANDING.
AS SUCH, WE ARE ABLE TO LIMIT CLASS SIZES VERY STRICTLY. IT ALLOWS OUR STUDENTS THE OPPORTUNITY TO ENJOY A GREAT DEAL OF ONE-ON-ONE INTERACTION WITH THEIR INSTRUCTORS.
FOLLOW ME, PLEASE.

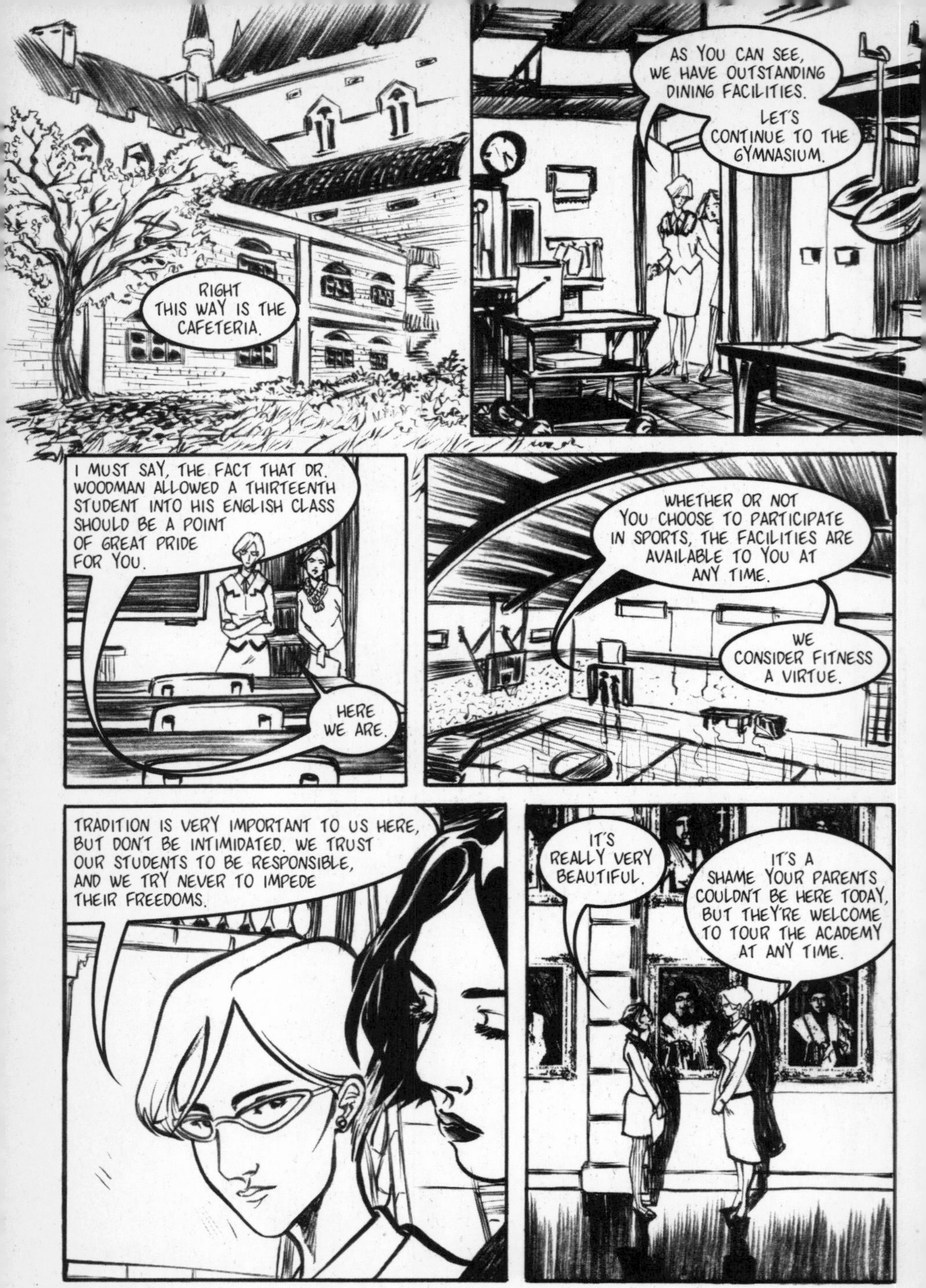
RIGHT THIS WAY IS THE CAFETERIA.
AS YOU CAN SEE, WE HAVE OUTSTANDING DINING FACILITIES.
LET'S CONTINUE TO THE GYMNASIUM.
I MUST SAY, THE FACT THAT DR. WOODMAN ALLOWED A THIRTEENTH STUDENT INTO HIS ENGLISH CLASS SHOULD BE A POINT OF GREAT PRIDE FOR YOU.
HERE WE ARE.
WHETHER OR NOT YOU CHOOSE TO PARTICIPATE IN SPORTS, THE FACILITIES ARE AVAILABLE TO YOU AT ANY TIME.
WE CONSIDER FITNESS A VIRTUE.
TRADITION IS VERY IMPORTANT TO US HERE, BUT DON'T BE INTIMIDATED. WE TRUST OUR STUDENTS TO BE RESPONSIBLE, AND WE TRY NEVER TO IMPEDE THEIR FREEDOMS.
IT'S REALLY VERY BEAUTIFUL.
IT'S A SHAME YOUR PARENTS COULDN'T BE HERE TODAY, BUT THEY'RE WELCOME TO TOUR THE ACADEMY AT ANY TIME.

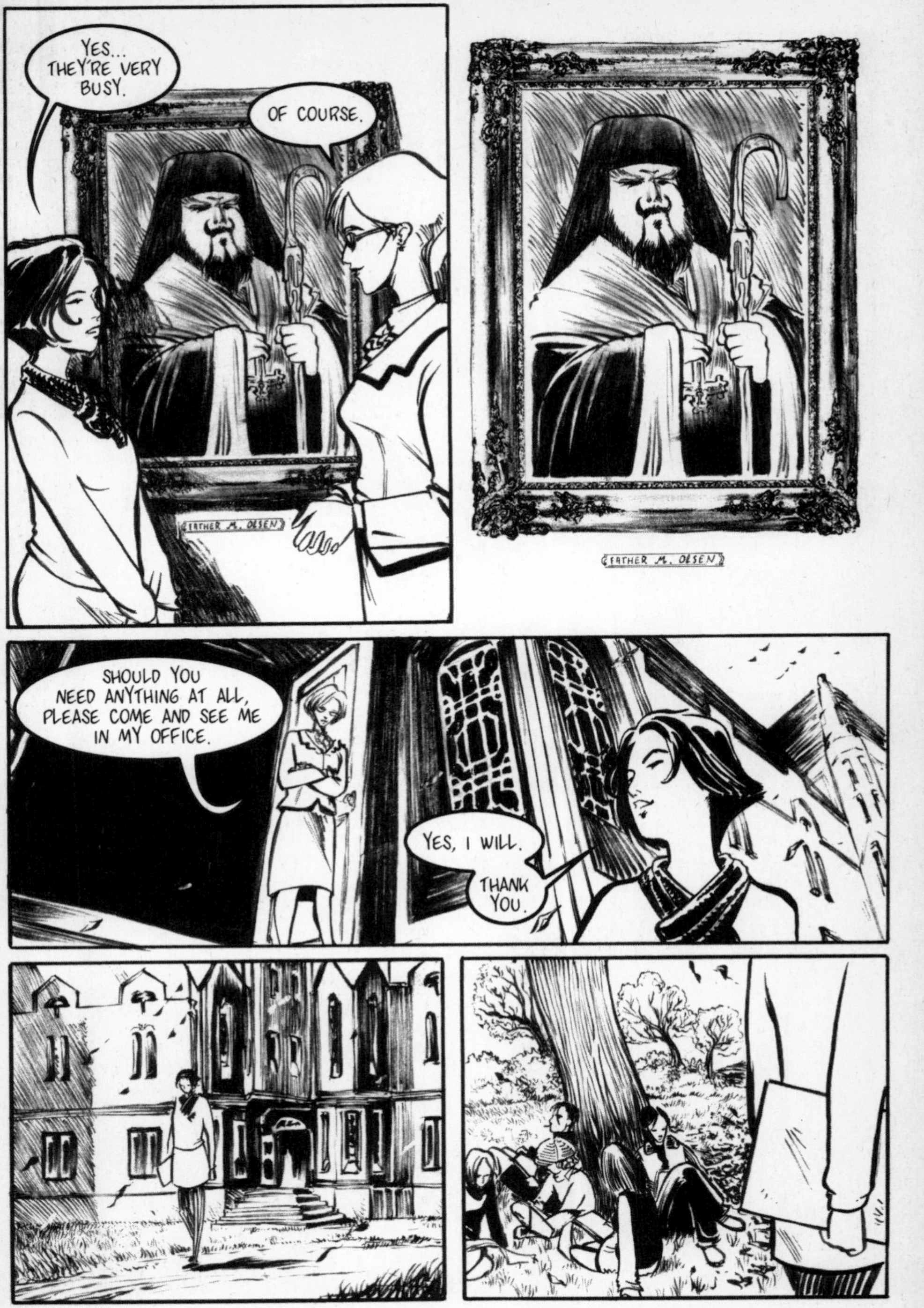
YES... THEY'RE VERY BUSY.
OF COURSE.
FATHER M. OLSEN
FATHER M. OLSEN
SHOULD YOU NEED ANYTHING AT ALL, PLEASE COME AND SEE ME IN MY OFFICE.
YES, I WILL.
THANK YOU.

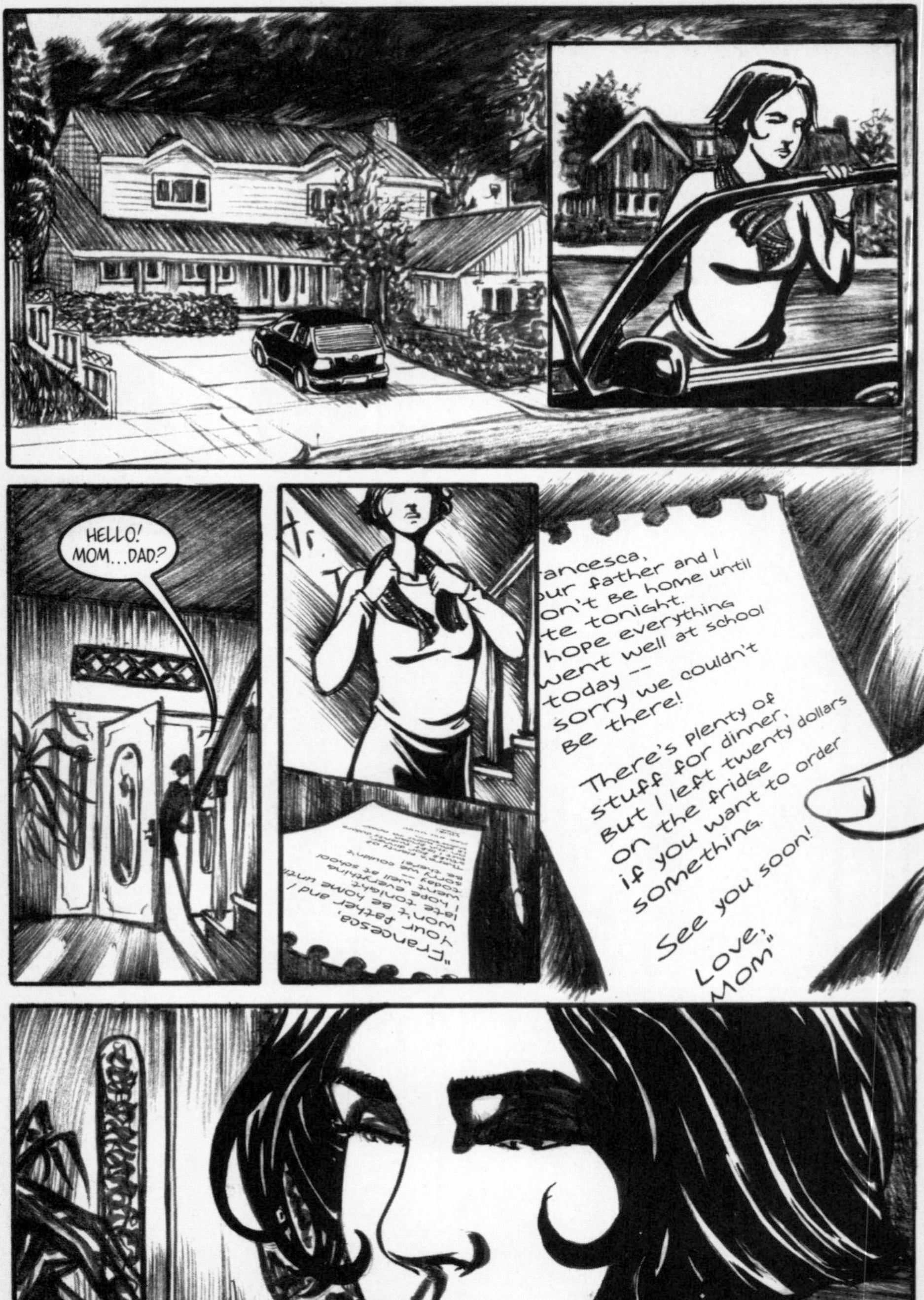
HELLO! MOM...DAD?
rancesca,
our father and I
on't be home until
te tonight.
hope everything
went well at school
today --
sorry we couldn't
Be there!
There's plenty of
stuff for dinner,
But I left twenty dollars
on the fridge
if you want to order
something.
See you soon!
Love,
MOM"

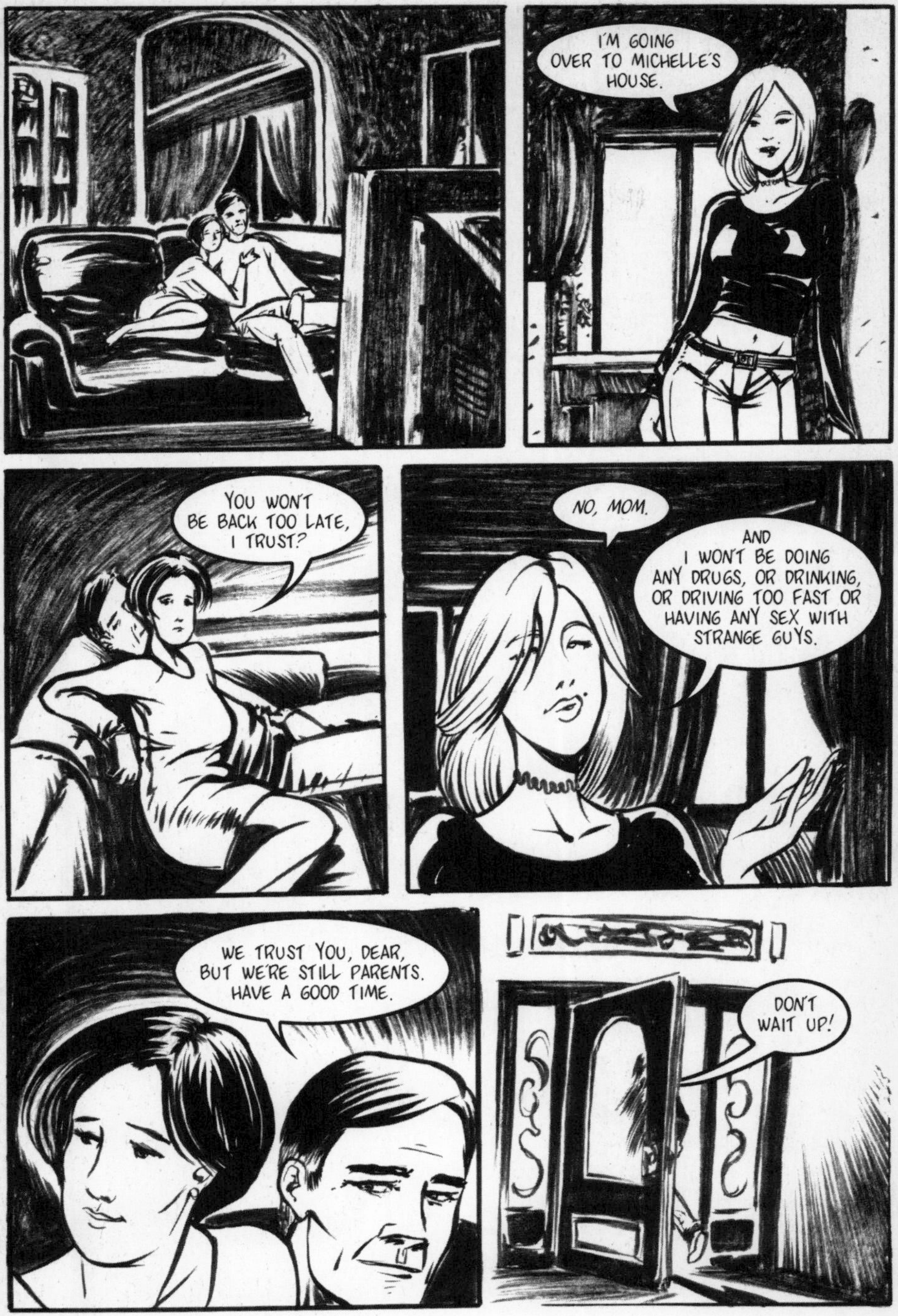
I'M GOING OVER TO MICHELLE'S HOUSE.
YOU WON'T BE BACK TOO LATE, I TRUST?
NO, MOM.
AND I WON'T BE DOING ANY DRUGS, OR DRINKING, OR DRIVING TOO FAST OR HAVING ANY SEX WITH STRANGE GUYS.
WE TRUST YOU, DEAR, BUT WE'RE STILL PARENTS. HAVE A GOOD TIME.
DON'T WAIT UP!

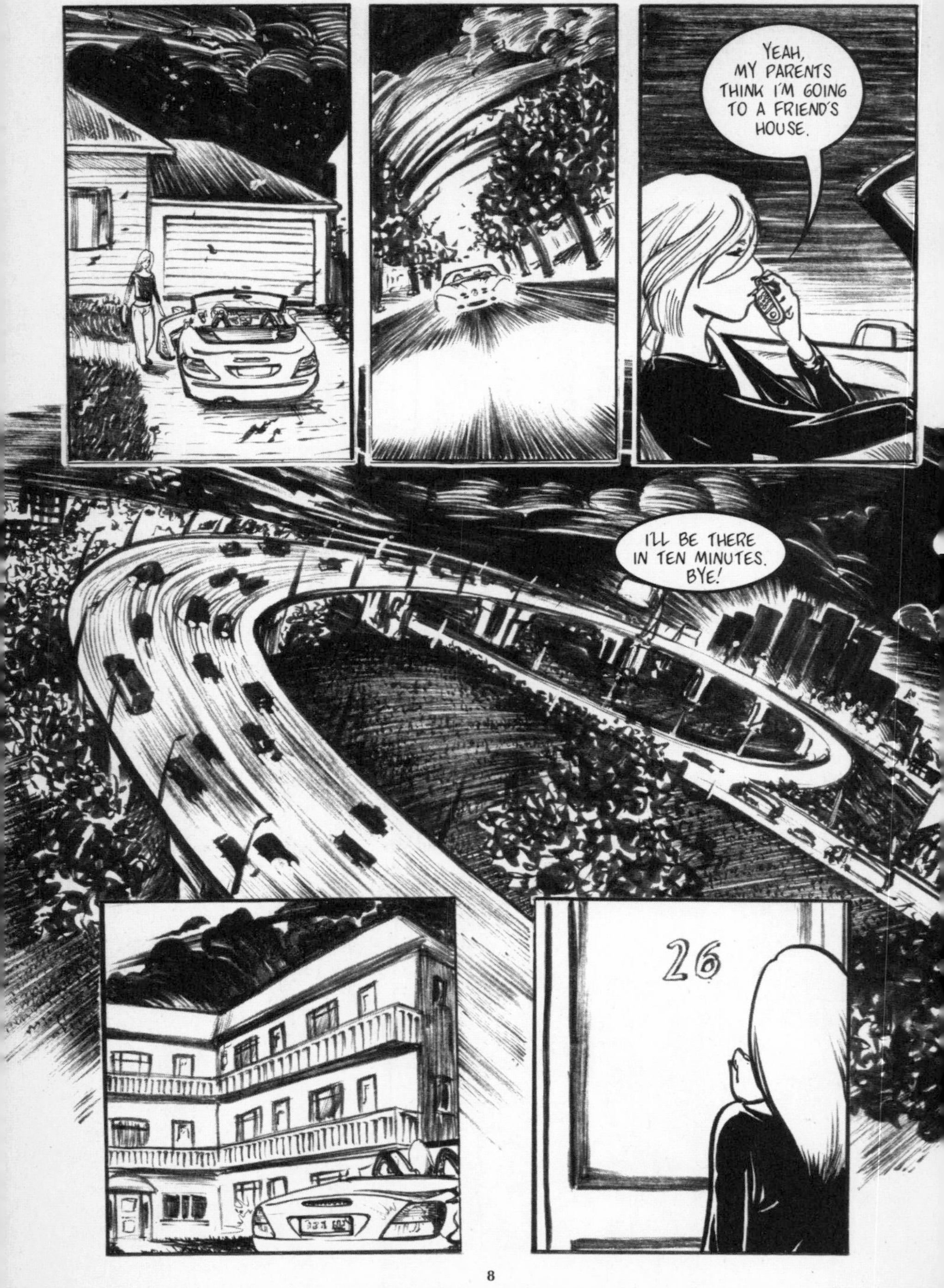
YEAH, MY PARENTS THINK I'M GOING TO A FRIEND'S HOUSE.
I'LL BE THERE IN TEN MINUTES. BYE!
26

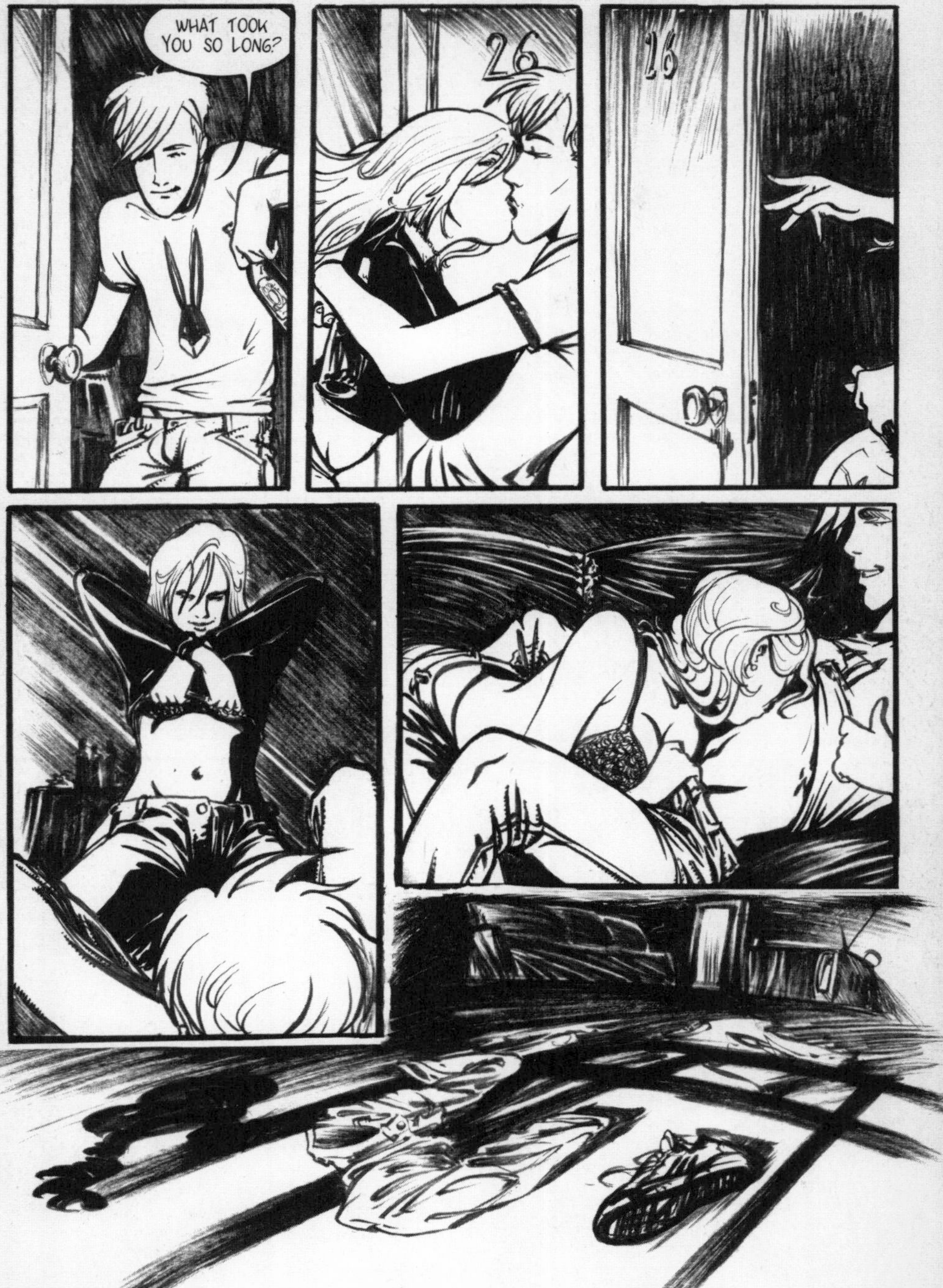
WHAT TOOK YOU SO LONG?
26
26

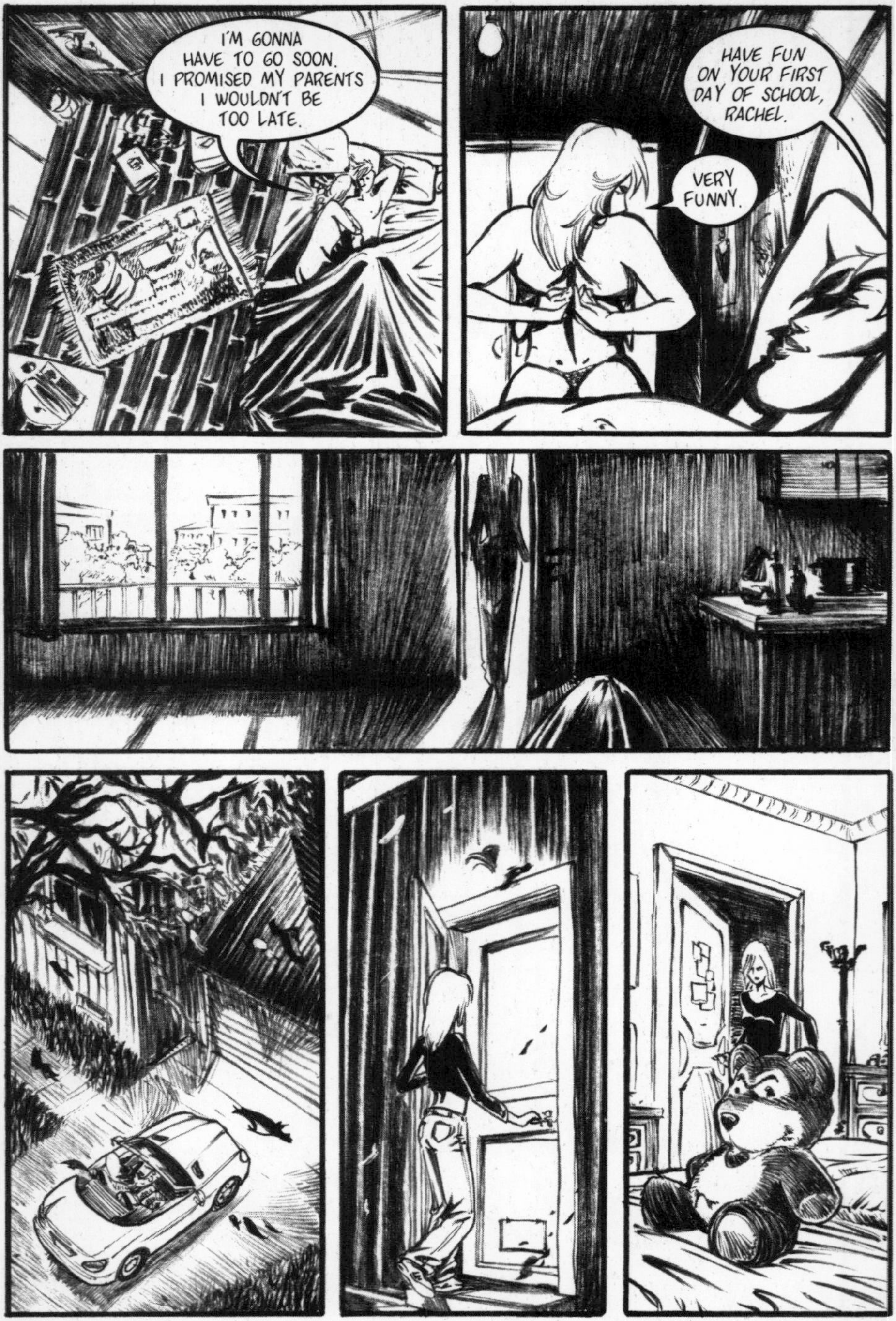
I'M GONNA HAVE TO GO SOON. I PROMISED MY PARENTS I WOULDN'T BE TOO LATE.
HAVE FUN ON YOUR FIRST DAY OF SCHOOL, RACHEL.
VERY FUNNY.

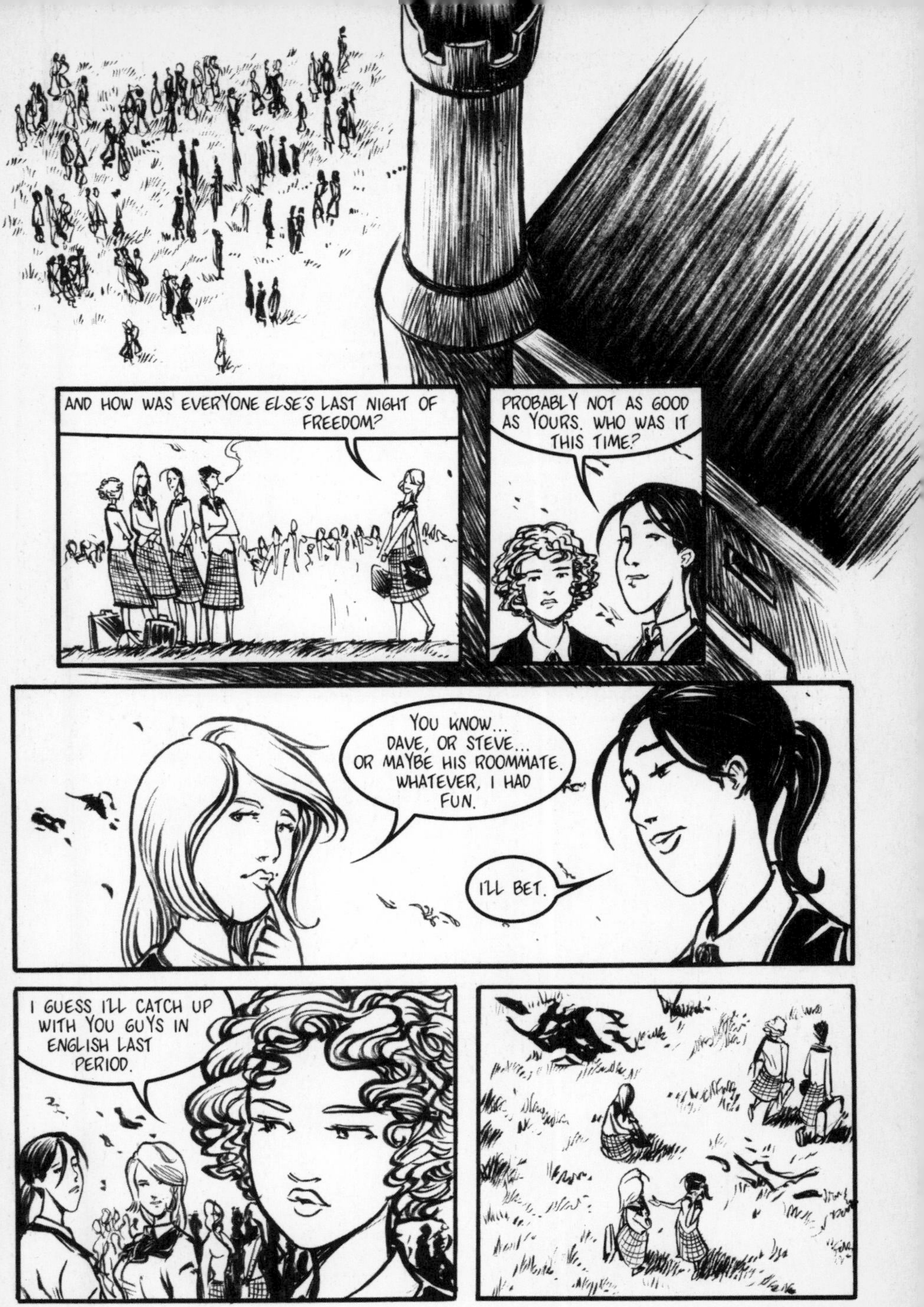
AND HOW WAS EVERYONE ELSE'S LAST NIGHT OF FREEDOM?
PROBABLY NOT AS GOOD AS YOURS. WHO WAS IT THIS TIME?
YOU KNOW... DAVE, OR STEVE... OR MAYBE HIS ROOMMATE. WHATEVER, I HAD FUN.
I'LL BET.
I GUESS I'LL CATCH UP WITH YOU GUYS IN ENGLISH LAST PERIOD.

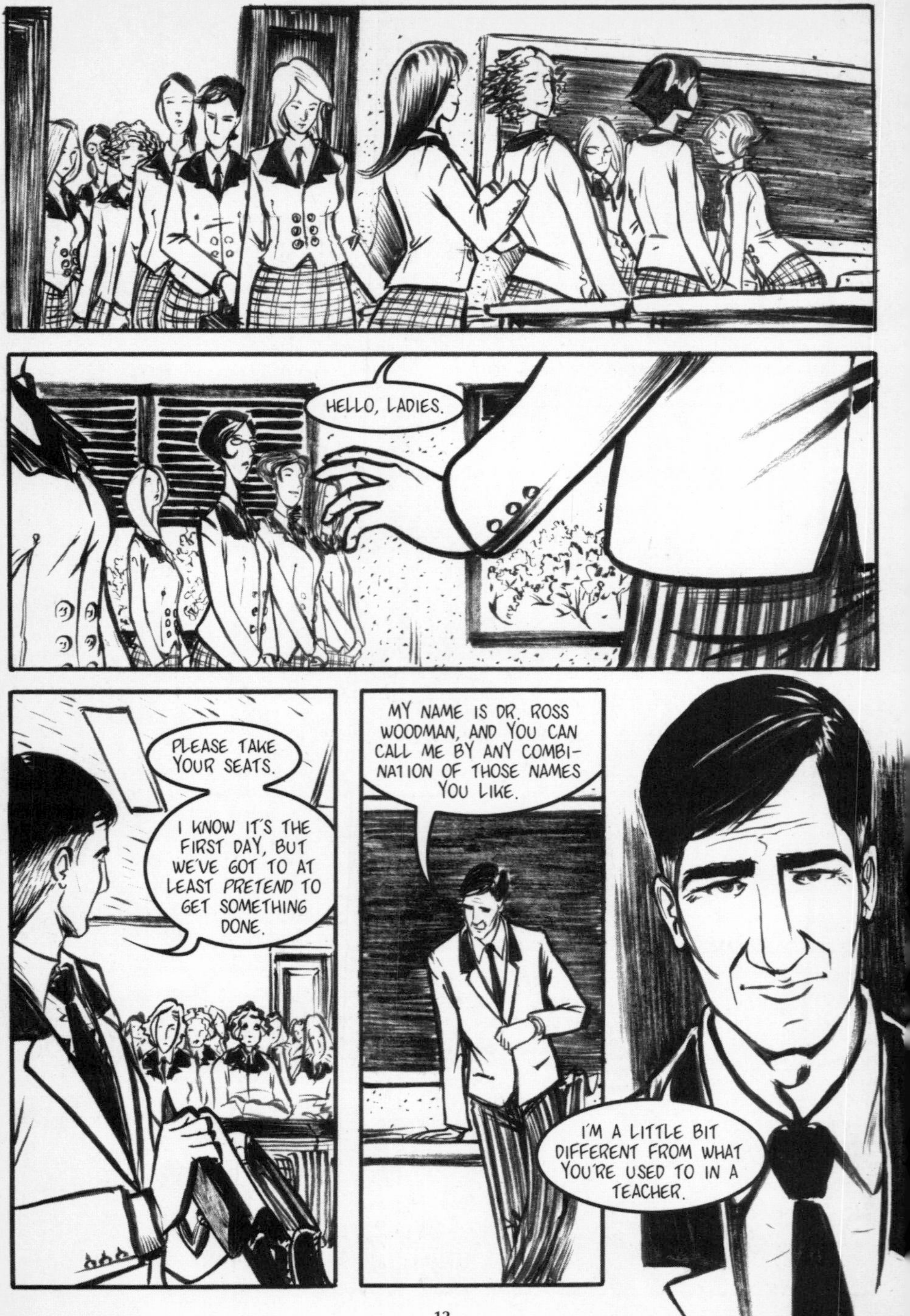
HELLO, LADIES.
PLEASE TAKE YOUR SEATS.
I KNOW IT'S THE FIRST DAY, BUT WE'VE GOT TO AT LEAST PRETEND TO GET SOMETHING DONE.
MY NAME IS DR. ROSS WOODMAN, AND YOU CAN CALL ME BY ANY COMBINATION OF THOSE NAMES YOU LIKE.
I'M A LITTLE BIT DIFFERENT FROM WHAT YOU'RE USED TO IN A TEACHER.

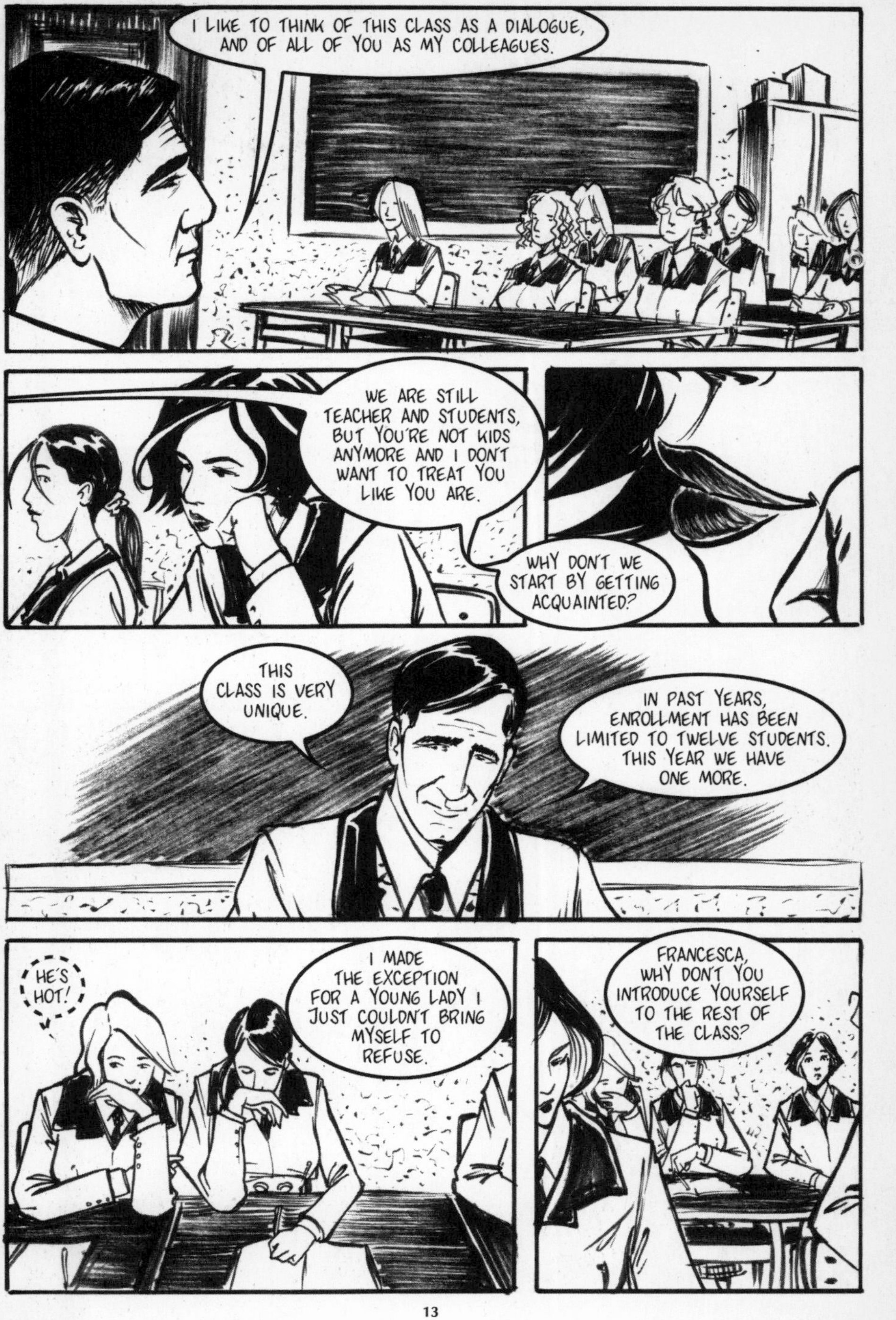
I LIKE TO THINK OF THIS CLASS AS A DIALOGUE, AND OF ALL OF YOU AS MY COLLEAGUES.
WE ARE STILL TEACHER AND STUDENTS, BUT YOU'RE NOT KIDS ANYMORE AND I DON'T WANT TO TREAT YOU LIKE YOU ARE.
WHY DON'T WE START BY GETTING ACQUAINTED?
THIS CLASS IS VERY UNIQUE.
IN PAST YEARS, ENROLLMENT HAS BEEN LIMITED TO TWELVE STUDENTS. THIS YEAR WE HAVE ONE MORE.
HE'S HOT!
I MADE THE EXCEPTION FOR A YOUNG LADY I JUST COULDN'T BRING MYSELF TO REFUSE.
FRANCESCA, WHY DON'T YOU INTRODUCE YOURSELF TO THE REST OF THE CLASS?

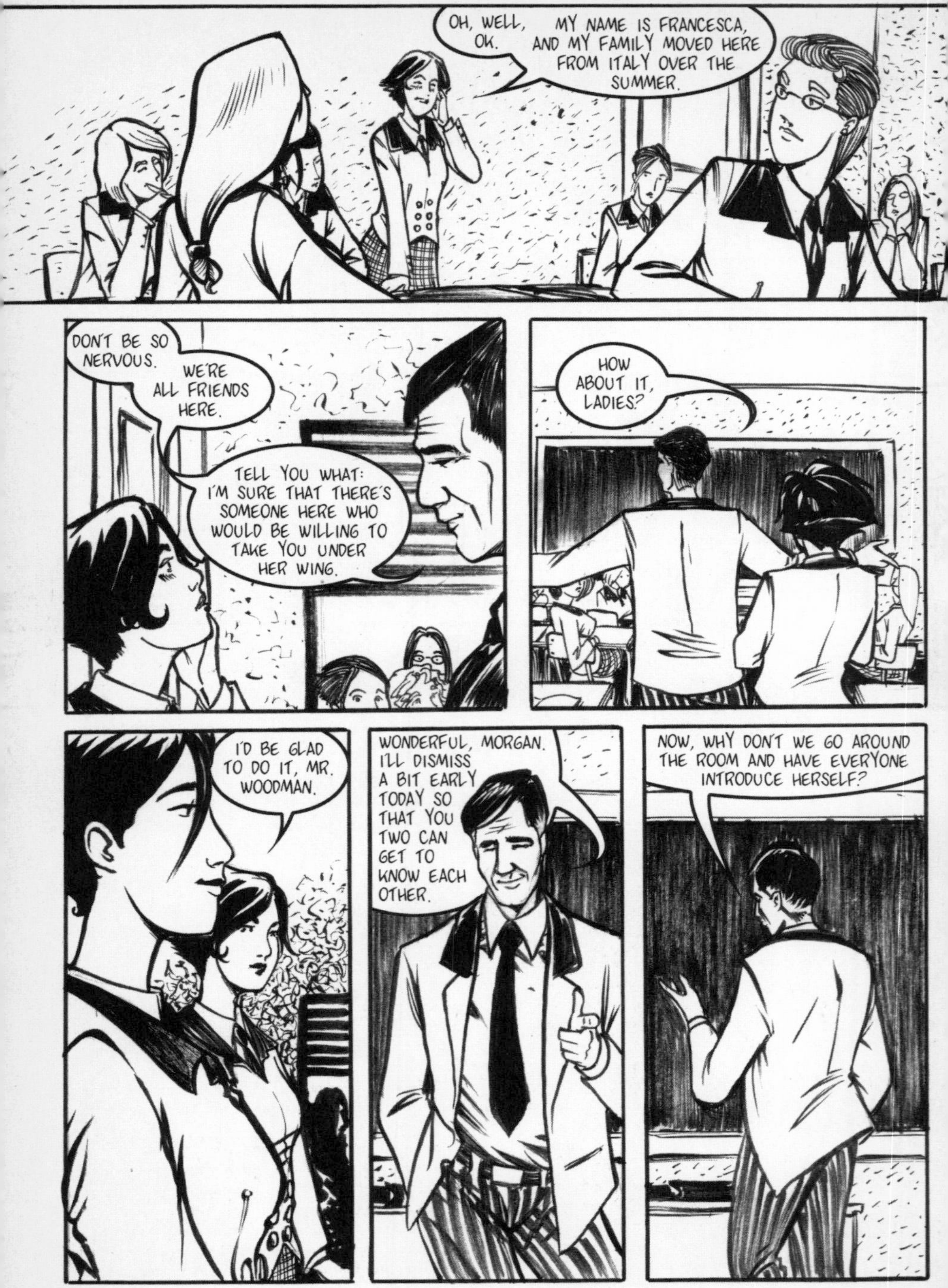
OH, WELL, OK.
MY NAME IS FRANCESCA, AND MY FAMILY MOVED HERE FROM ITALY OVER THE SUMMER.
DON'T BE SO NERVOUS.
WE'RE ALL FRIENDS HERE.
TELL YOU WHAT: I'M SURE THAT THERE'S SOMEONE HERE WHO WOULD BE WILLING TO TAKE YOU UNDER HER WING.
HOW ABOUT IT, LADIES?
I'D BE GLAD TO DO IT, MR. WOODMAN.
WONDERFUL, MORGAN. I'LL DISMISS A BIT EARLY TODAY SO THAT YOU TWO CAN GET TO KNOW EACH OTHER.
NOW, WHY DON'T WE GO AROUND THE ROOM AND HAVE EVERYONE INTRODUCE HERSELF?

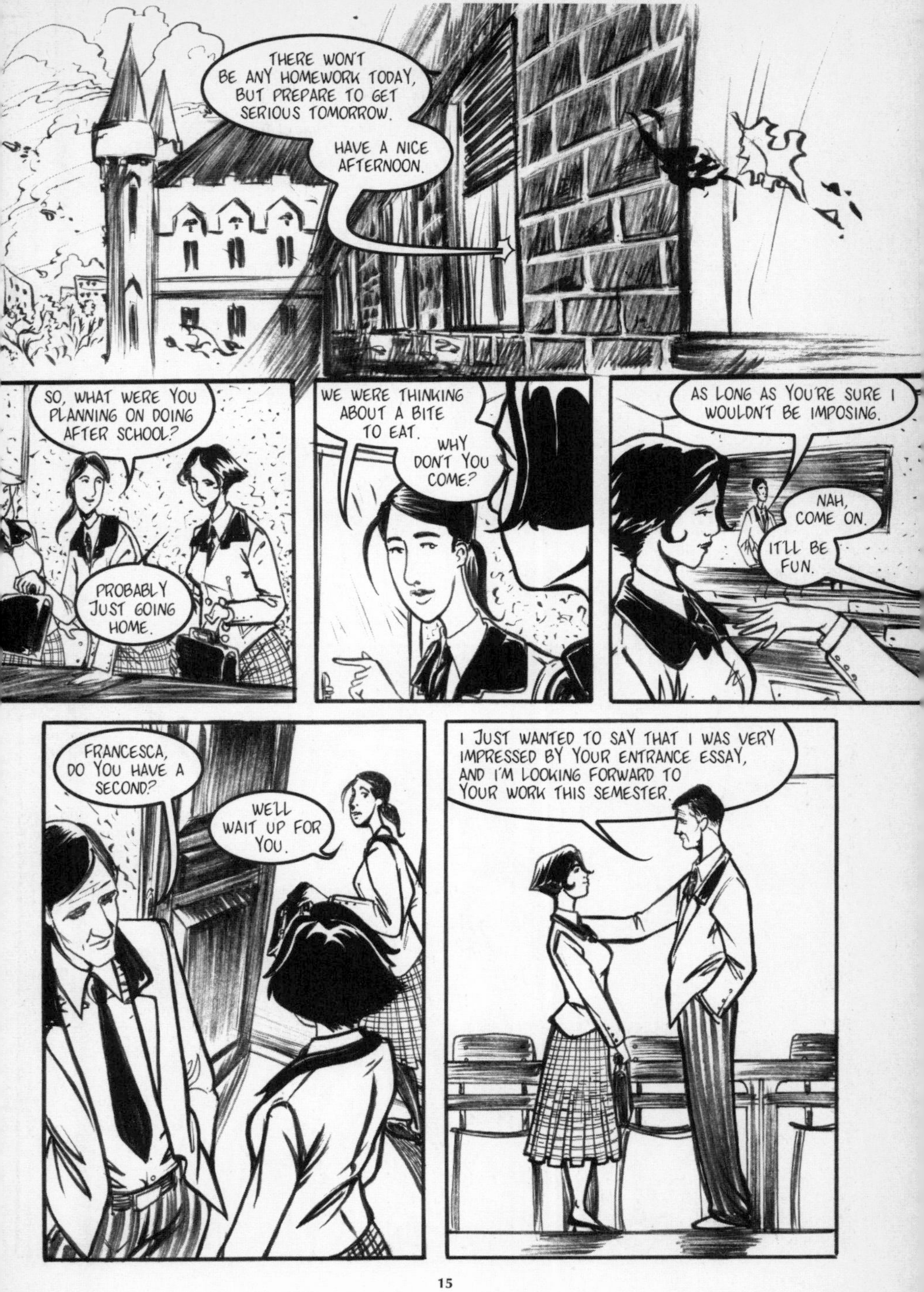
THERE WON'T BE ANY HOMEWORK TODAY, BUT PREPARE TO GET SERIOUS TOMORROW.
HAVE A NICE AFTERNOON.
SO, WHAT WERE YOU PLANNING ON DOING AFTER SCHOOL?
PROBABLY JUST GOING HOME.
WE WERE THINKING ABOUT A BITE TO EAT.
WHY DON'T YOU COME?
AS LONG AS YOU'RE SURE I WOULDN'T BE IMPOSING.
NAH, COME ON.
IT'LL BE FUN.
FRANCESCA, DO YOU HAVE A SECOND?
WE'LL WAIT UP FOR YOU.
I JUST WANTED TO SAY THAT I WAS VERY IMPRESSED BY YOUR ENTRANCE ESSAY, AND I'M LOOKING FORWARD TO YOUR WORK THIS SEMESTER.

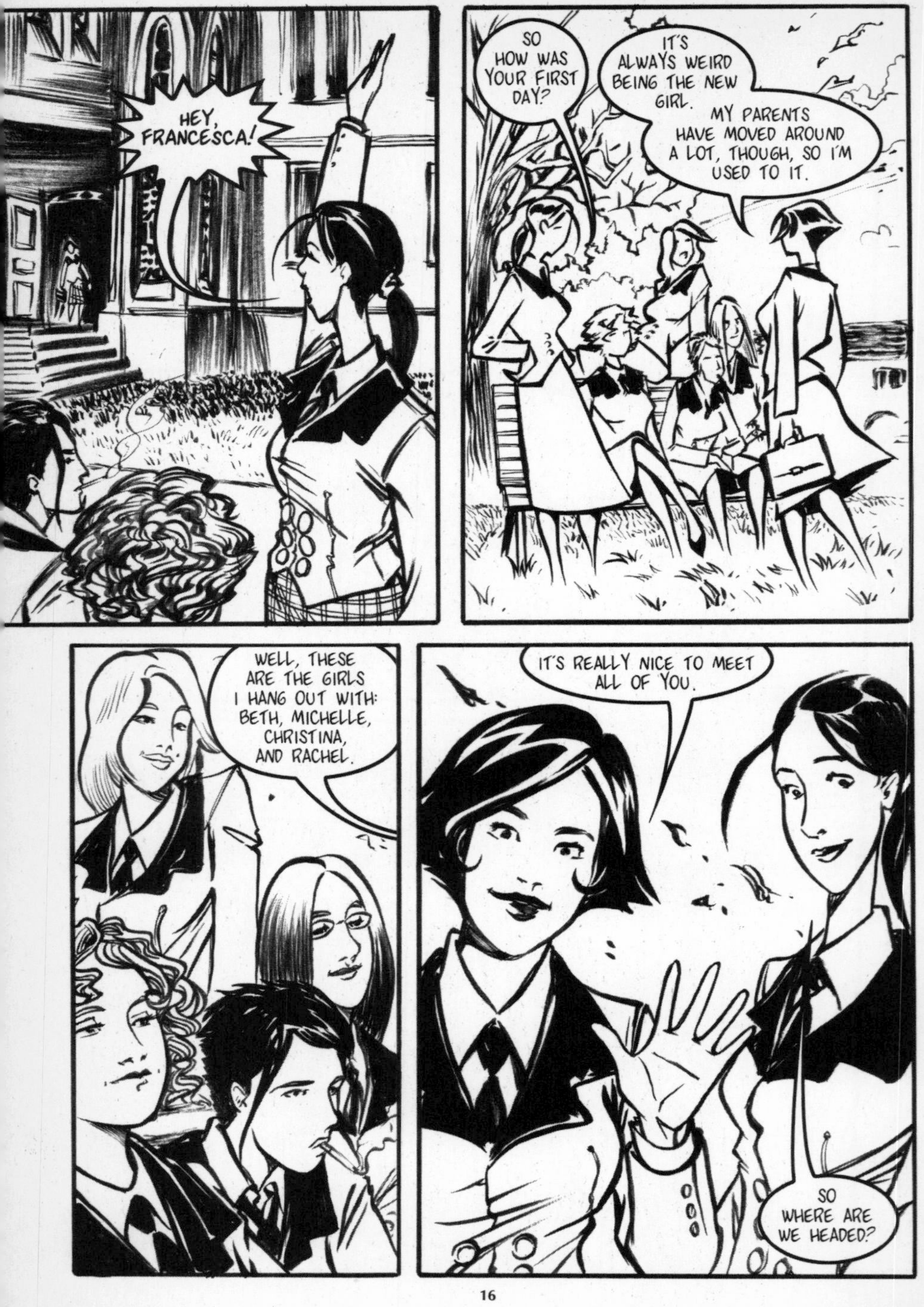
HEY, FRANCESCA!
SO HOW WAS YOUR FIRST DAY?
IT'S ALWAYS WEIRD BEING THE NEW GIRL.
MY PARENTS HAVE MOVED AROUND A LOT, THOUGH, SO I'M USED TO IT.
WELL, THESE ARE THE GIRLS I HANG OUT WITH: BETH, MICHELLE, CHRISTINA, AND RACHEL.
IT'S REALLY NICE TO MEET ALL OF YOU.
SO WHERE ARE WE HEADED?

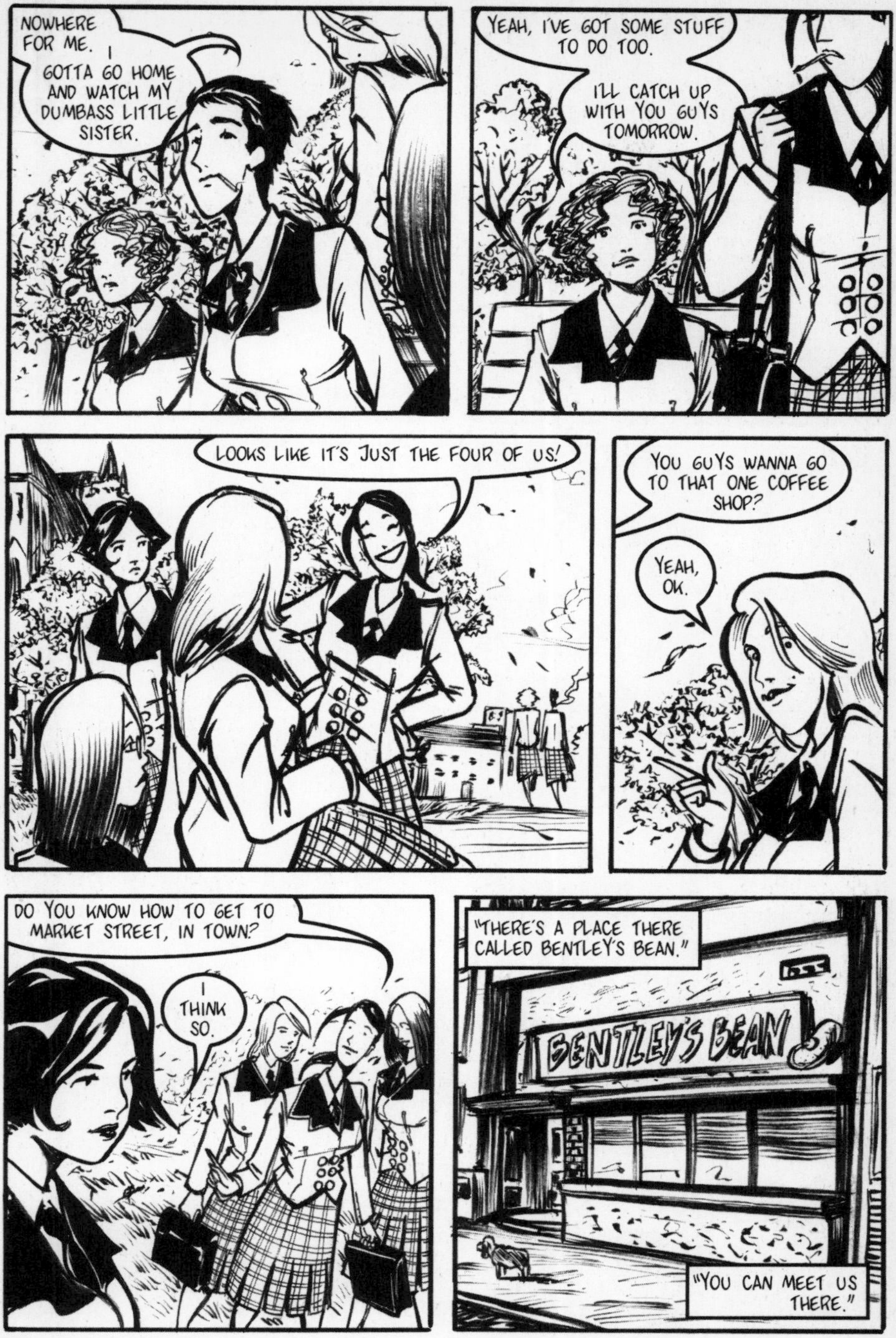
NOWHERE FOR ME.
I GOTTA GO HOME AND WATCH MY DUMBASS LITTLE SISTER.
YEAH, I'VE GOT SOME STUFF TO DO TOO.
I'LL CATCH UP WITH YOU GUYS TOMORROW.
LOOKS LIKE IT'S JUST THE FOUR OF US!
YOU GUYS WANNA GO TO THAT ONE COFFEE SHOP?
YEAH, OK.
DO YOU KNOW HOW TO GET TO MARKET STREET, IN TOWN?
I THINK SO.
"THERE'S A PLACE THERE CALLED BENTLEY'S BEAN."
BENTLEY'S BEAN
"YOU CAN MEET US THERE."

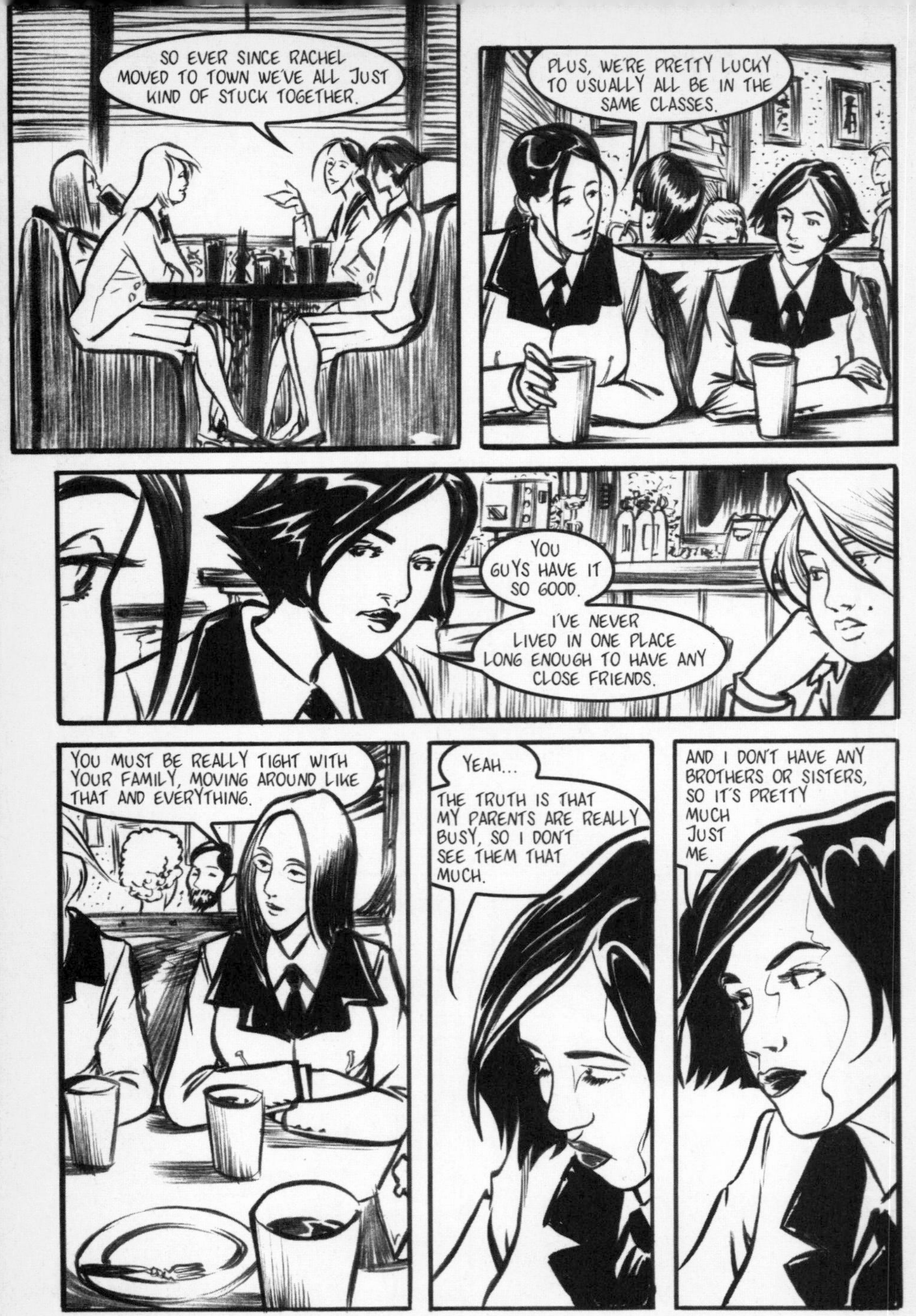

SO EVER SINCE RACHEL MOVED TO TOWN WE'VE ALL JUST KIND OF STUCK TOGETHER.
PLUS, WE'RE PRETTY LUCKY TO USUALLY ALL BE IN THE SAME CLASSES.
YOU GUYS HAVE IT SO GOOD.
I'VE NEVER LIVED IN ONE PLACE LONG ENOUGH TO HAVE ANY CLOSE FRIENDS.
YOU MUST BE REALLY TIGHT WITH YOUR FAMILY, MOVING AROUND LIKE THAT AND EVERYTHING.
YEAH...
THE TRUTH IS THAT MY PARENTS ARE REALLY BUSY, SO I DON'T SEE THEM THAT MUCH.
AND I DON'T HAVE ANY BROTHERS OR SISTERS, SO IT'S PRETTY MUCH JUST ME.

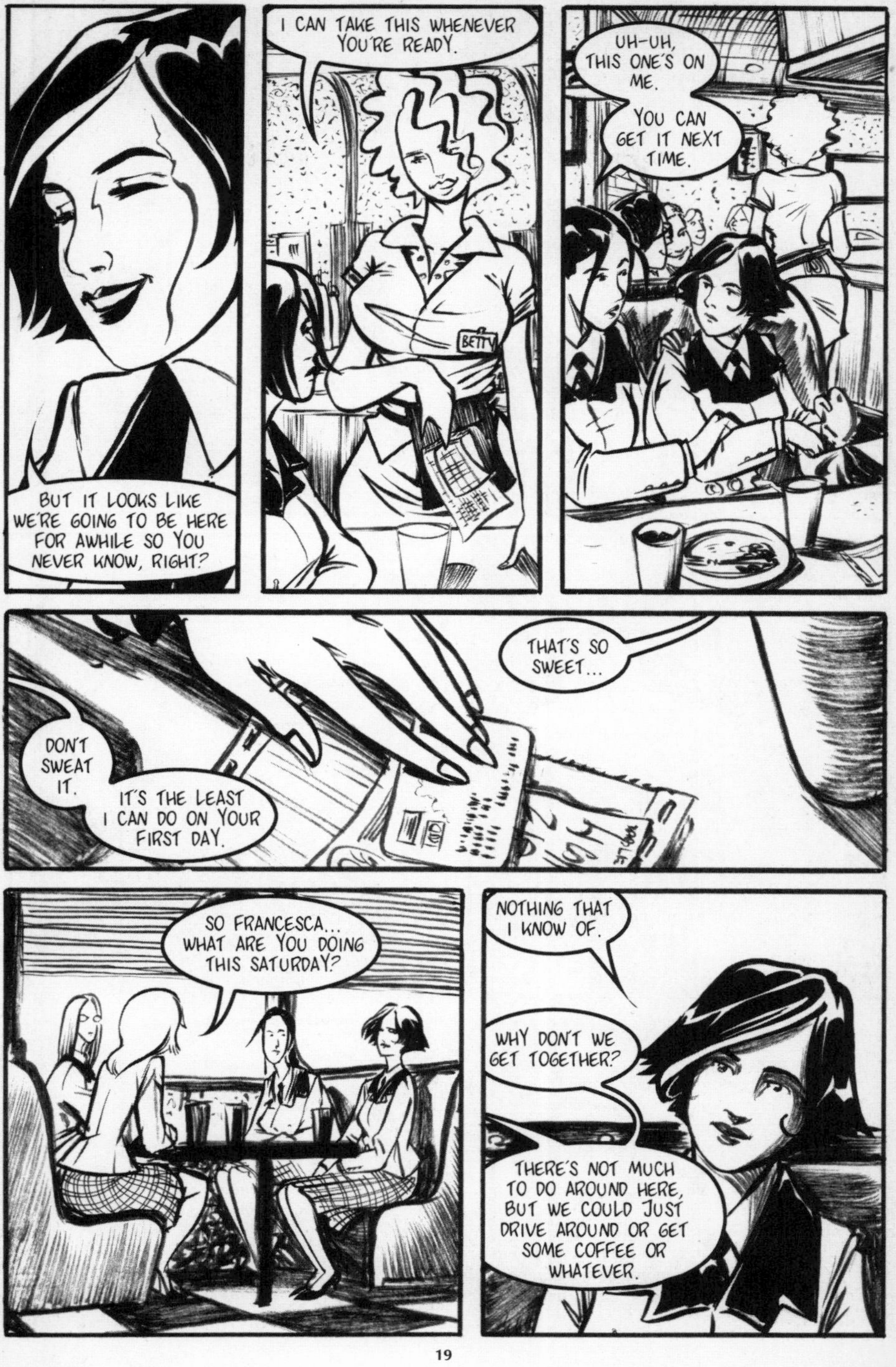

BUT IT LOOKS LIKE WE'RE GOING TO BE HERE FOR AWHILE SO YOU NEVER KNOW, RIGHT?
I CAN TAKE THIS WHENEVER YOU'RE READY.
BETTY
UH-UH, THIS ONE'S ON ME.
YOU CAN GET IT NEXT TIME.
THAT'S SO SWEET...
DON'T SWEAT IT.
IT'S THE LEAST I CAN DO ON YOUR FIRST DAY.
SO FRANCESCA... WHAT ARE YOU DOING THIS SATURDAY?
NOTHING THAT I KNOW OF.
WHY DON'T WE GET TOGETHER?
THERE'S NOT MUCH TO DO AROUND HERE, BUT WE COULD JUST DRIVE AROUND OR GET SOME COFFEE OR WHATEVER.

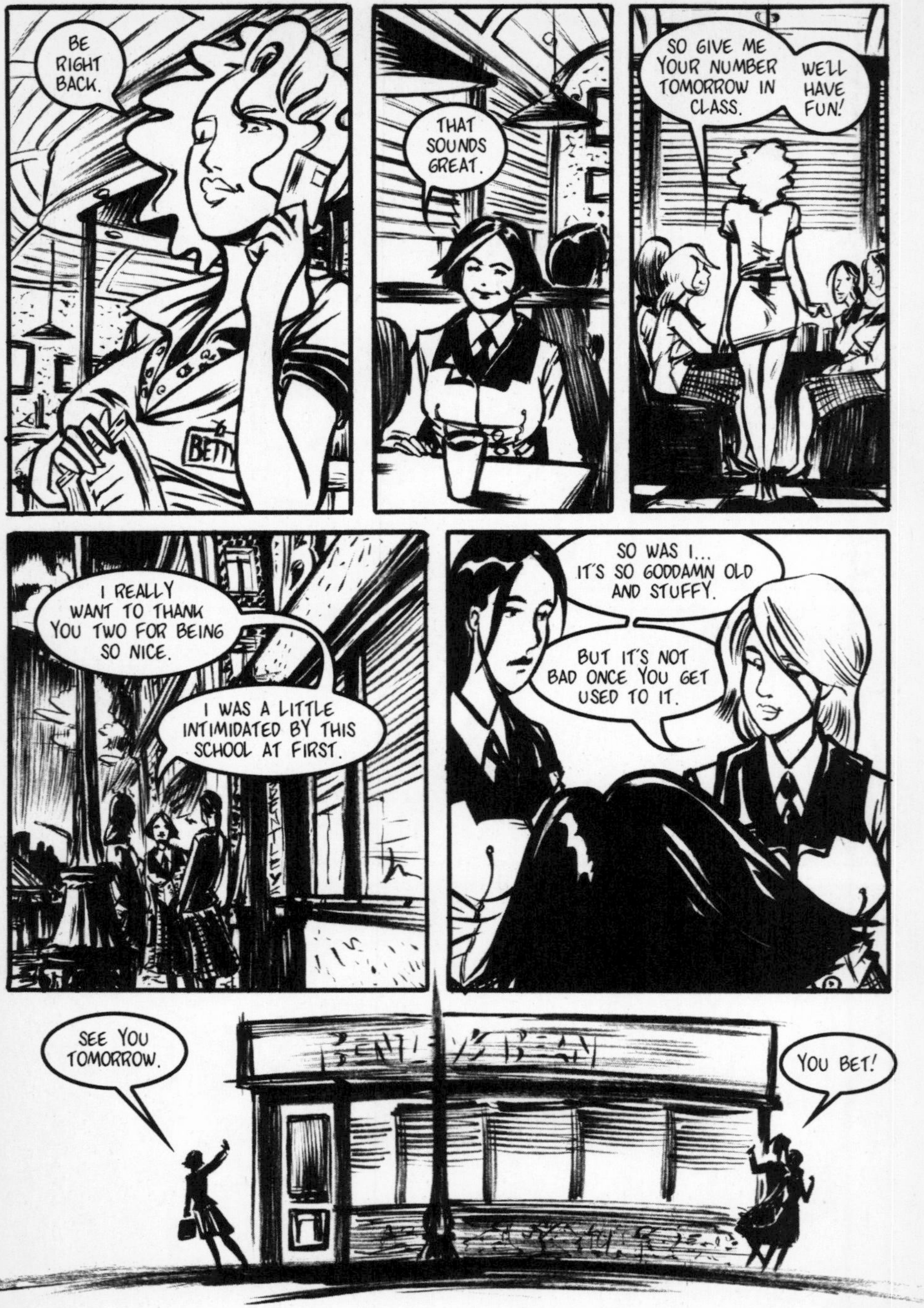
BE RIGHT BACK.
BETTY
THAT SOUNDS GREAT.
SO GIVE ME YOUR NUMBER TOMORROW IN CLASS.
WE'LL HAVE FUN!
I REALLY WANT TO THANK YOU TWO FOR BEING SO NICE.
I WAS A LITTLE INTIMIDATED BY THIS SCHOOL AT FIRST.
SO WAS I... IT'S SO GODDAMN OLD AND STUFFY.
BUT IT'S NOT BAD ONCE YOU GET USED TO IT.
SEE YOU TOMORROW.
YOU BET!

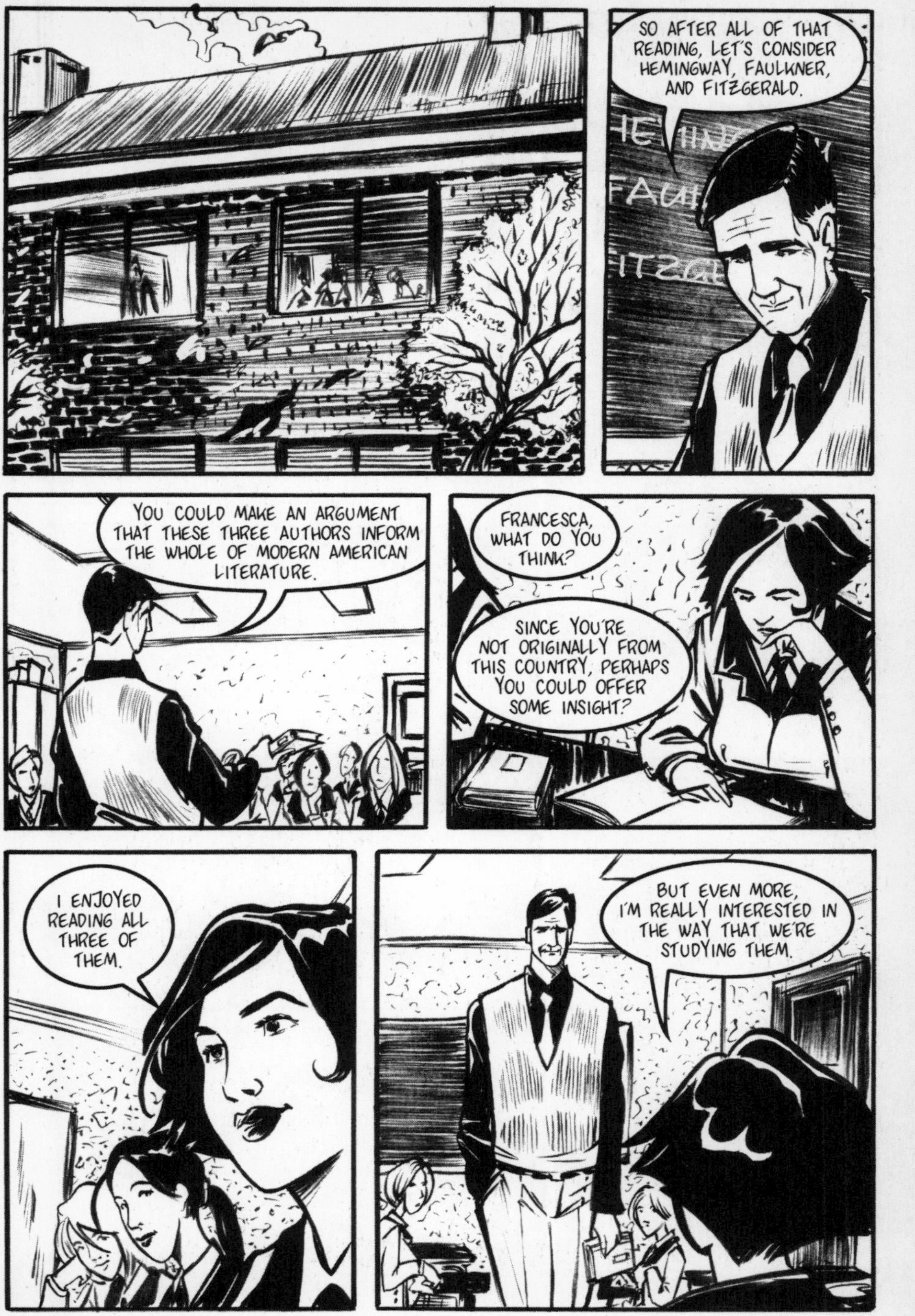
SO AFTER ALL OF THAT READING, LET'S CONSIDER HEMINGWAY, FAULKNER, AND FITZGERALD.
YOU COULD MAKE AN ARGUMENT THAT THESE THREE AUTHORS INFORM THE WHOLE OF MODERN AMERICAN LITERATURE.
FRANCESCA, WHAT DO YOU THINK?
SINCE YOU'RE NOT ORIGINALLY FROM THIS COUNTRY, PERHAPS YOU COULD OFFER SOME INSIGHT?
I ENJOYED READING ALL THREE OF THEM.
BUT EVEN MORE, I'M REALLY INTERESTED IN THE WAY THAT WE'RE STUDYING THEM.

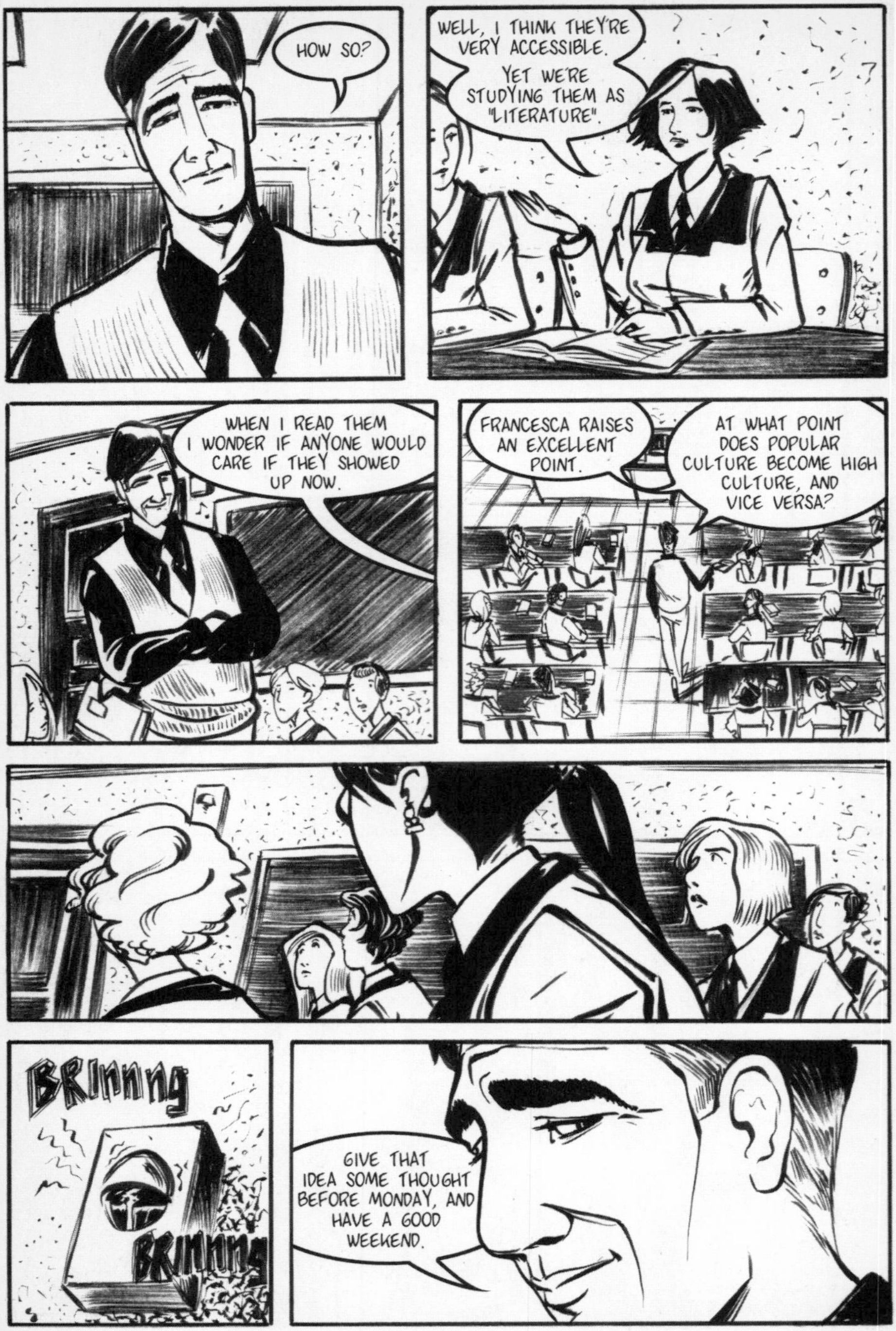
HOW SO?
WELL, I THINK THEY'RE VERY ACCESSIBLE.
YET WE'RE STUDYING THEM AS "LITERATURE".
WHEN I READ THEM I WONDER IF ANYONE WOULD CARE IF THEY SHOWED UP NOW.
FRANCESCA RAISES AN EXCELLENT POINT.
AT WHAT POINT DOES POPULAR CULTURE BECOME HIGH CULTURE, AND VICE VERSA?
BRInnng
BRInnng
GIVE THAT IDEA SOME THOUGHT BEFORE MONDAY, AND HAVE A GOOD WEEKEND.

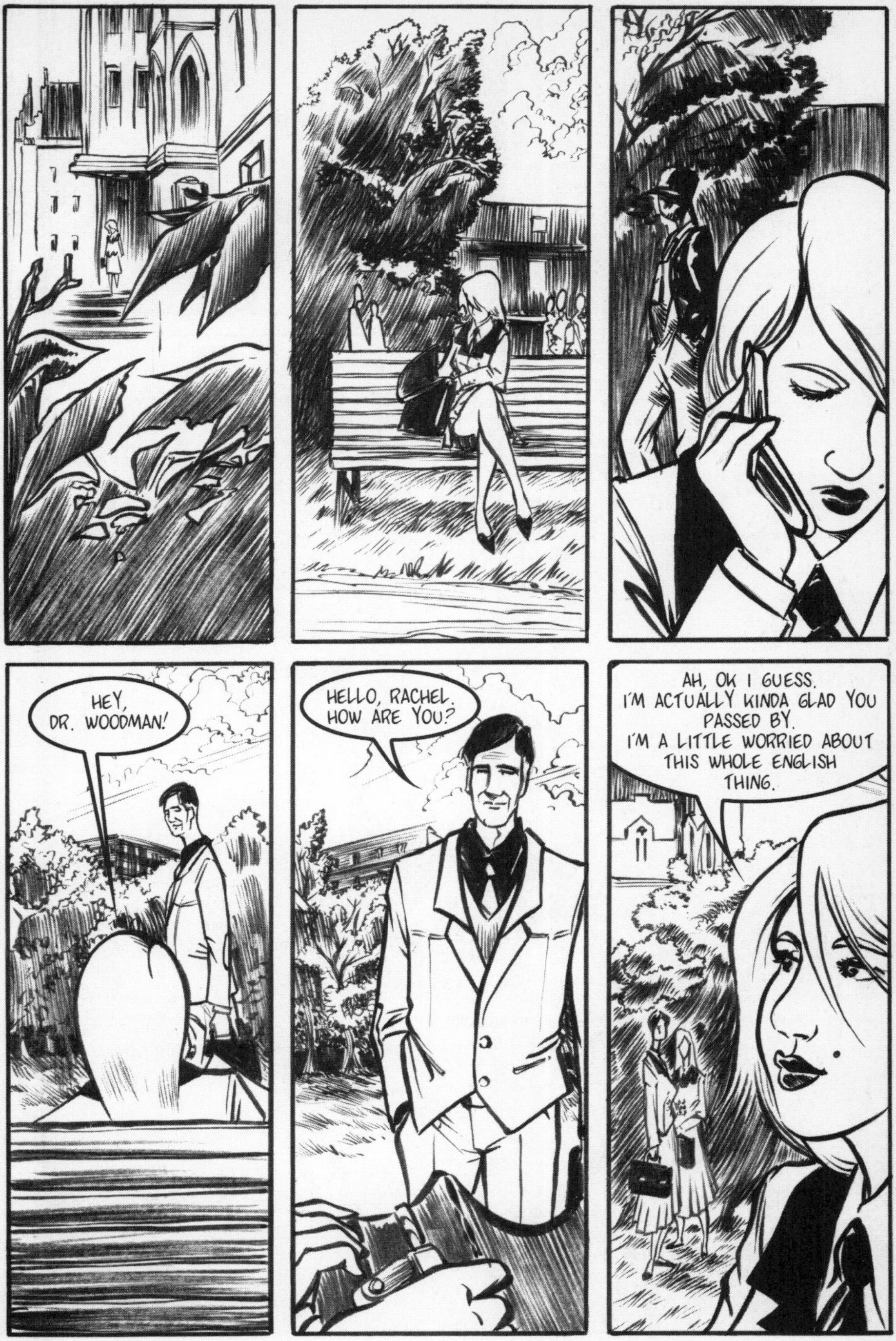
HEY, DR. WOODMAN!
HELLO, RACHEL. HOW ARE YOU?
AH, OK I GUESS. I'M ACTUALLY KINDA GLAD YOU PASSED BY. I'M A LITTLE WORRIED ABOUT THIS WHOLE ENGLISH THING.

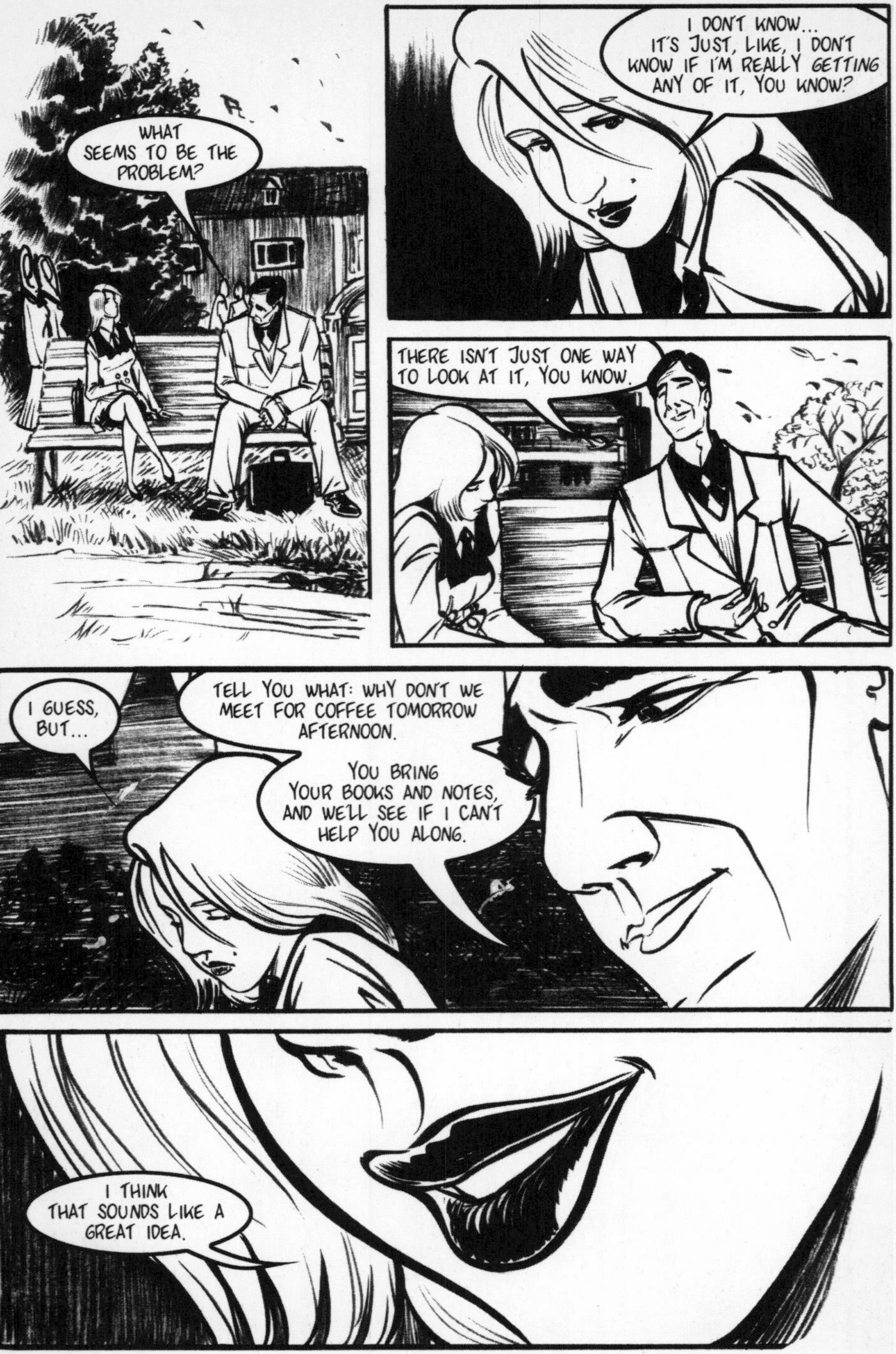
WHAT SEEMS TO BE THE PROBLEM?
I DON'T KNOW... IT'S JUST, LIKE, I DON'T KNOW IF I'M REALLY GETTING ANY OF IT, YOU KNOW?
THERE ISN'T JUST ONE WAY TO LOOK AT IT, YOU KNOW.
I GUESS, BUT...
TELL YOU WHAT: WHY DON'T WE MEET FOR COFFEE TOMORROW AFTERNOON.
YOU BRING YOUR BOOKS AND NOTES, AND WE'LL SEE IF I CAN'T HELP YOU ALONG.
I THINK THAT SOUNDS LIKE A GREAT IDEA.

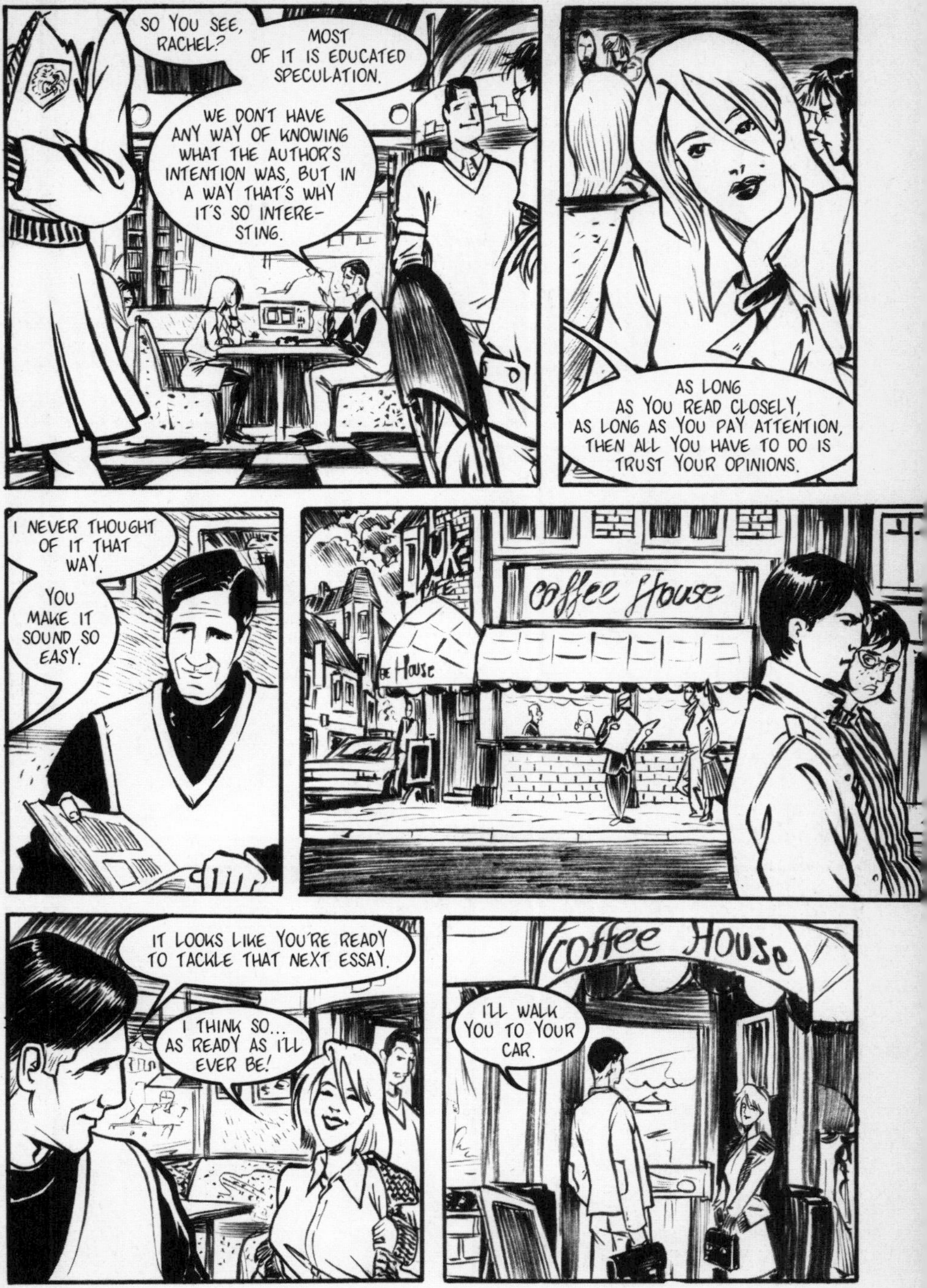
SO YOU SEE, RACHEL?
MOST OF IT IS EDUCATED SPECULATION.
WE DON'T HAVE ANY WAY OF KNOWING WHAT THE AUTHOR'S INTENTION WAS, BUT IN A WAY THAT'S WHY IT'S SO INTERE-STING.
AS LONG AS YOU READ CLOSELY, AS LONG AS YOU PAY ATTENTION, THEN ALL YOU HAVE TO DO IS TRUST YOUR OPINIONS.
I NEVER THOUGHT OF IT THAT WAY.
YOU MAKE IT SOUND SO EASY.
Coffee House
IT LOOKS LIKE YOU'RE READY TO TACKLE THAT NEXT ESSAY.
I THINK SO... AS READY AS I'LL EVER BE!
coffee House
I'LL WALK YOU TO YOUR CAR.

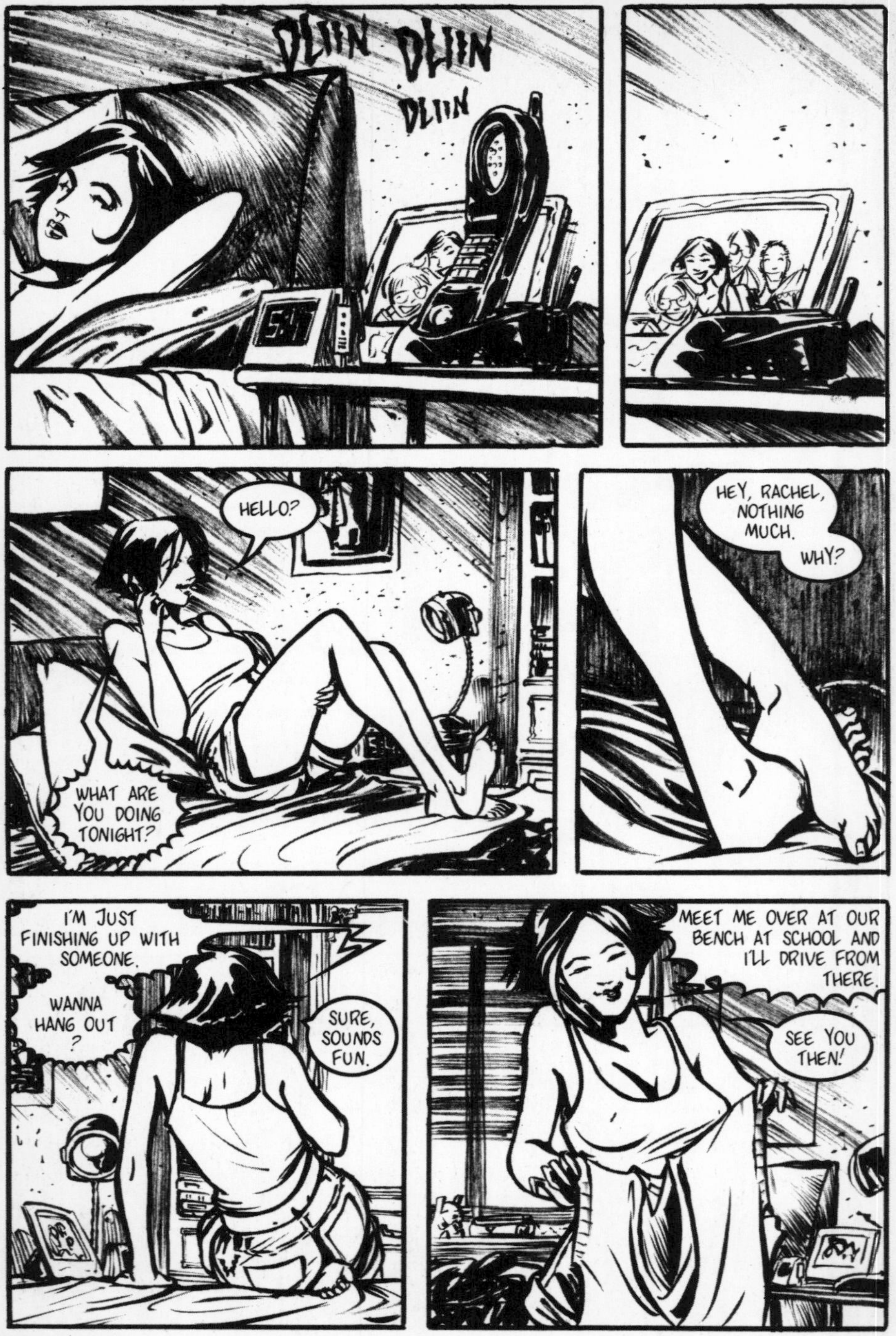
DLIIN DLIIN
DLIIN
HELLO?
WHAT ARE YOU DOING TONIGHT?
HEY, RACHEL, NOTHING MUCH.
WHY?
I'M JUST FINISHING UP WITH SOMEONE.
WANNA HANG OUT?
SURE, SOUNDS FUN.
MEET ME OVER AT OUR BENCH AT SCHOOL AND I'LL DRIVE FROM THERE.
SEE YOU THEN!

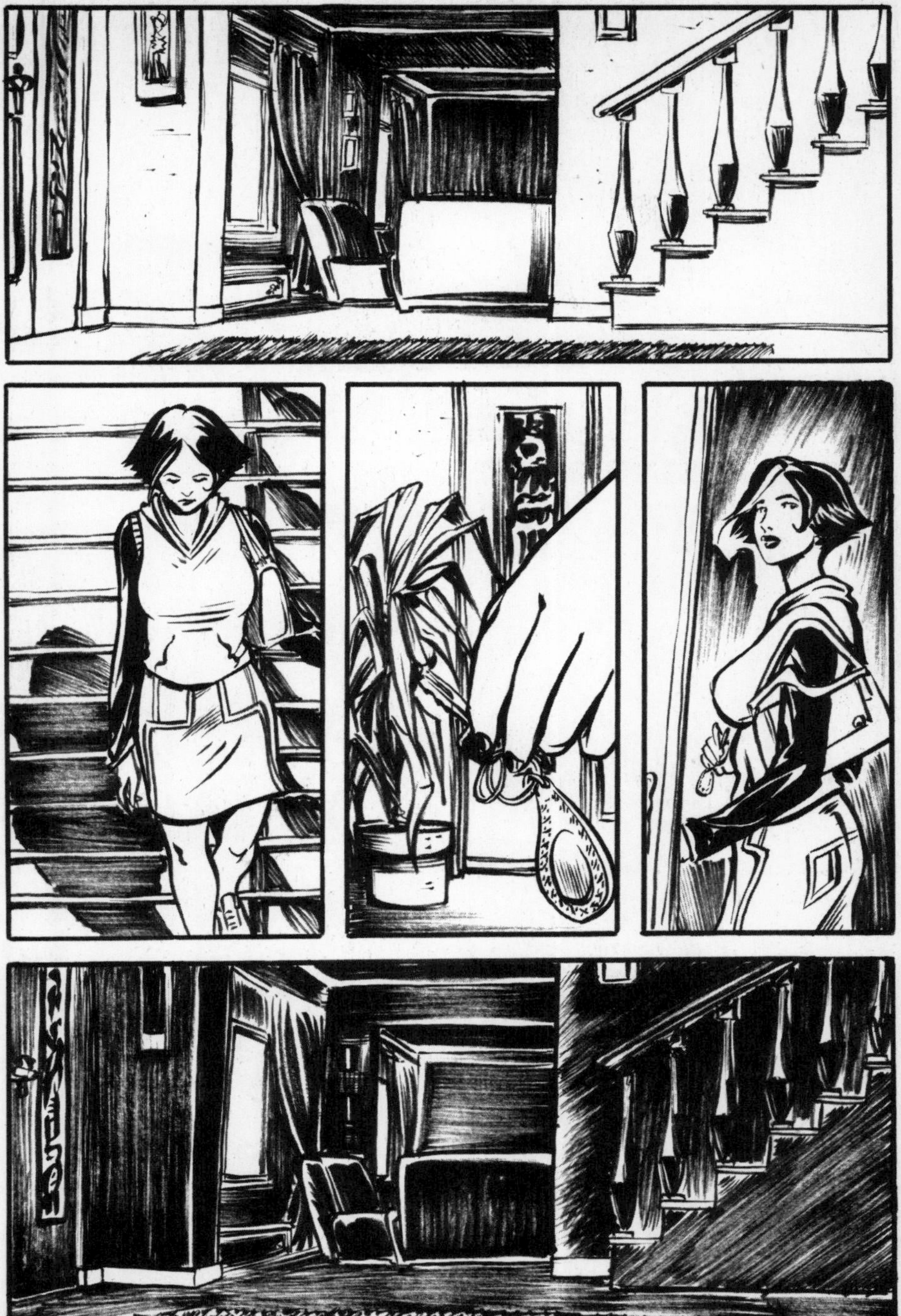

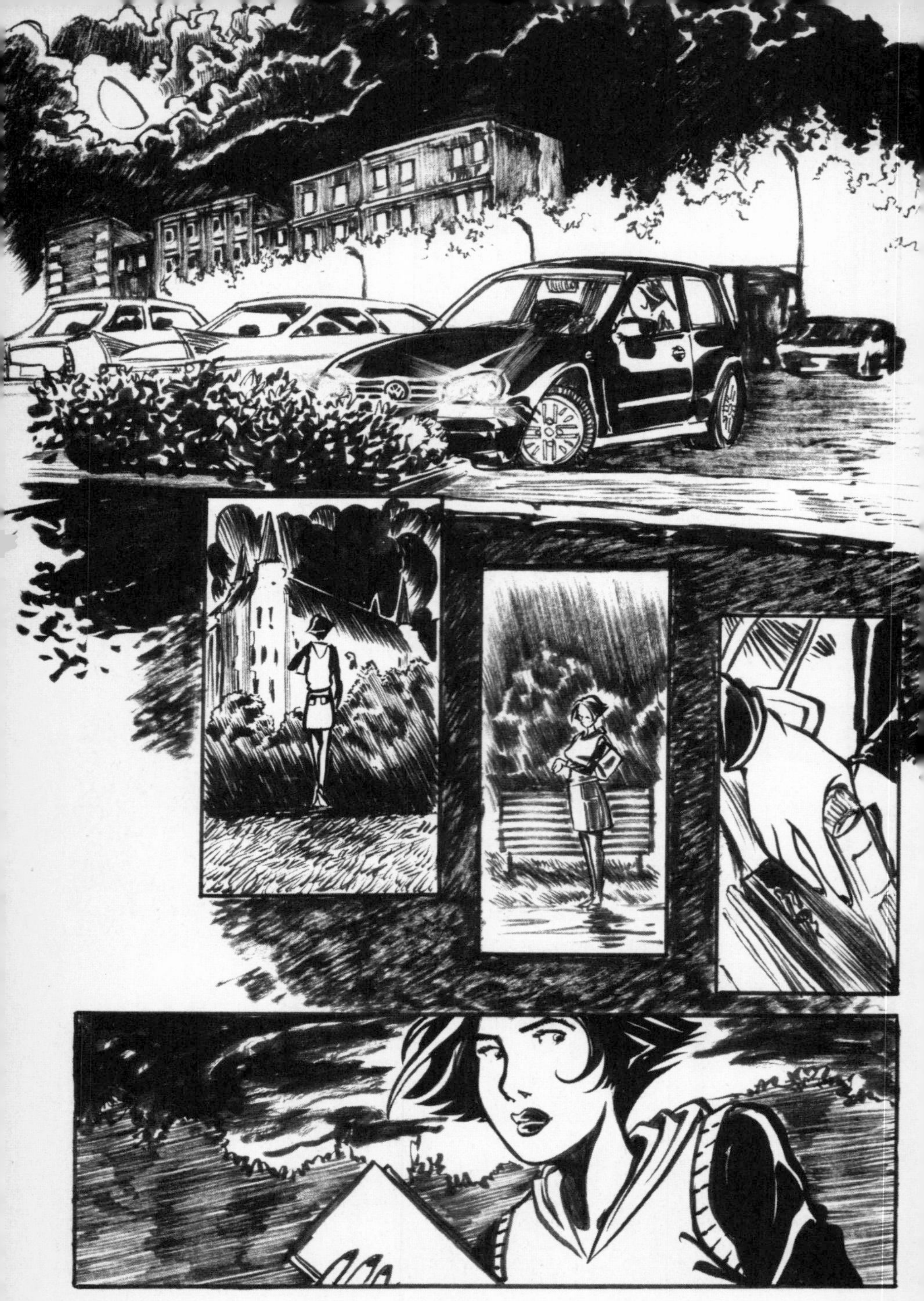

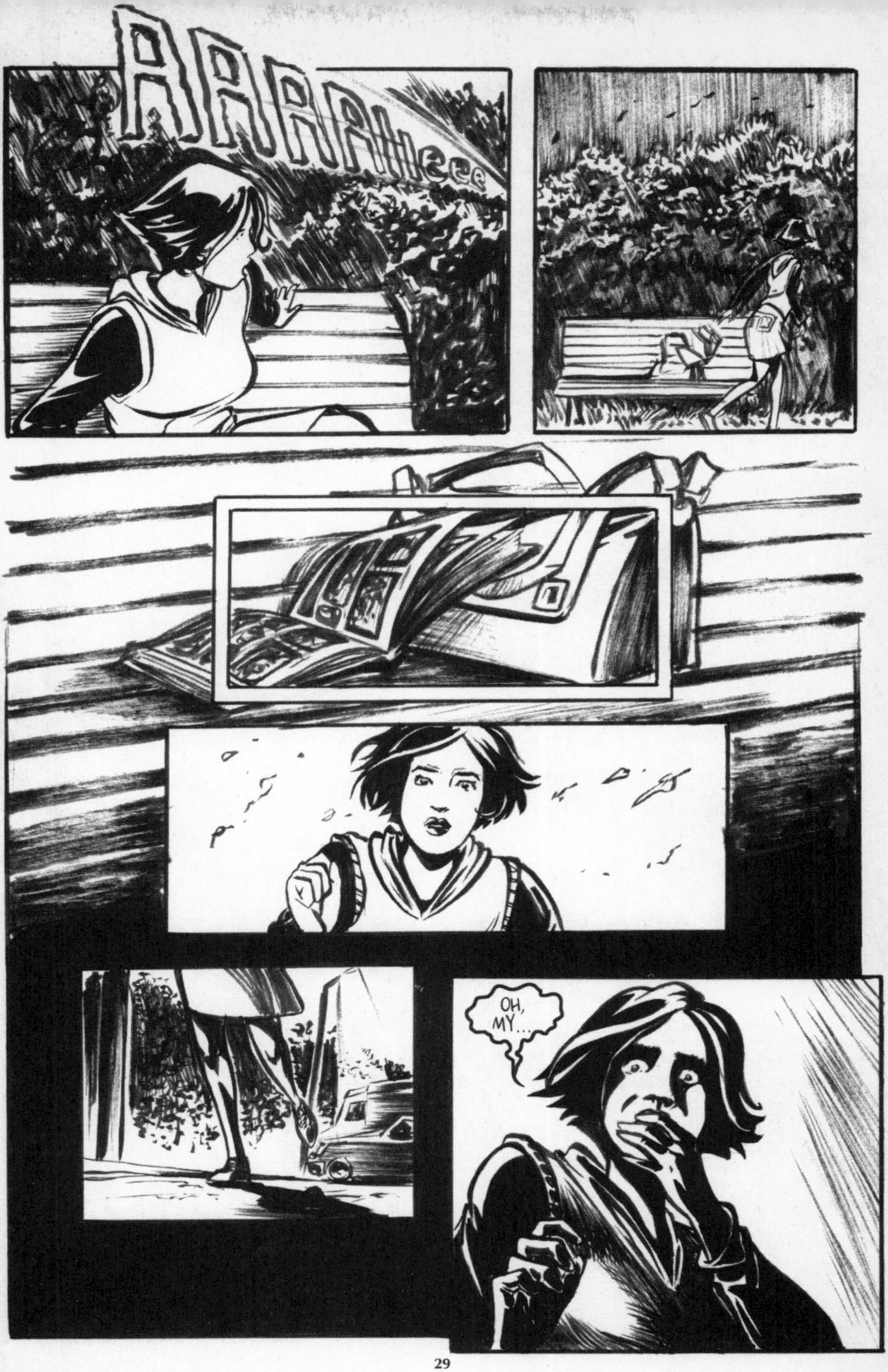
AAARRRHeee
OH, MY...

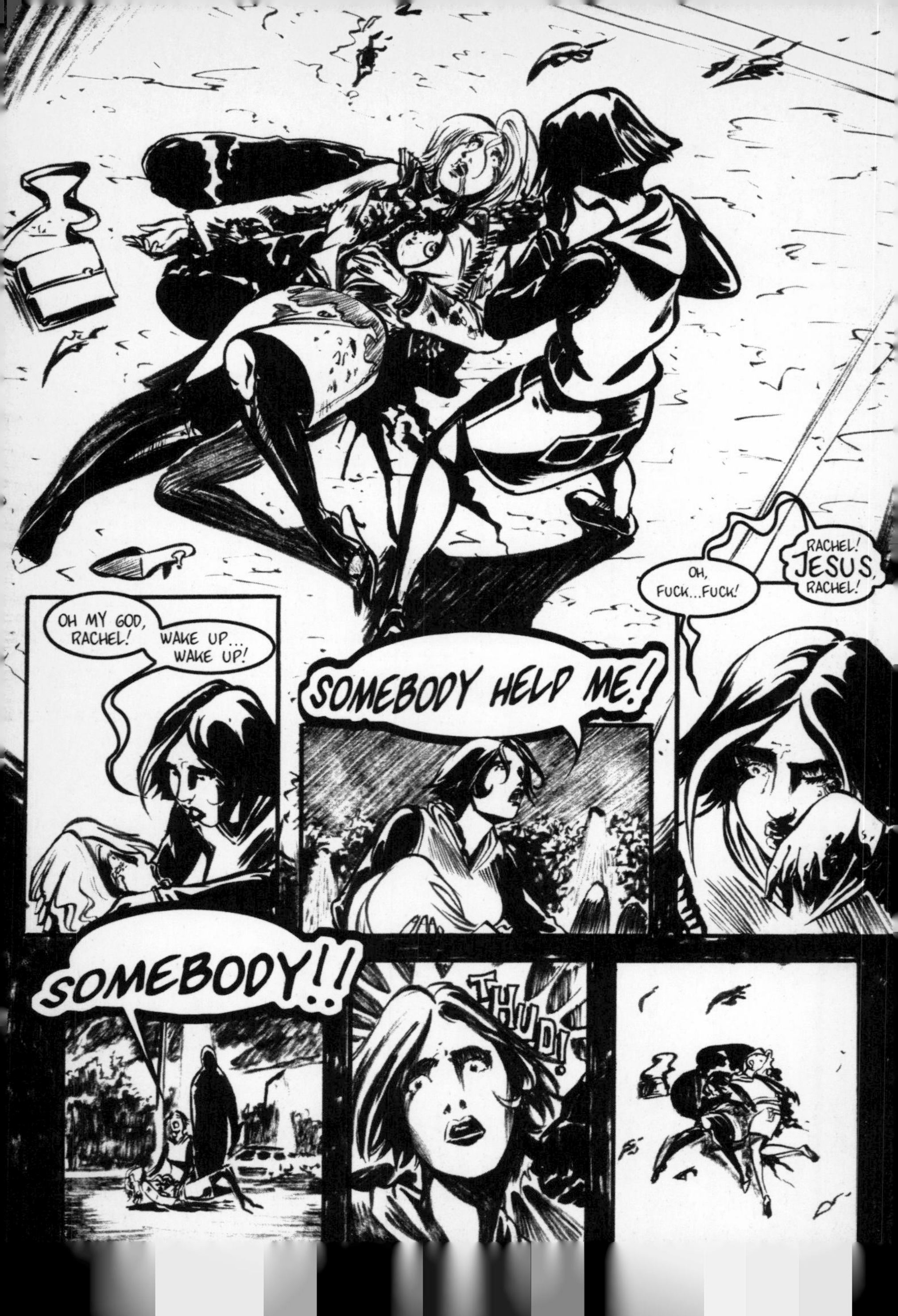
RACHEL! JESUS, RACHEL!
OH, FUCK...FUCK!
OH MY GOD, RACHEL!
WAKE UP... WAKE UP!
SOMEBODY HELP ME!
SOMEBODY!!
THUD!

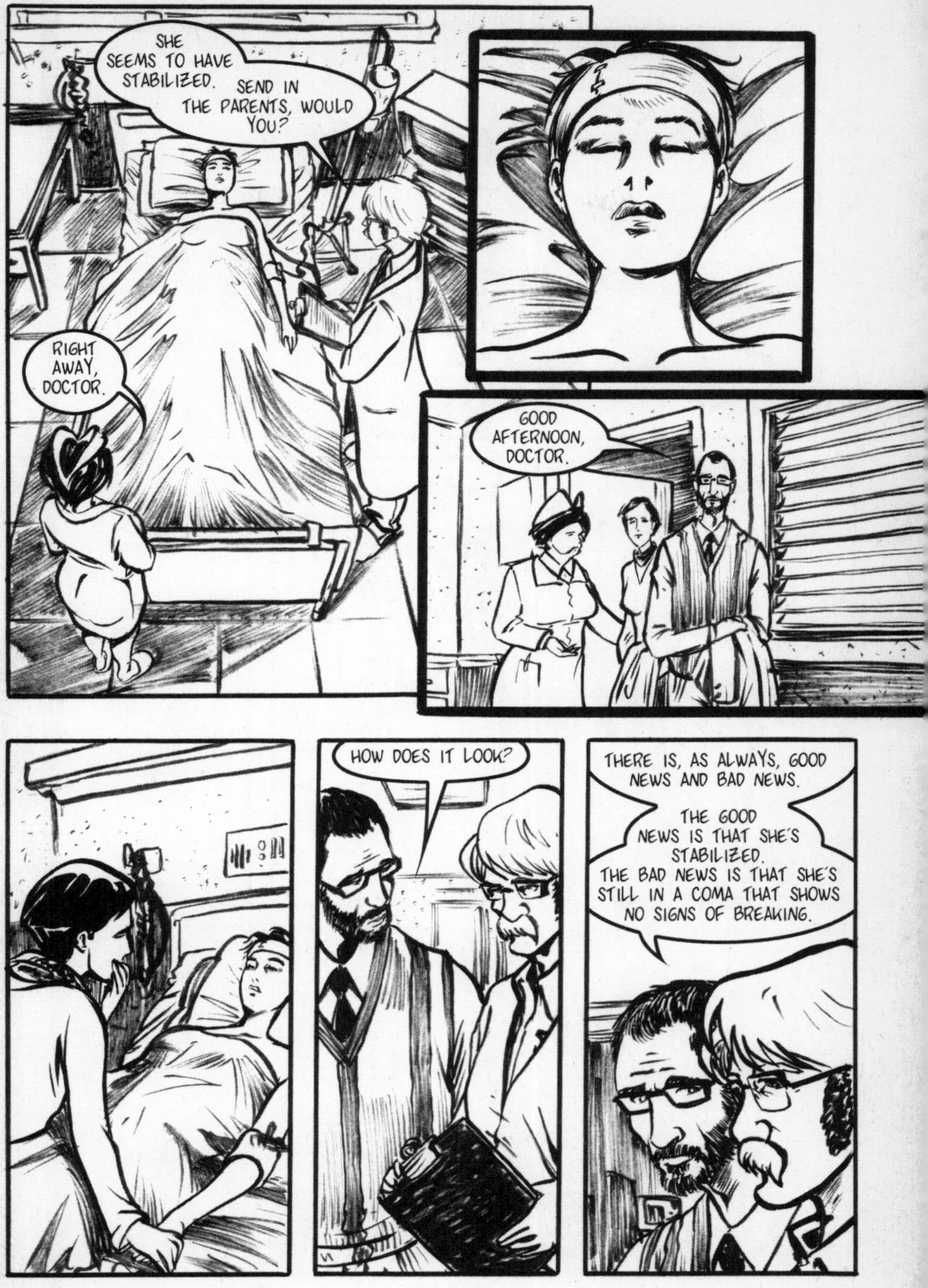
SHE SEEMS TO HAVE STABILIZED. SEND IN THE PARENTS, WOULD YOU?
RIGHT AWAY, DOCTOR.
GOOD AFTERNOON, DOCTOR.
HOW DOES IT LOOK?
THERE IS, AS ALWAYS, GOOD NEWS AND BAD NEWS.
THE GOOD NEWS IS THAT SHE'S STABILIZED.
THE BAD NEWS IS THAT SHE'S STILL IN A COMA THAT SHOWS NO SIGNS OF BREAKING.

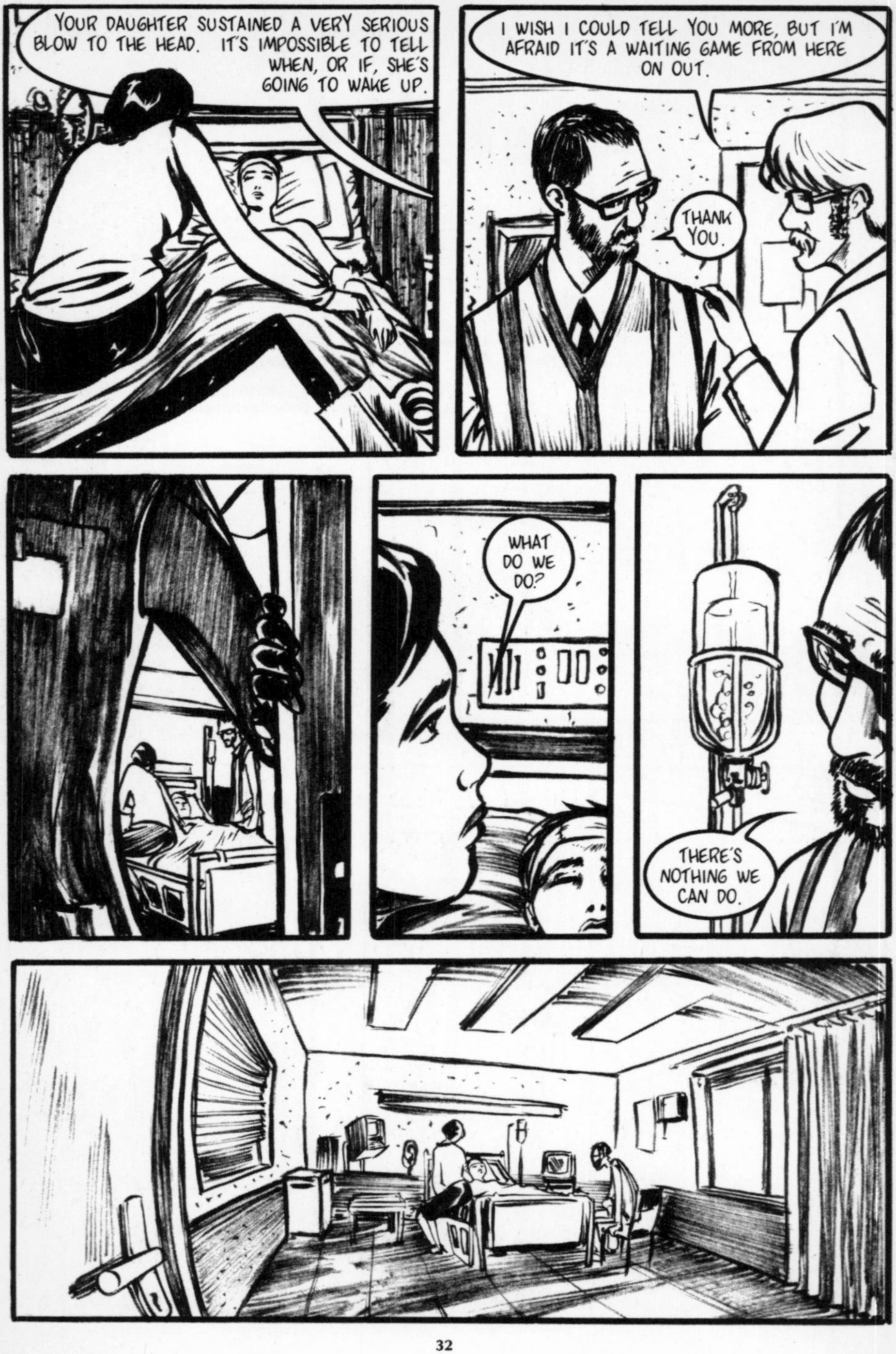
YOUR DAUGHTER SUSTAINED A VERY SERIOUS BLOW TO THE HEAD. IT'S IMPOSSIBLE TO TELL WHEN, OR IF, SHE'S GOING TO WAKE UP.
I WISH I COULD TELL YOU MORE, BUT I'M AFRAID IT'S A WAITING GAME FROM HERE ON OUT.
THANK YOU.
WHAT DO WE DO?
THERE'S NOTHING WE CAN DO.

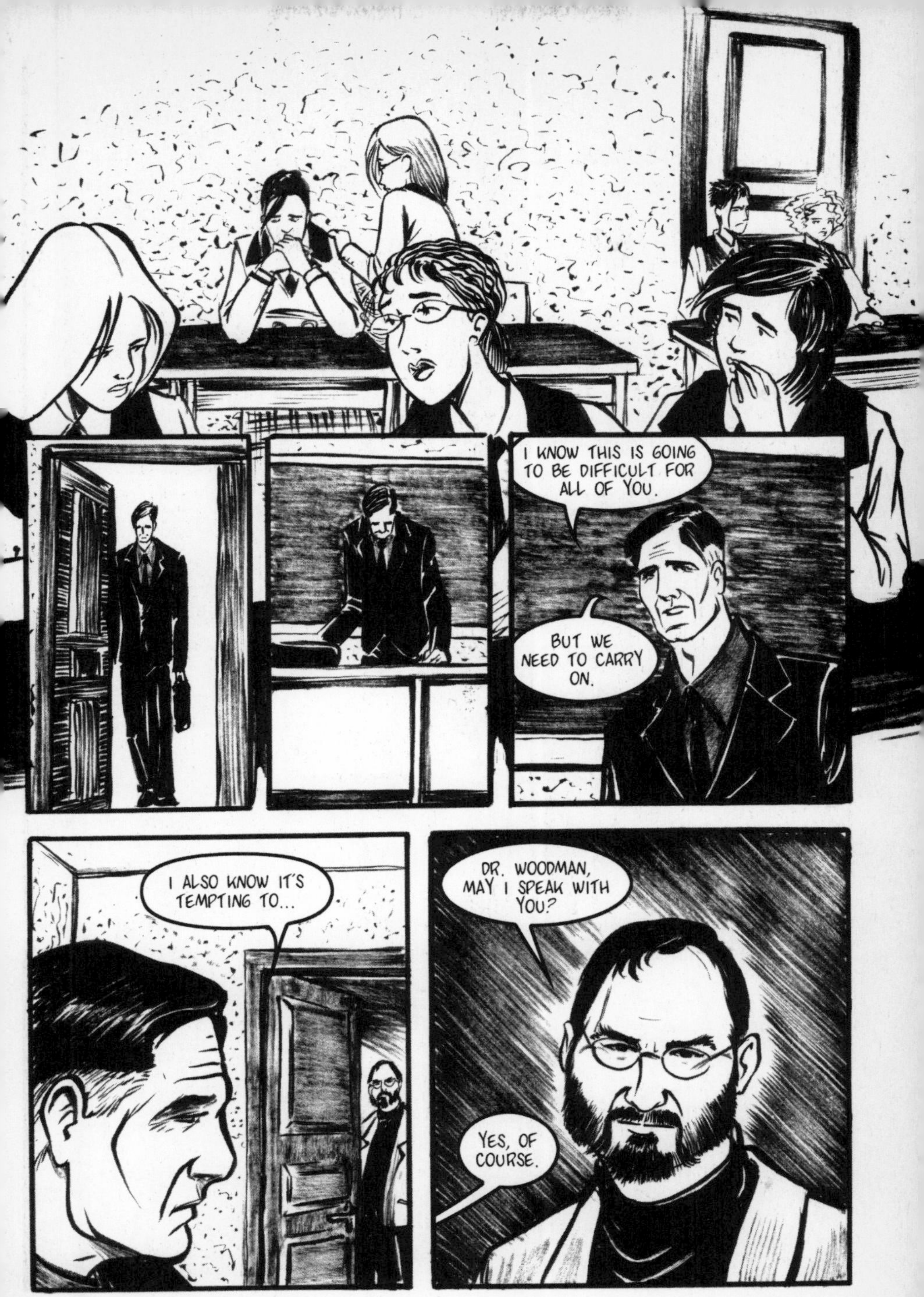
I KNOW THIS IS GOING TO BE DIFFICULT FOR ALL OF YOU.
BUT WE NEED TO CARRY ON.
I ALSO KNOW IT'S TEMPTING TO...
DR. WOODMAN, MAY I SPEAK WITH YOU?
YES, OF COURSE.

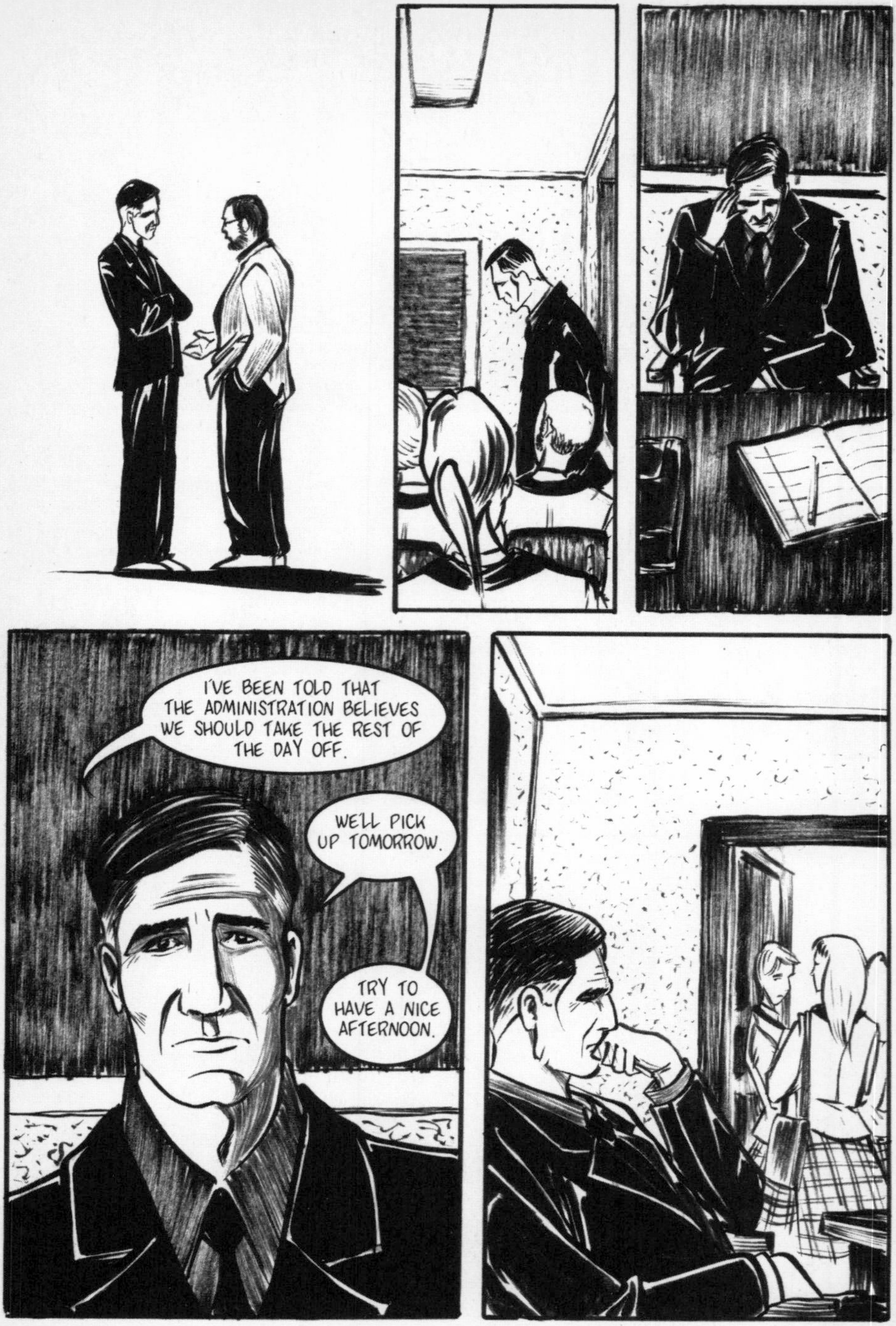
I'VE BEEN TOLD THAT THE ADMINISTRATION BELIEVES WE SHOULD TAKE THE REST OF THE DAY OFF.
WE'LL PICK UP TOMORROW.
TRY TO HAVE A NICE AFTERNOON.

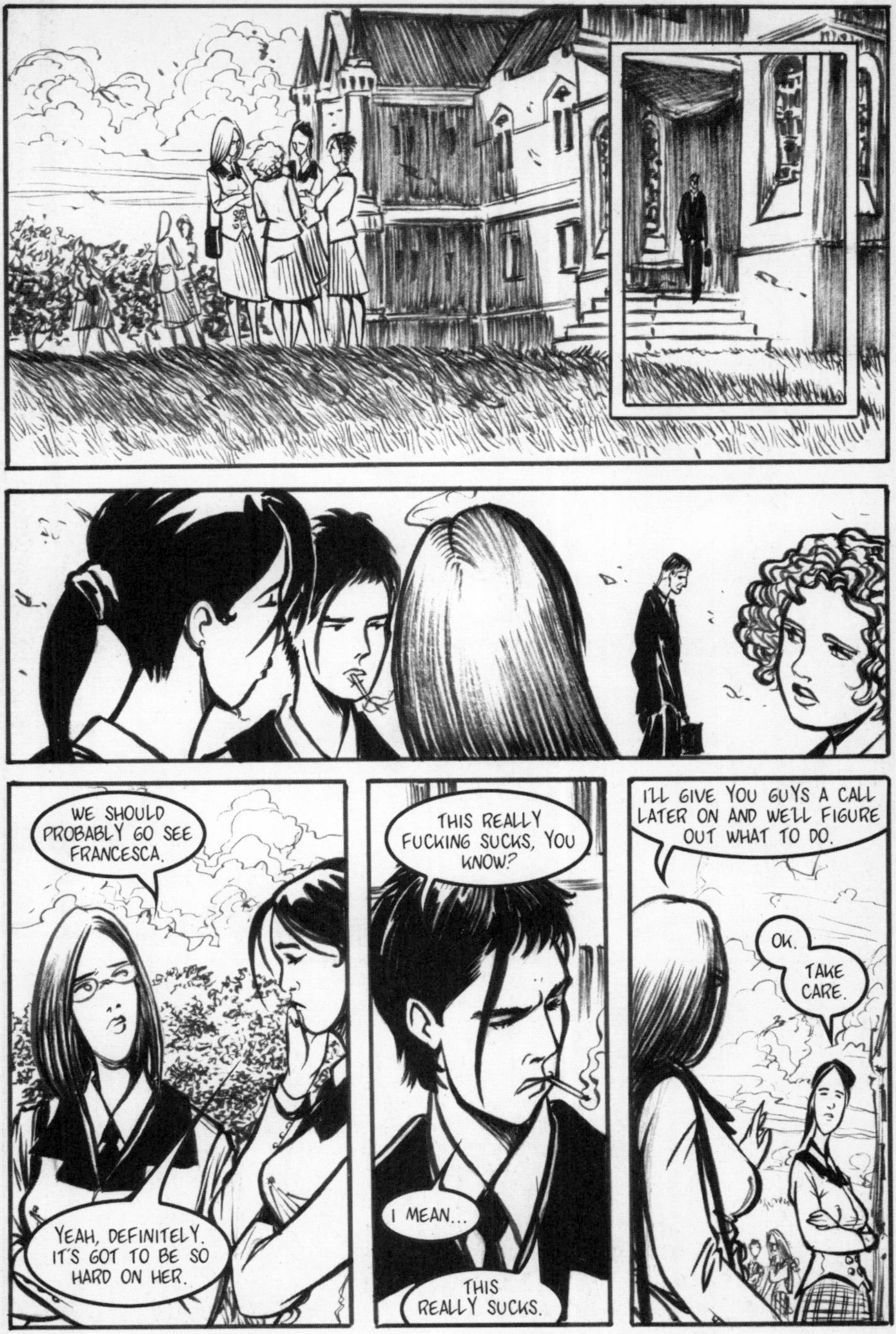
WE SHOULD PROBABLY GO SEE FRANCESCA.
YEAH, DEFINITELY. IT'S GOT TO BE SO HARD ON HER.
THIS REALLY FUCKING SUCKS, YOU KNOW?
I MEAN...
THIS REALLY SUCKS.
I'LL GIVE YOU GUYS A CALL LATER ON AND WE'LL FIGURE OUT WHAT TO DO.
OK.
TAKE CARE.

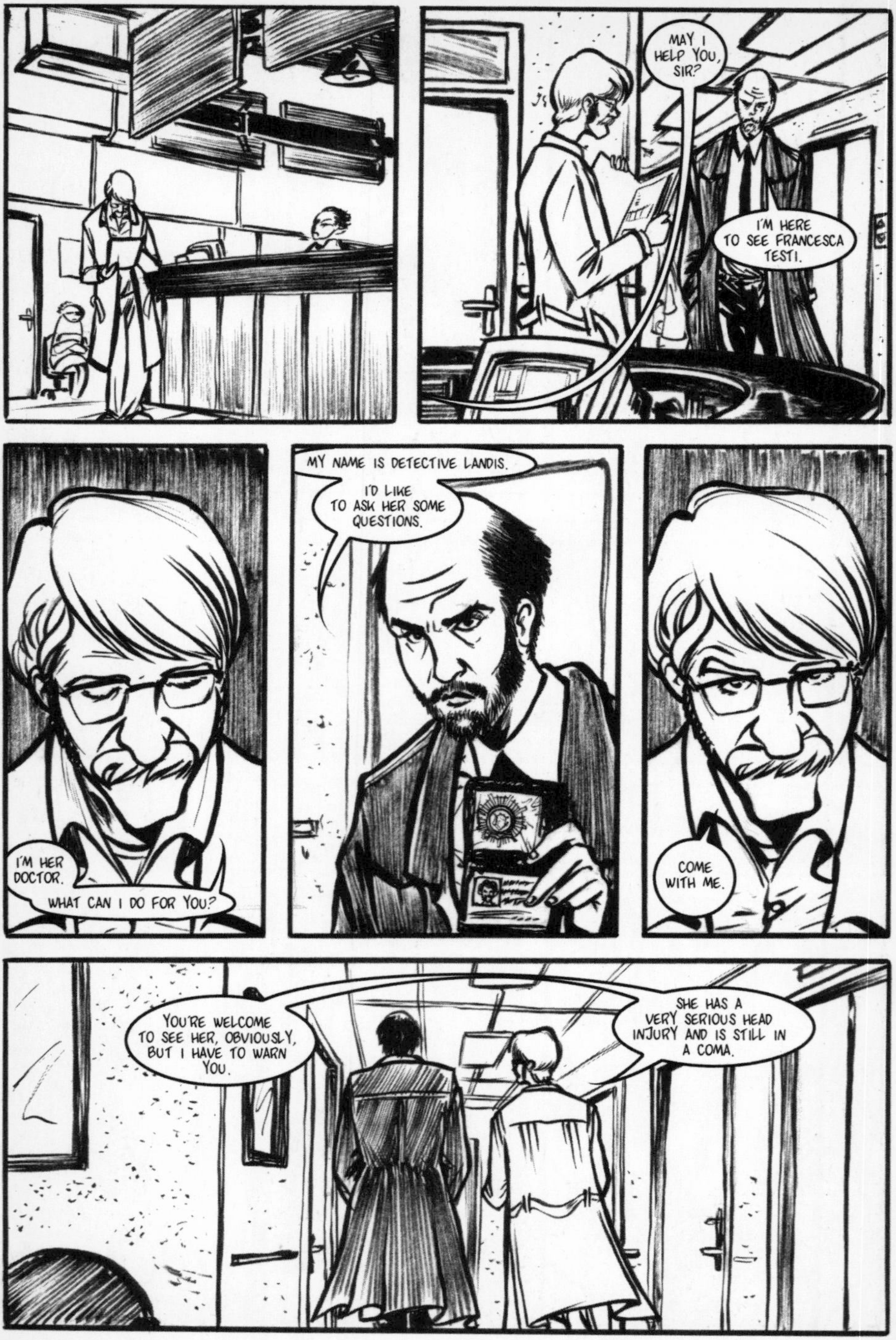
MAY I HELP YOU, SIR?
I'M HERE TO SEE FRANCESCA TESTI.
I'M HER DOCTOR.
WHAT CAN I DO FOR YOU?
MY NAME IS DETECTIVE LANDIS.
I'D LIKE TO ASK HER SOME QUESTIONS.
COME WITH ME.
YOU'RE WELCOME TO SEE HER, OBVIOUSLY, BUT I HAVE TO WARN YOU.
SHE HAS A VERY SERIOUS HEAD INJURY AND IS STILL IN A COMA.

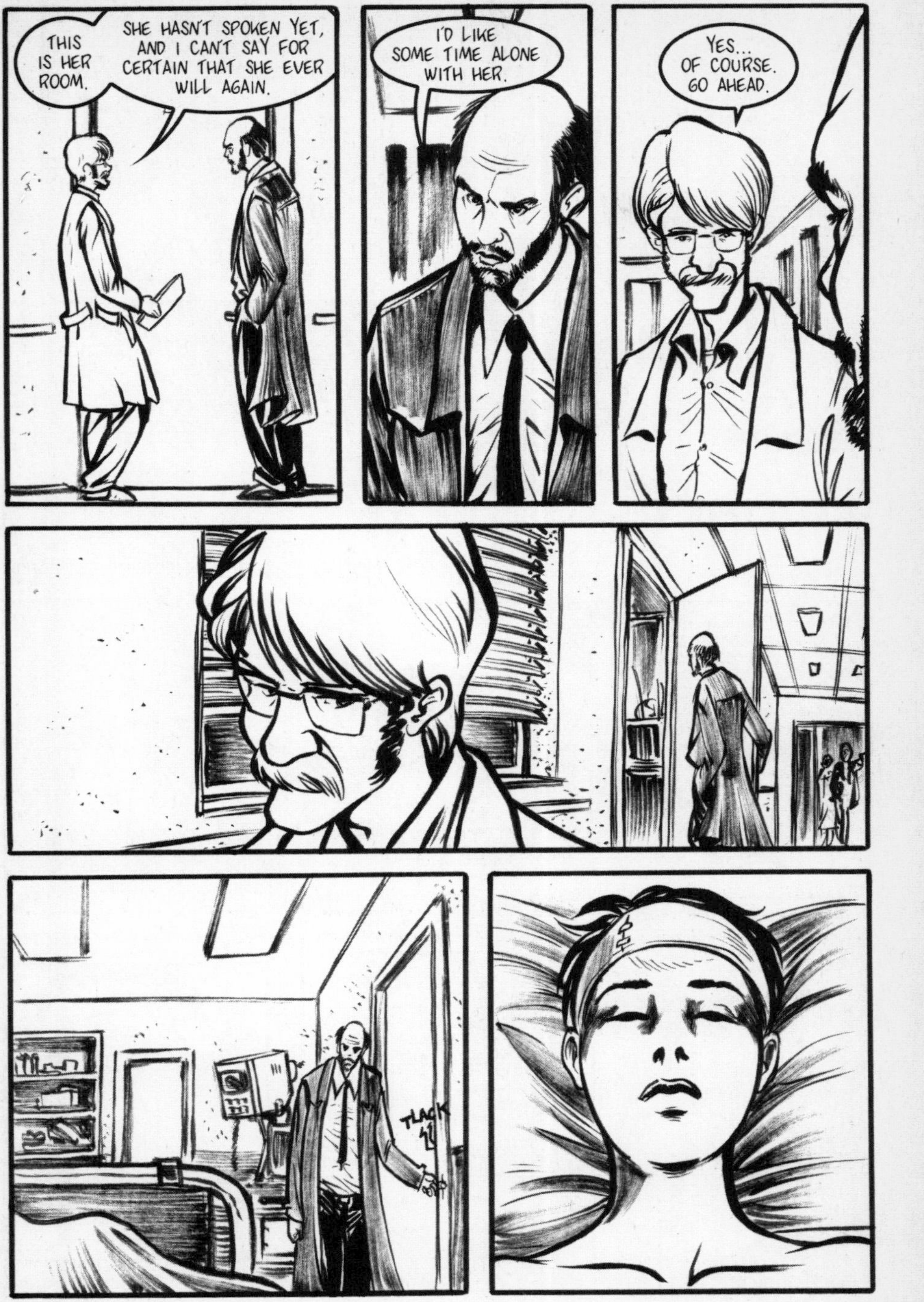
THIS IS HER ROOM.
SHE HASN'T SPOKEN YET, AND I CAN'T SAY FOR CERTAIN THAT SHE EVER WILL AGAIN.
I'D LIKE SOME TIME ALONE WITH HER.
YES... OF COURSE. GO AHEAD.
TLACK

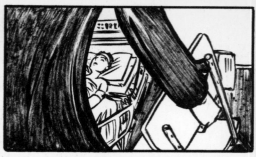

YOU'RE THE ONLY ONE WHO KNOWS.

TLACK

BETH...

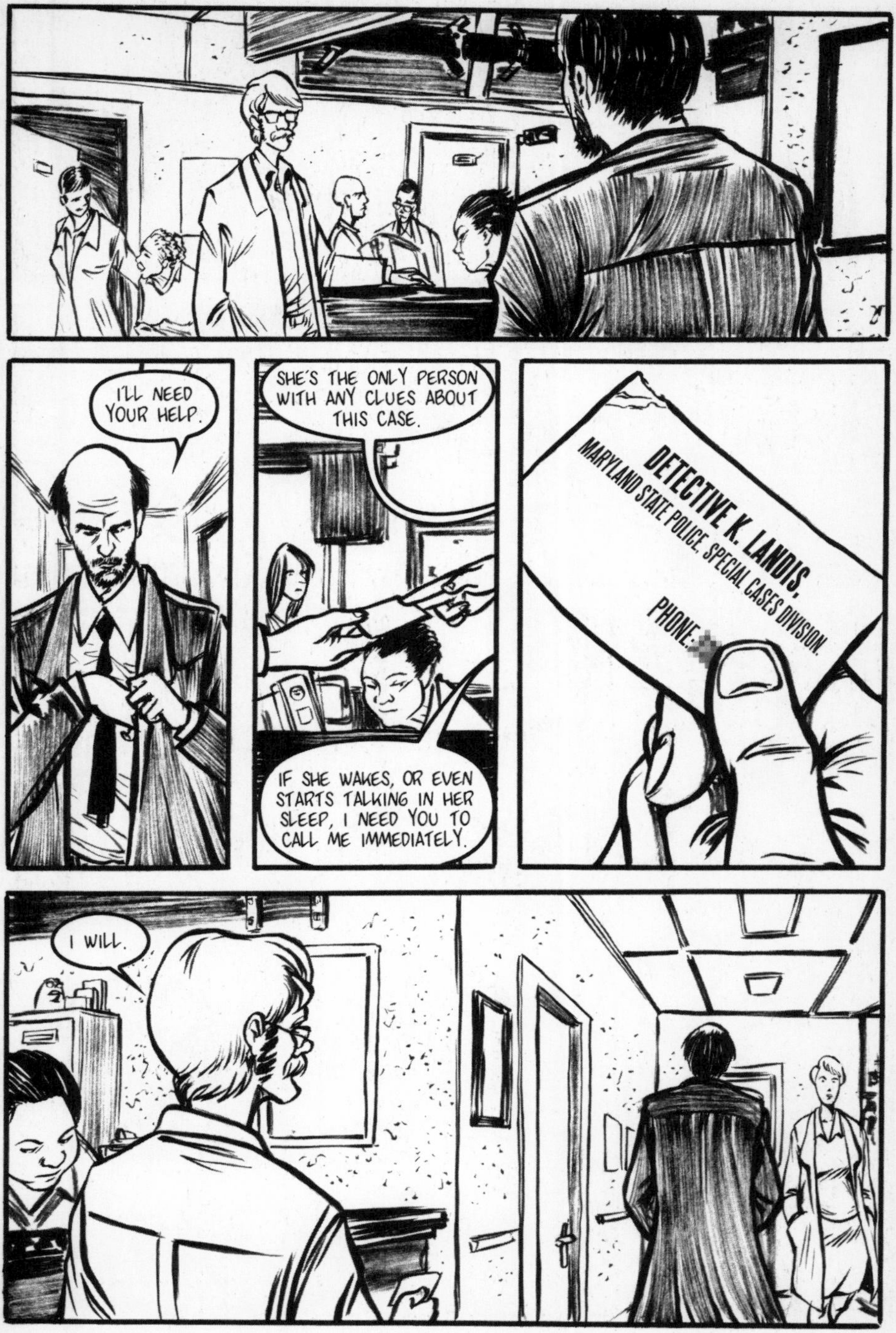
I'LL NEED YOUR HELP.
SHE'S THE ONLY PERSON WITH ANY CLUES ABOUT THIS CASE.
IF SHE WAKES, OR EVEN STARTS TALKING IN HER SLEEP, I NEED YOU TO CALL ME IMMEDIATELY.
DETECTIVE K. LANDIS.
MARYLAND STATE POLICE, SPECIAL CASES DIVISION.
PHONE:
I WILL.

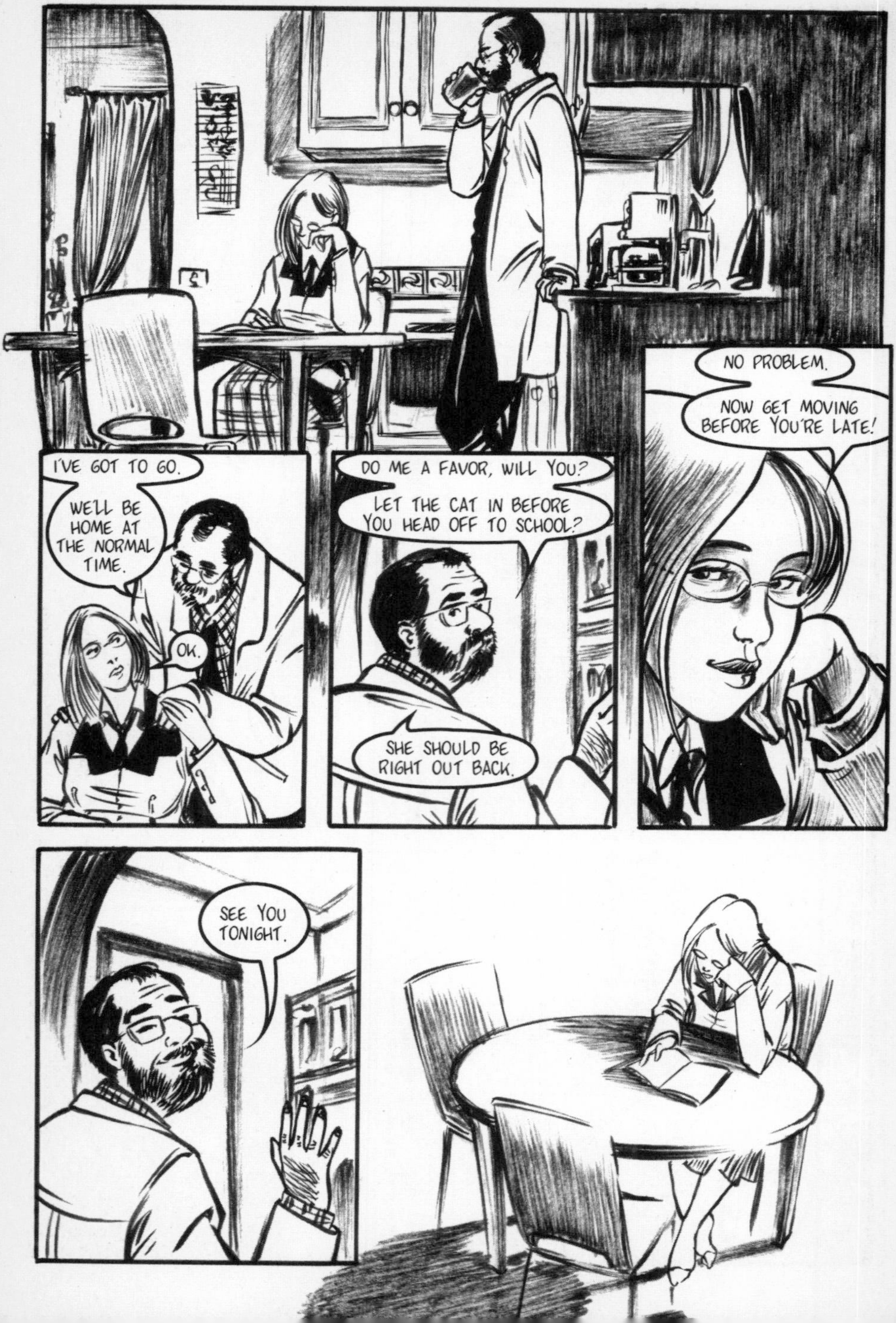

I'VE GOT TO GO.
WE'LL BE HOME AT THE NORMAL TIME.
OK.
DO ME A FAVOR, WILL YOU?
LET THE CAT IN BEFORE YOU HEAD OFF TO SCHOOL?
SHE SHOULD BE RIGHT OUT BACK.
NO PROBLEM.
NOW GET MOVING BEFORE YOU'RE LATE!
SEE YOU TONIGHT.

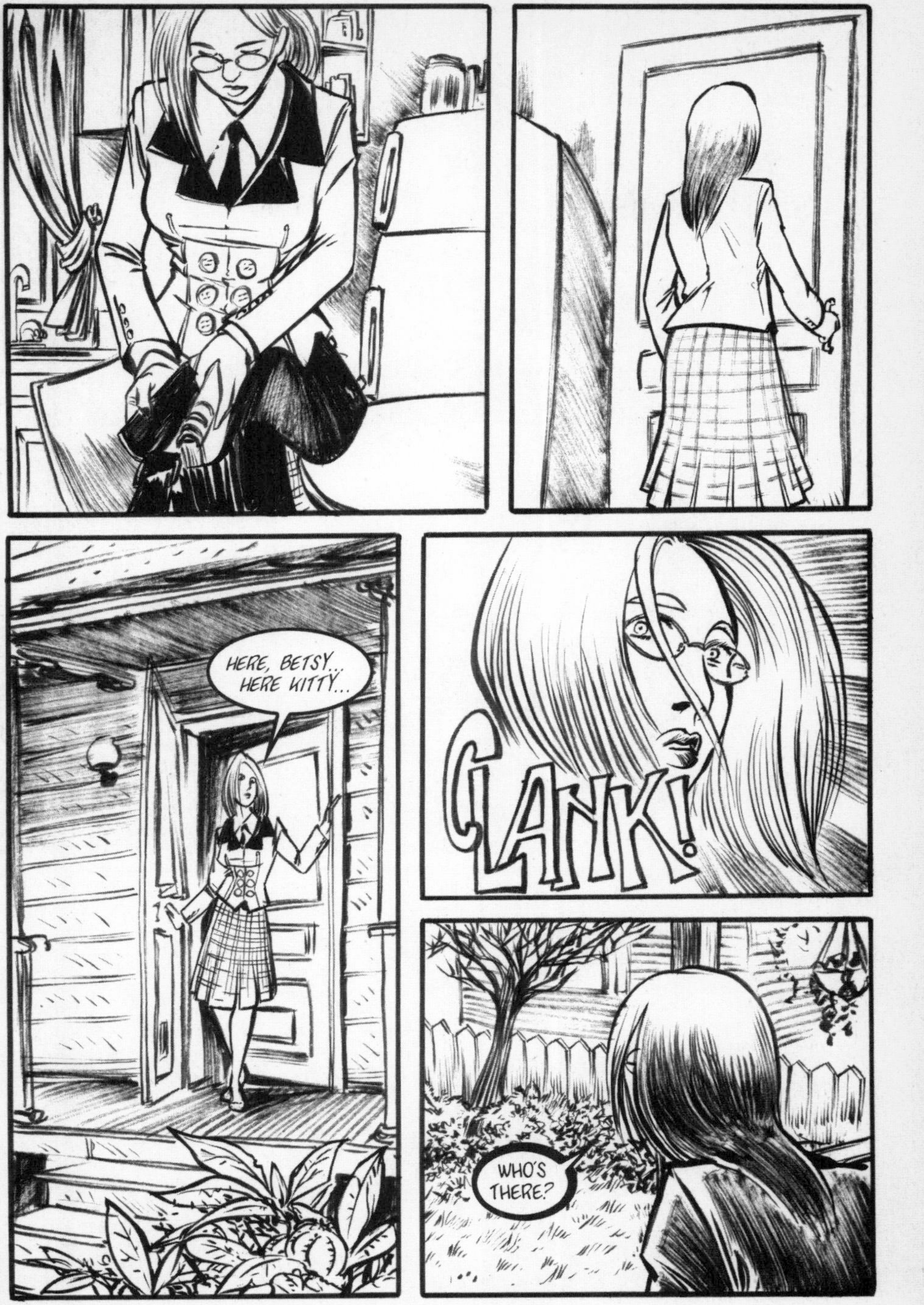
HERE, BETSY...
HERE KITTY...
CLANK!
WHO'S THERE?

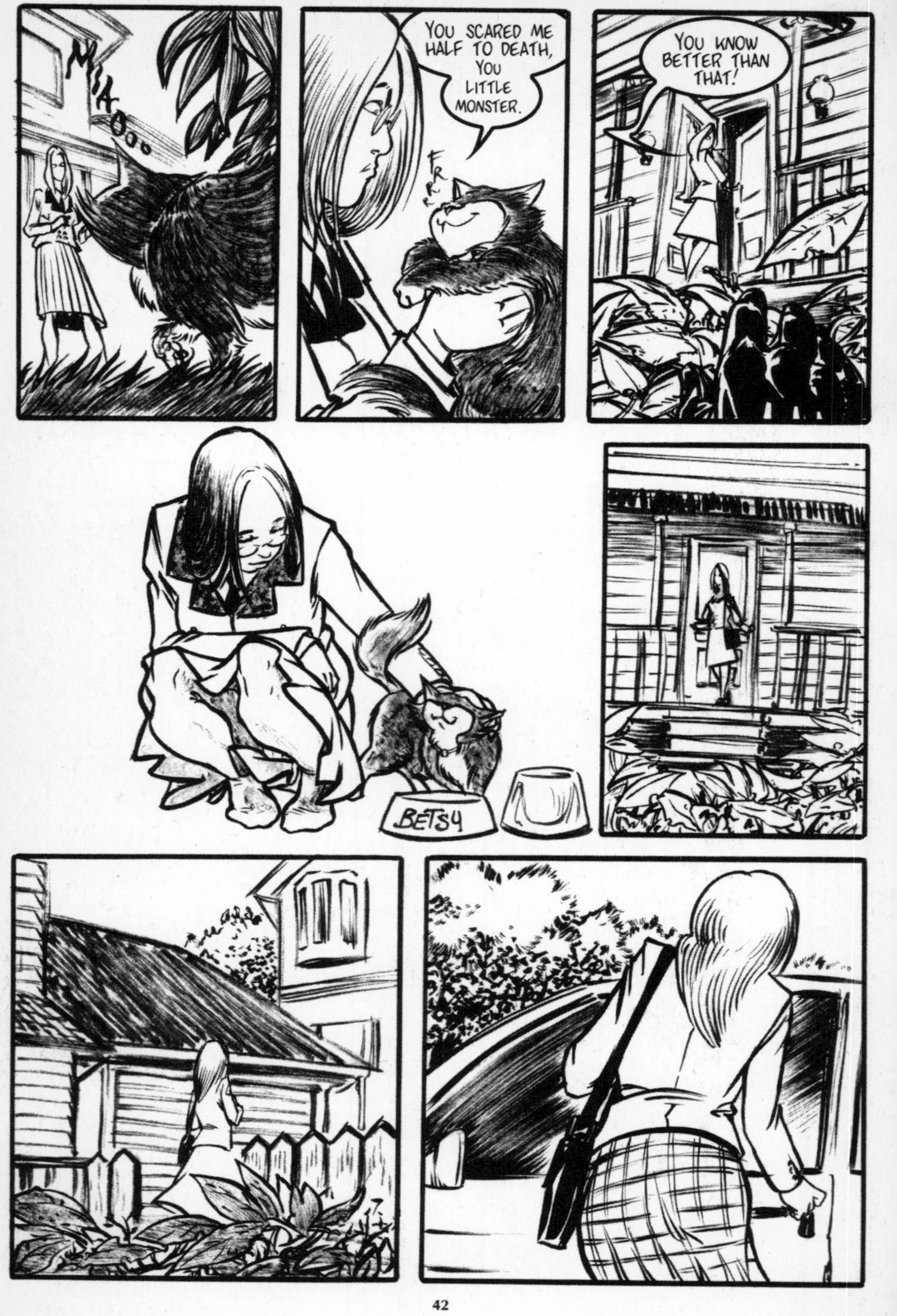
MIAOoo
YOU SCARED ME HALF TO DEATH, YOU LITTLE MONSTER.
YOU KNOW BETTER THAN THAT!
BETSY

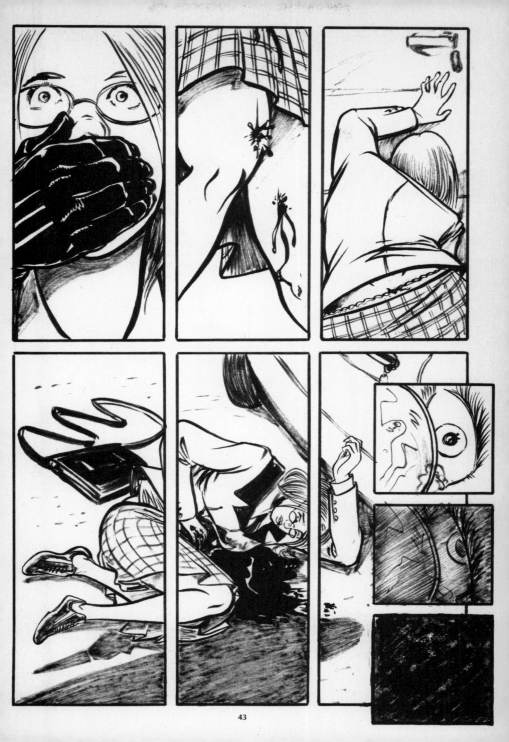

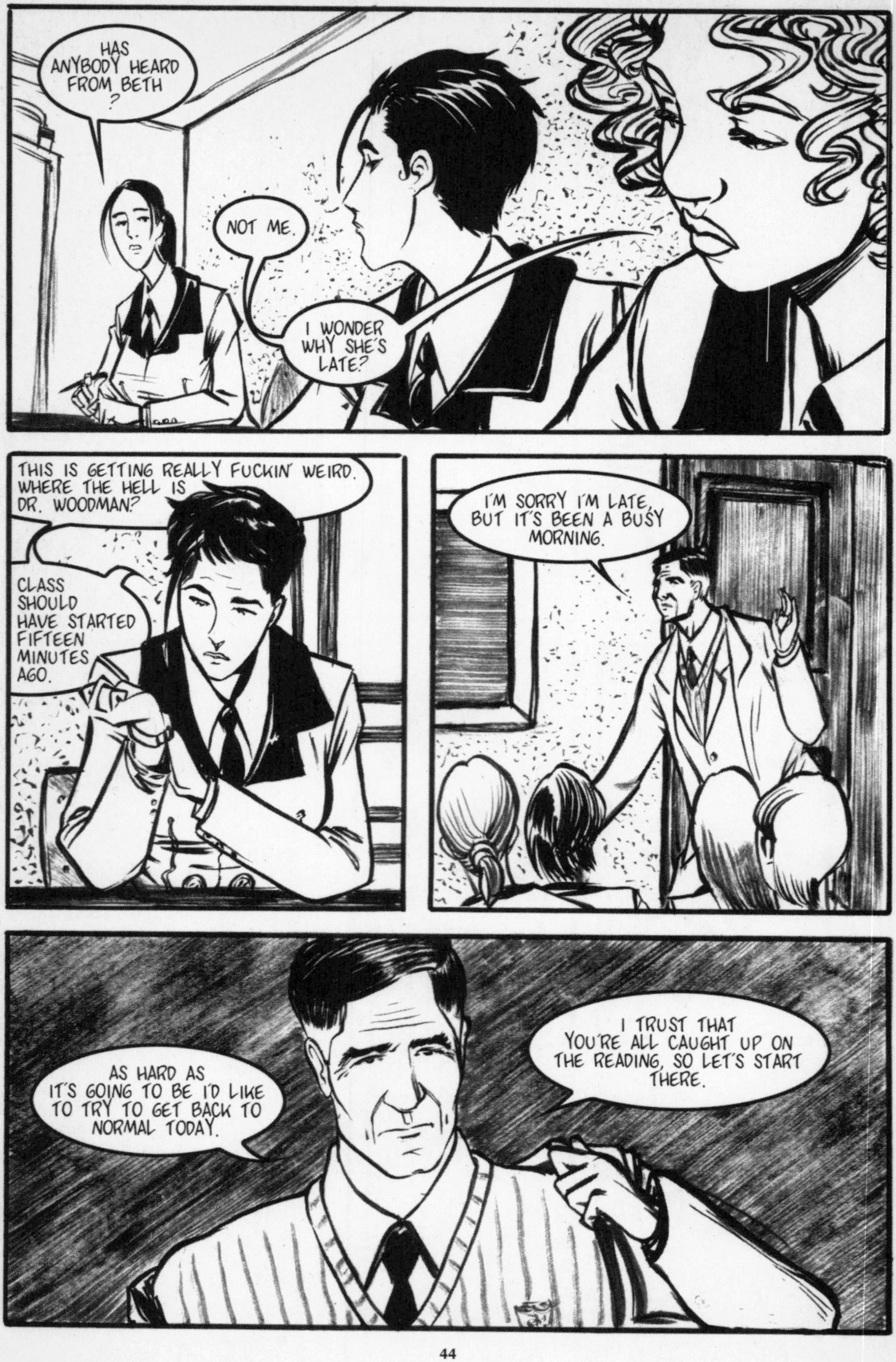
HAS ANYBODY HEARD FROM BETH ?
NOT ME.
I WONDER WHY SHE'S LATE?
THIS IS GETTING REALLY FUCKIN' WEIRD. WHERE THE HELL IS DR. WOODMAN?
CLASS SHOULD HAVE STARTED FIFTEEN MINUTES AGO.
I'M SORRY I'M LATE, BUT IT'S BEEN A BUSY MORNING.
AS HARD AS IT'S GOING TO BE I'D LIKE TO TRY TO GET BACK TO NORMAL TODAY.
I TRUST THAT YOU'RE ALL CAUGHT UP ON THE READING, SO LET'S START THERE.

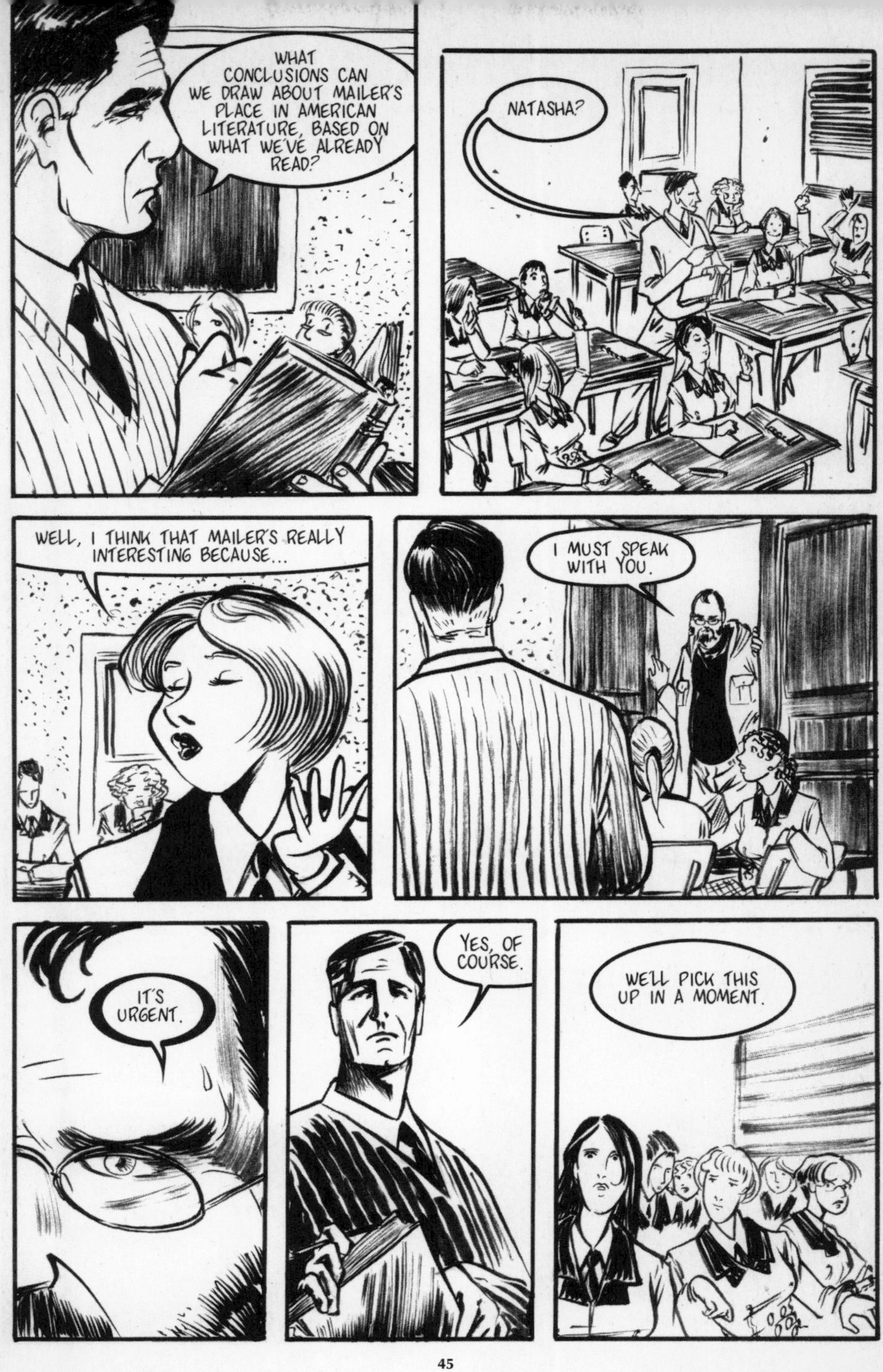
WHAT CONCLUSIONS CAN WE DRAW ABOUT MAILER'S PLACE IN AMERICAN LITERATURE, BASED ON WHAT WE'VE ALREADY READ?
NATASHA?
WELL, I THINK THAT MAILER'S REALLY INTERESTING BECAUSE...
I MUST SPEAK WITH YOU.
IT'S URGENT.
YES, OF COURSE.
WE'LL PICK THIS UP IN A MOMENT.

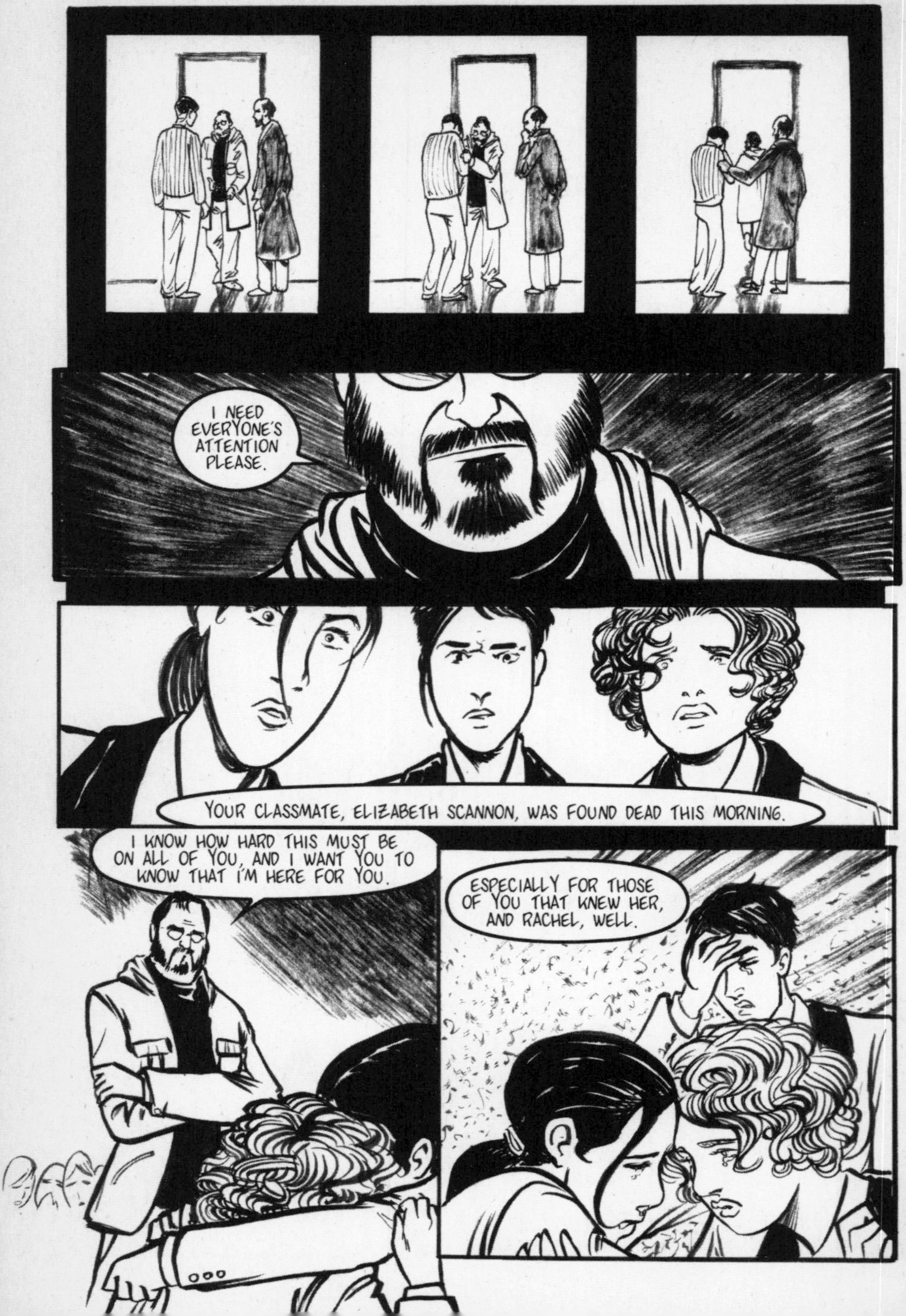
I NEED EVERYONE'S ATTENTION PLEASE.
YOUR CLASSMATE, ELIZABETH SCANNON, WAS FOUND DEAD THIS MORNING.
I KNOW HOW HARD THIS MUST BE ON ALL OF YOU, AND I WANT YOU TO KNOW THAT I'M HERE FOR YOU.
ESPECIALLY FOR THOSE OF YOU THAT KNEW HER, AND RACHEL, WELL.

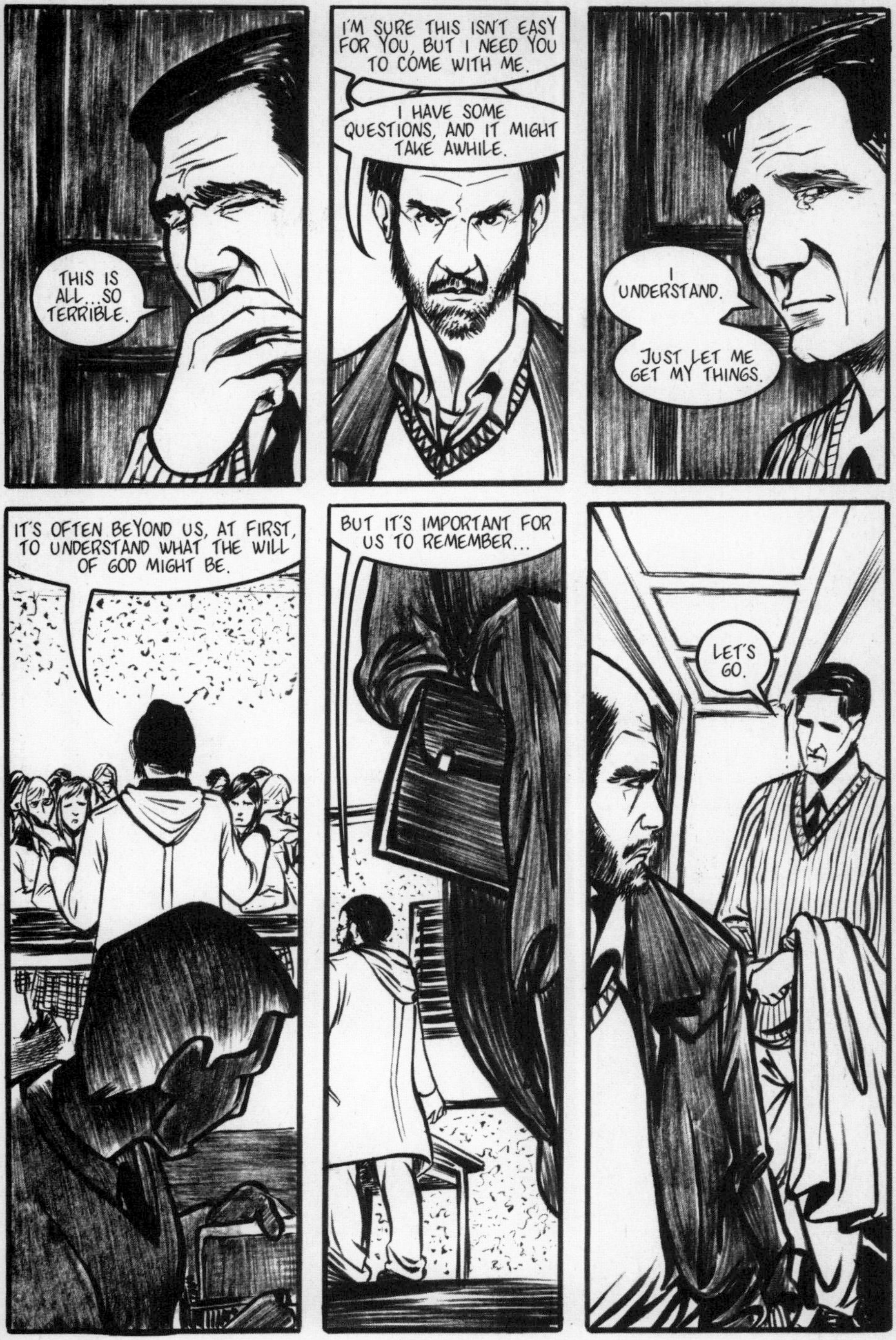
THIS IS ALL...SO TERRIBLE.
I'M SURE THIS ISN'T EASY FOR YOU, BUT I NEED YOU TO COME WITH ME.
I HAVE SOME QUESTIONS, AND IT MIGHT TAKE AWHILE.
I UNDERSTAND.
JUST LET ME GET MY THINGS.
IT'S OFTEN BEYOND US, AT FIRST, TO UNDERSTAND WHAT THE WILL OF GOD MIGHT BE.
BUT IT'S IMPORTANT FOR US TO REMEMBER...
LET'S GO.

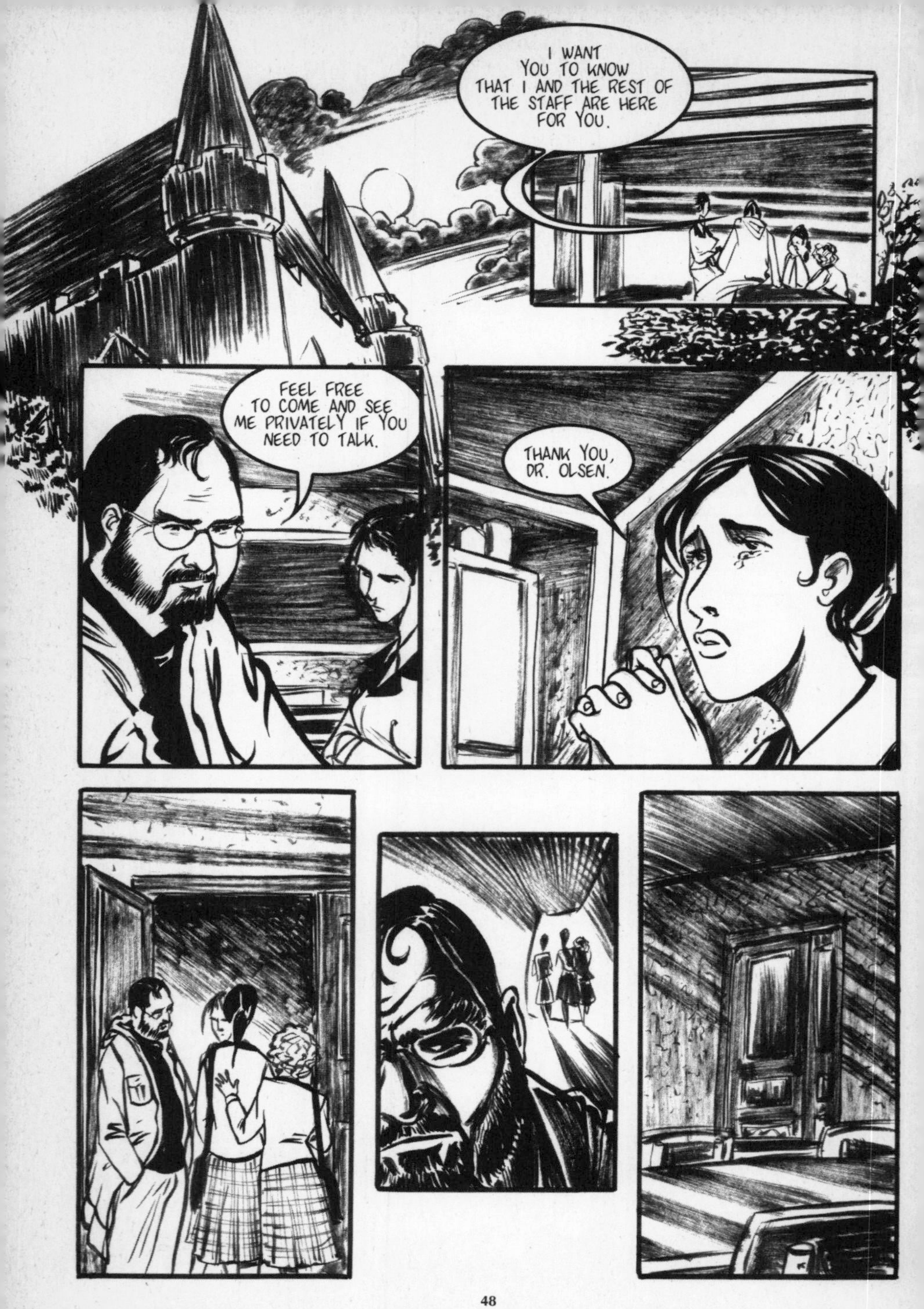
I WANT YOU TO KNOW THAT I AND THE REST OF THE STAFF ARE HERE FOR YOU.
FEEL FREE TO COME AND SEE ME PRIVATELY IF YOU NEED TO TALK.
THANK YOU, DR. OLSEN.

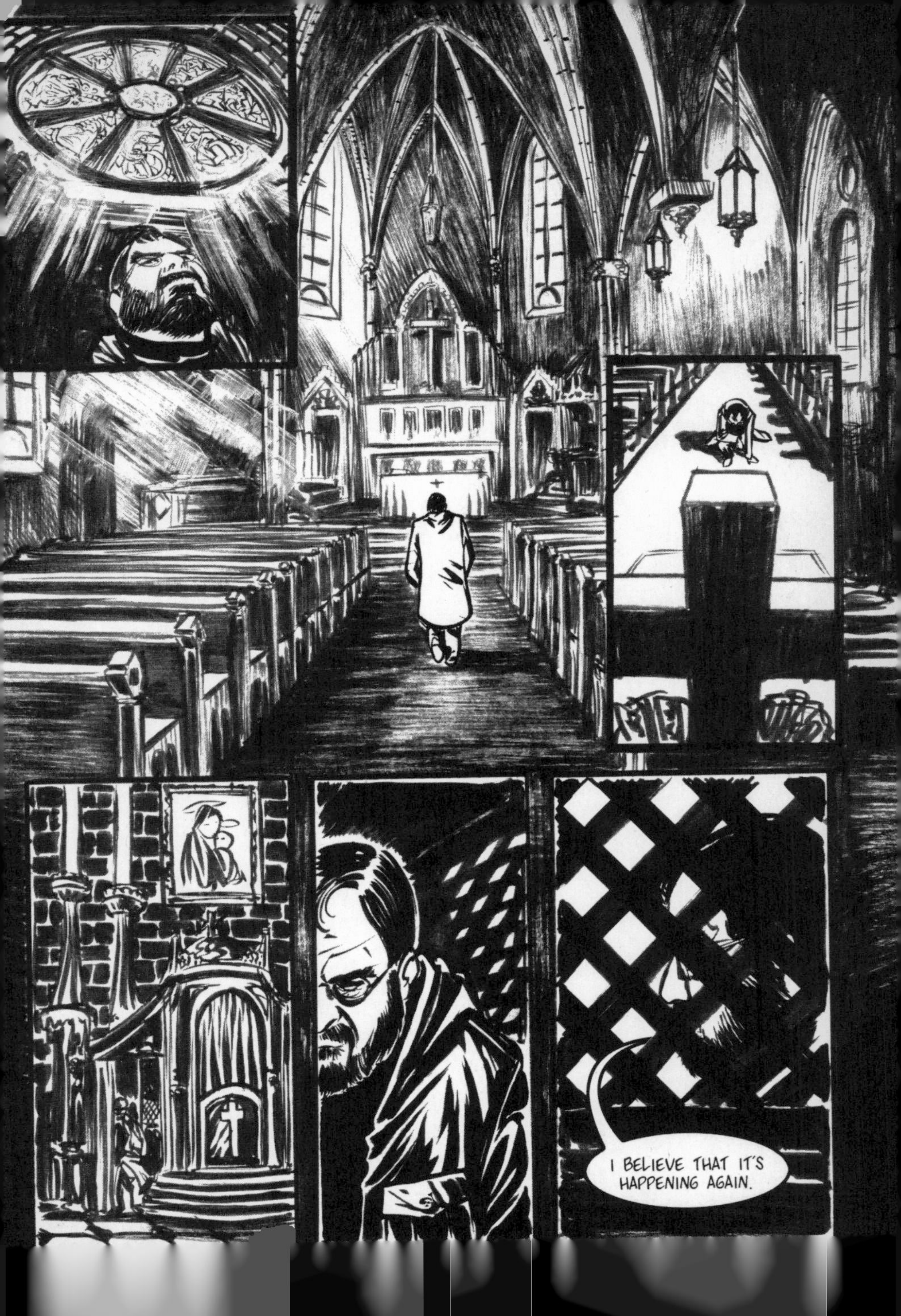
I BELIEVE THAT IT'S HAPPENING AGAIN.

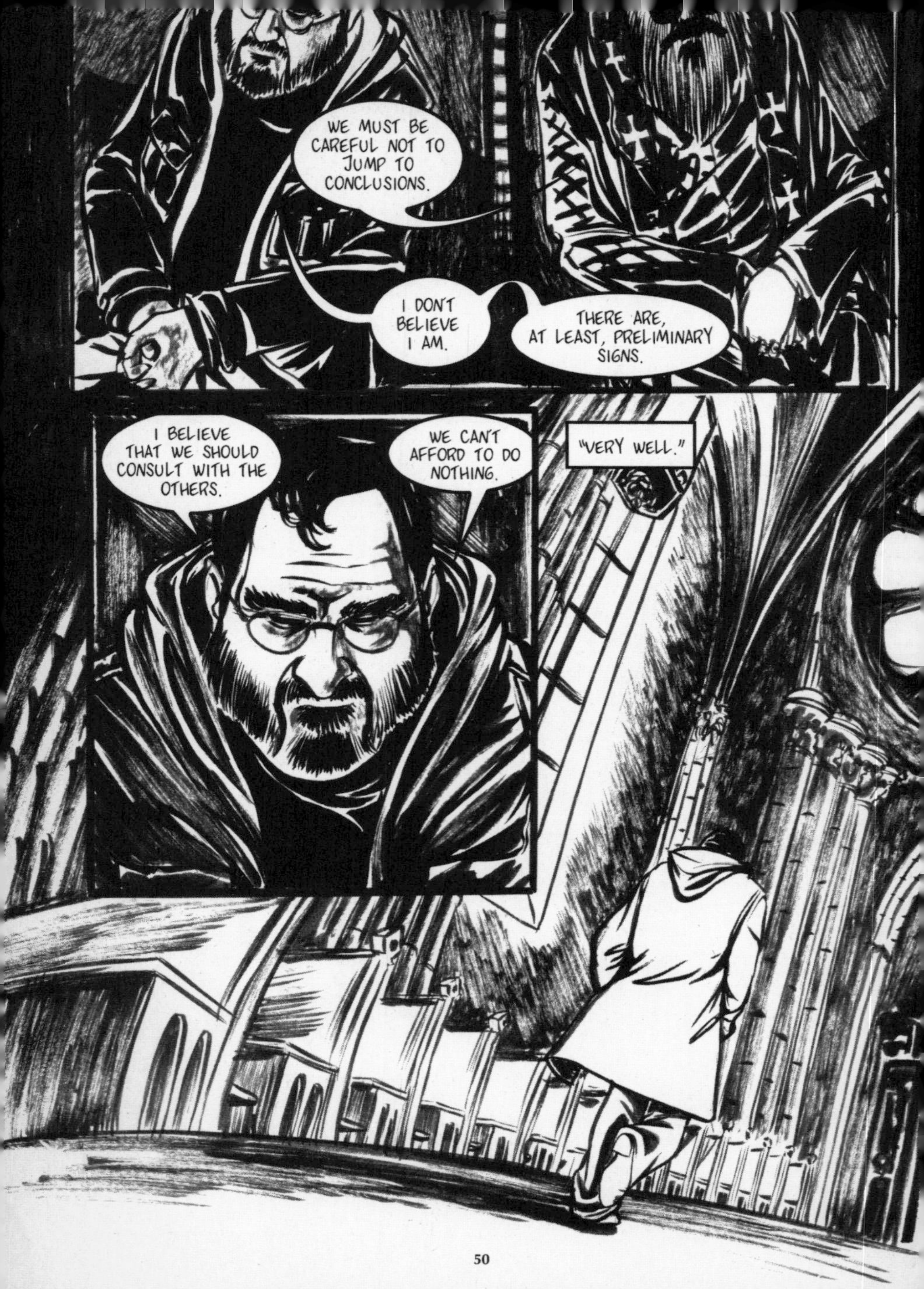
WE MUST BE CAREFUL NOT TO JUMP TO CONCLUSIONS.
I DON'T BELIEVE I AM.
THERE ARE, AT LEAST, PRELIMINARY SIGNS.
I BELIEVE THAT WE SHOULD CONSULT WITH THE OTHERS.
WE CAN'T AFFORD TO DO NOTHING.
"VERY WELL."

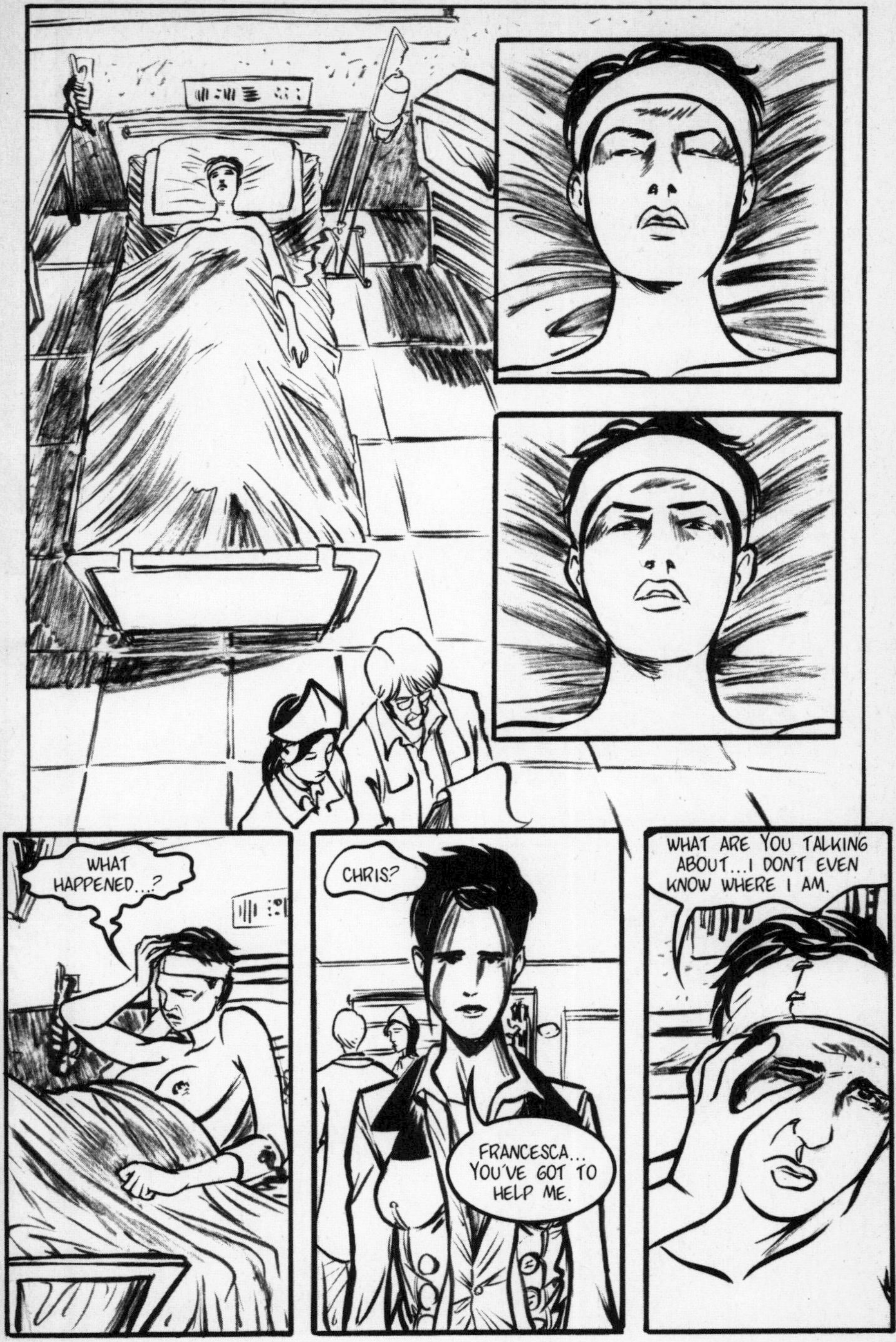
WHAT HAPPENED...?
CHRIS?
FRANCESCA... YOU'VE GOT TO HELP ME.
WHAT ARE YOU TALKING ABOUT...I DON'T EVEN KNOW WHERE I AM.

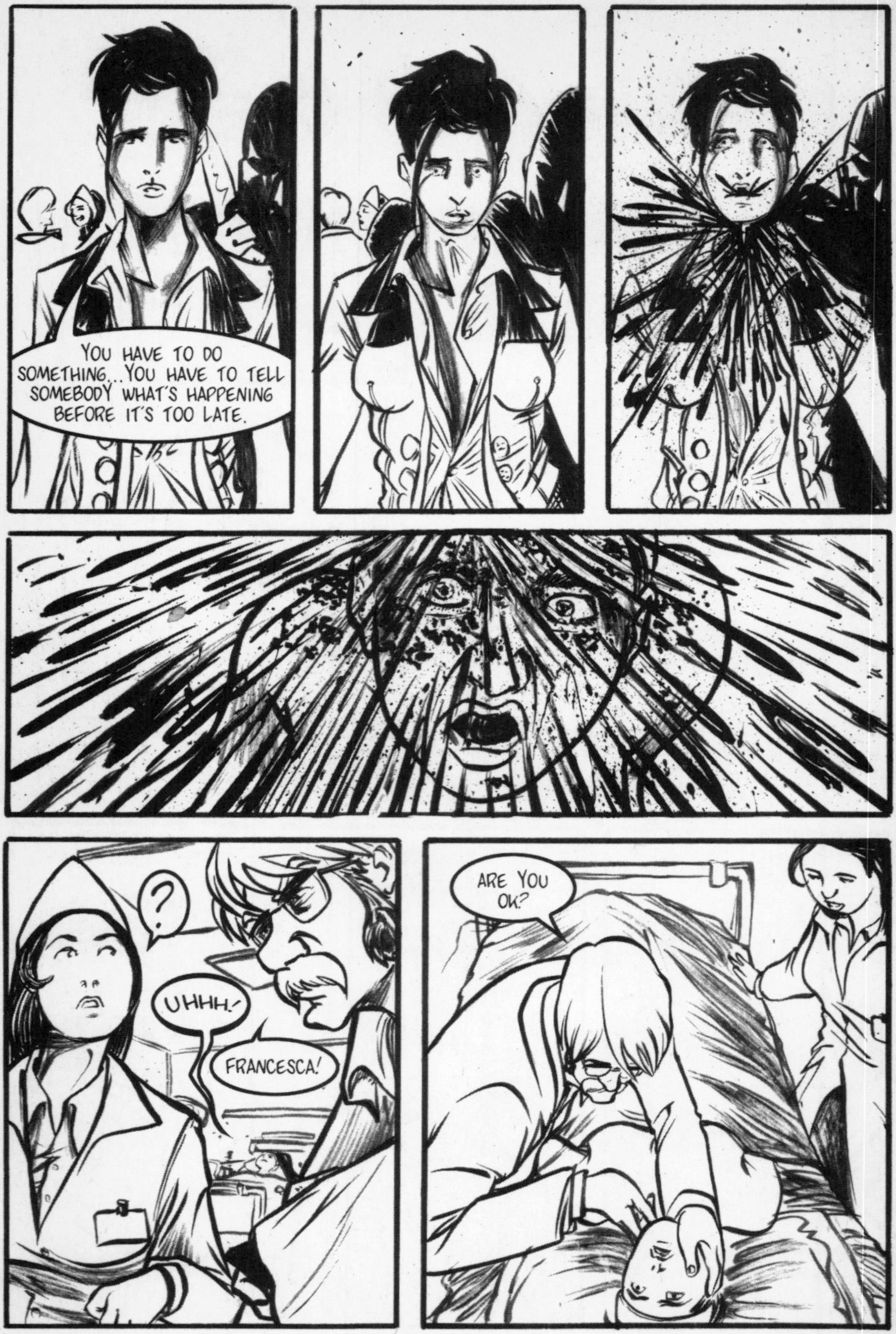
YOU HAVE TO DO SOMETHING...YOU HAVE TO TELL SOMEBODY WHAT'S HAPPENING BEFORE IT'S TOO LATE.
?
UHHH!
FRANCESCA!
ARE YOU OK?

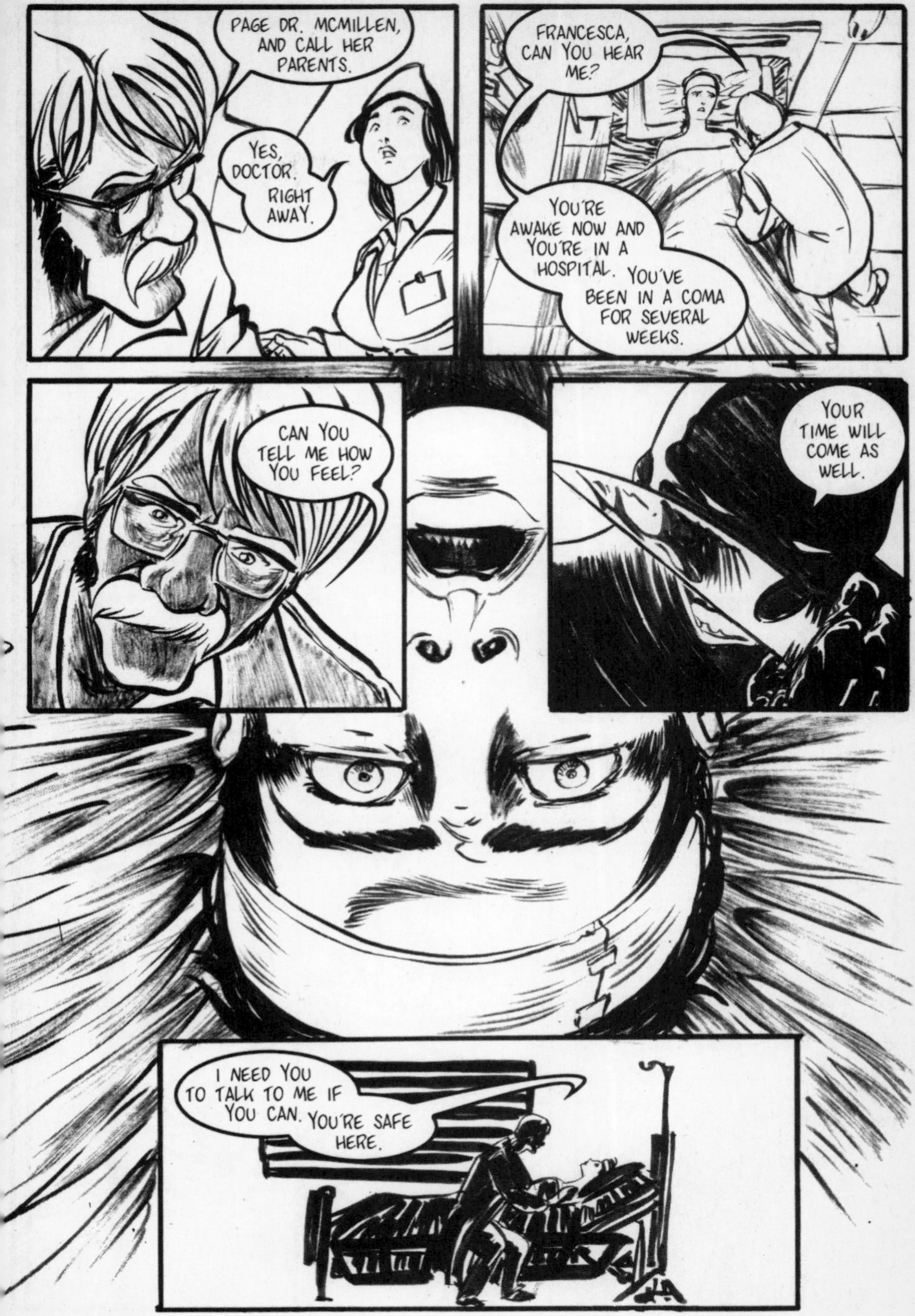
PAGE DR. MCMILLEN, AND CALL HER PARENTS.
YES, DOCTOR. RIGHT AWAY.
FRANCESCA, CAN YOU HEAR ME?
YOU'RE AWAKE NOW AND YOU'RE IN A HOSPITAL. YOU'VE BEEN IN A COMA FOR SEVERAL WEEKS.
CAN YOU TELL ME HOW YOU FEEL?
YOUR TIME WILL COME AS WELL.
I NEED YOU TO TALK TO ME IF YOU CAN. YOU'RE SAFE HERE.

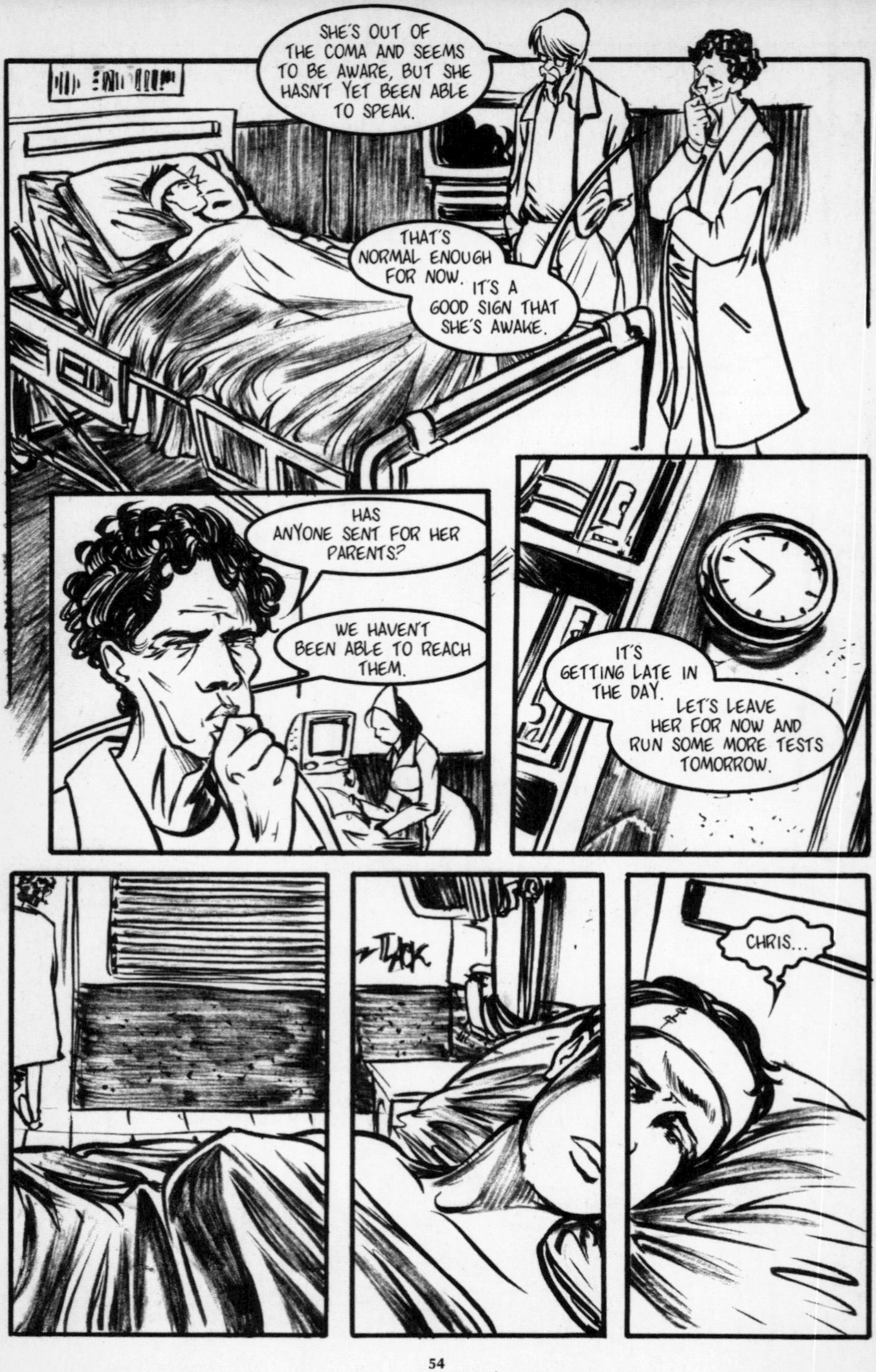
SHE'S OUT OF THE COMA AND SEEMS TO BE AWARE, BUT SHE HASN'T YET BEEN ABLE TO SPEAK.
THAT'S NORMAL ENOUGH FOR NOW.
IT'S A GOOD SIGN THAT SHE'S AWAKE.
HAS ANYONE SENT FOR HER PARENTS?
WE HAVEN'T BEEN ABLE TO REACH THEM.
IT'S GETTING LATE IN THE DAY.
LET'S LEAVE HER FOR NOW AND RUN SOME MORE TESTS TOMORROW.
TLACK
CHRIS...

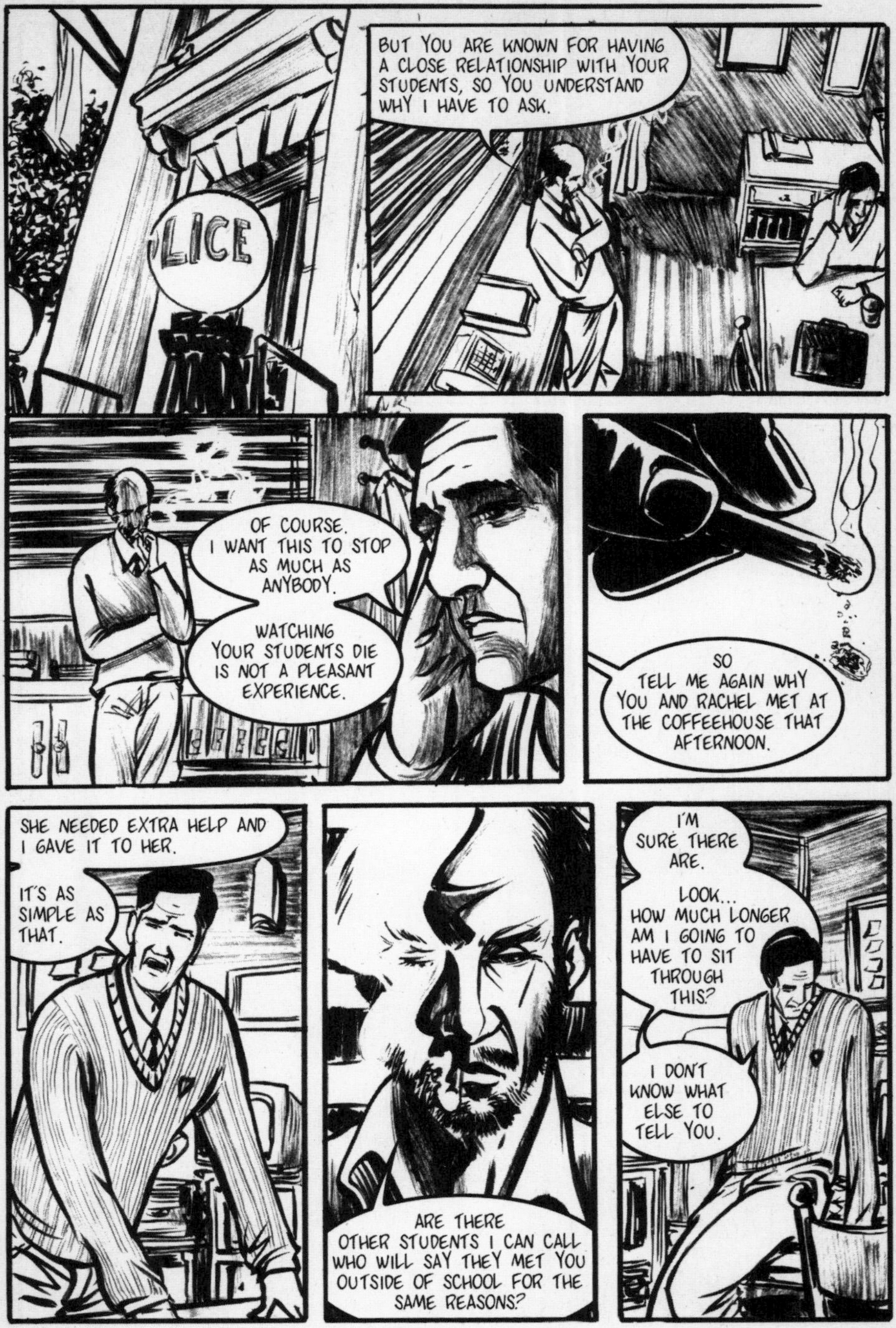
LICE
BUT YOU ARE KNOWN FOR HAVING A CLOSE RELATIONSHIP WITH YOUR STUDENTS, SO YOU UNDERSTAND WHY I HAVE TO ASK.
OF COURSE. I WANT THIS TO STOP AS MUCH AS ANYBODY.
WATCHING YOUR STUDENTS DIE IS NOT A PLEASANT EXPERIENCE.
SO TELL ME AGAIN WHY YOU AND RACHEL MET AT THE COFFEEHOUSE THAT AFTERNOON.
SHE NEEDED EXTRA HELP AND I GAVE IT TO HER.
IT'S AS SIMPLE AS THAT.
ARE THERE OTHER STUDENTS I CAN CALL WHO WILL SAY THEY MET YOU OUTSIDE OF SCHOOL FOR THE SAME REASONS?
I'M SURE THERE ARE.
LOOK... HOW MUCH LONGER AM I GOING TO HAVE TO SIT THROUGH THIS?
I DON'T KNOW WHAT ELSE TO TELL YOU.

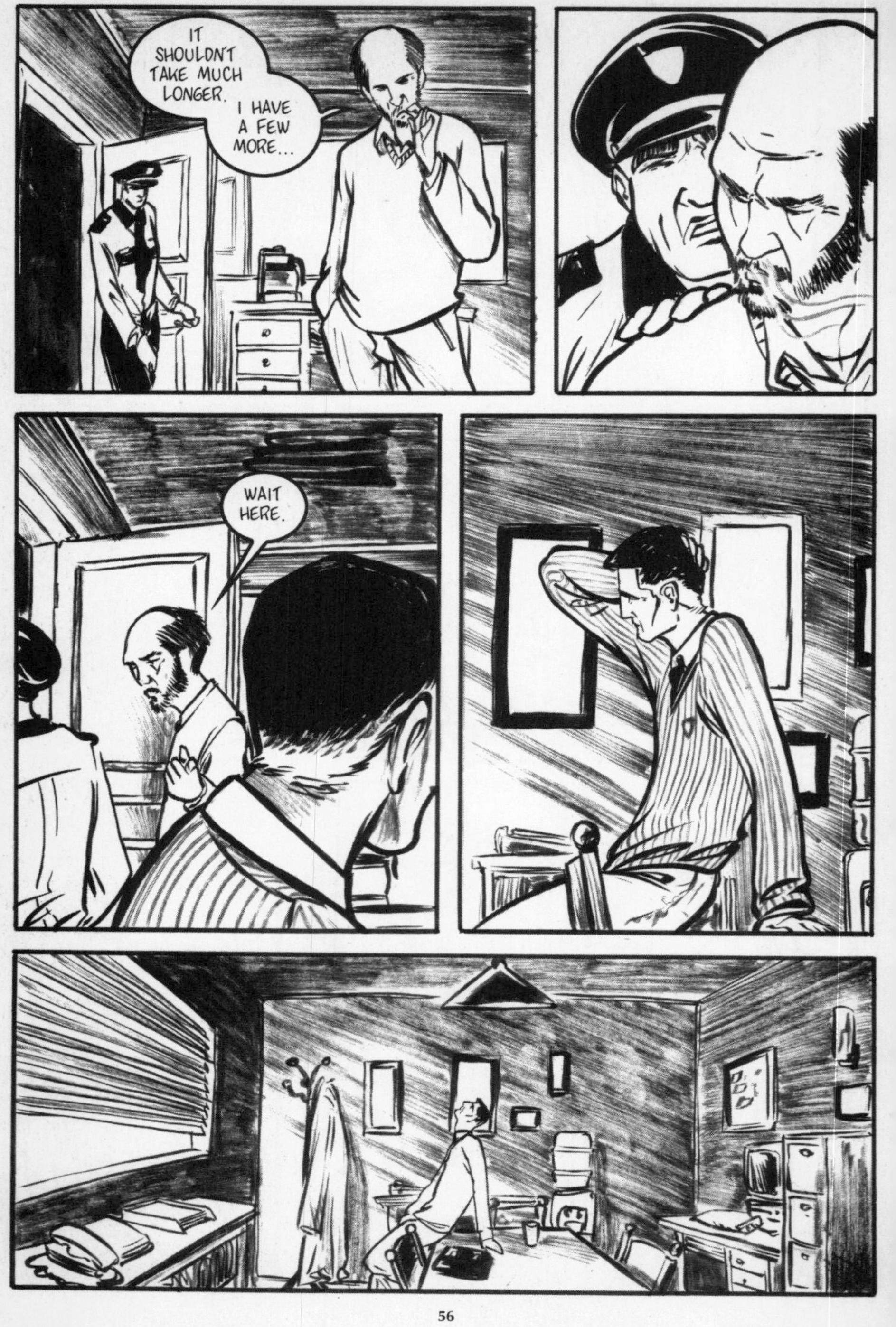
IT SHOULDN'T TAKE MUCH LONGER.
I HAVE A FEW MORE...
WAIT HERE.

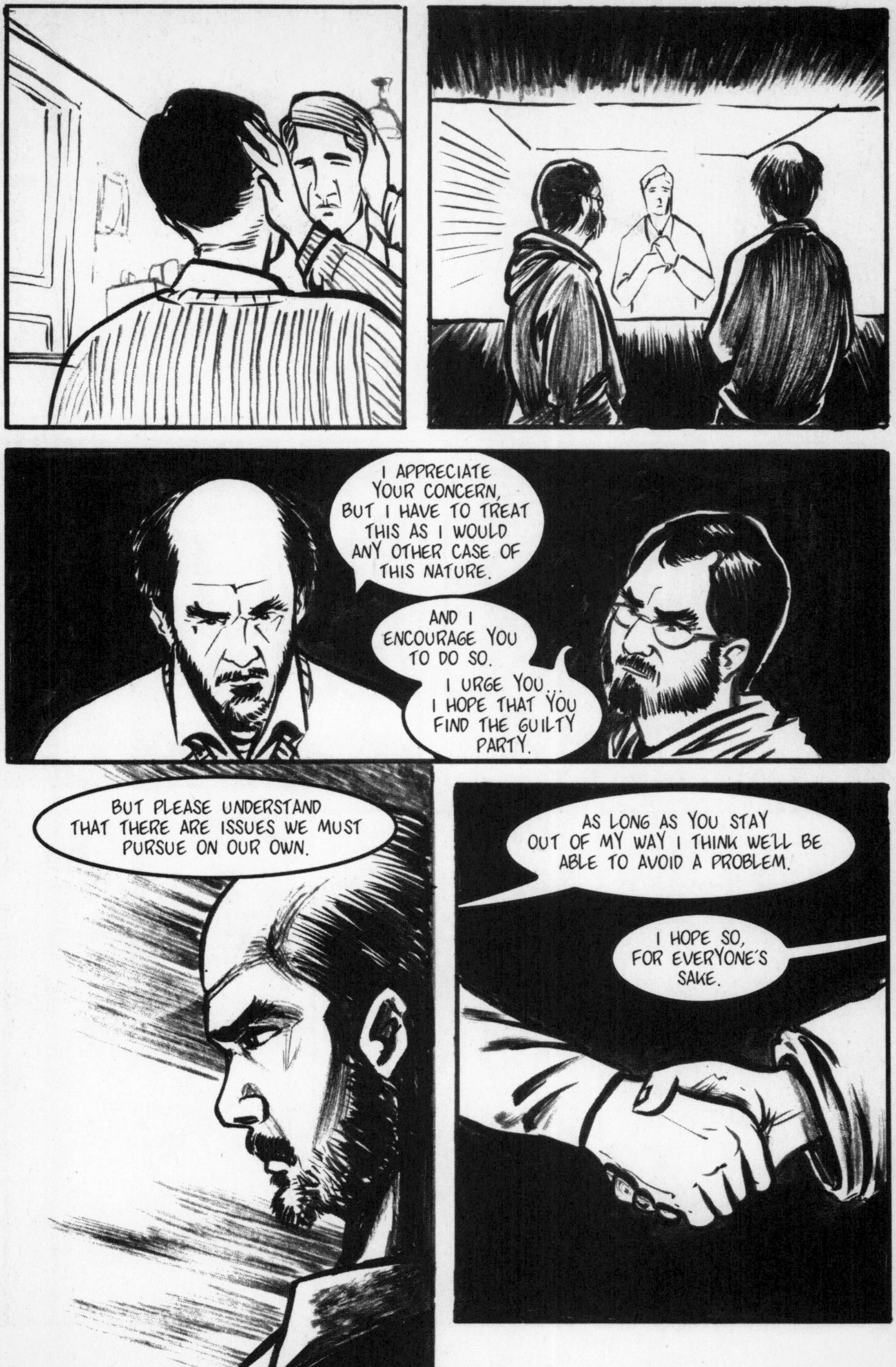
I APPRECIATE YOUR CONCERN, BUT I HAVE TO TREAT THIS AS I WOULD ANY OTHER CASE OF THIS NATURE.
AND I ENCOURAGE YOU TO DO SO.
I URGE YOU... I HOPE THAT YOU FIND THE GUILTY PARTY.
BUT PLEASE UNDERSTAND THAT THERE ARE ISSUES WE MUST PURSUE ON OUR OWN.
AS LONG AS YOU STAY OUT OF MY WAY I THINK WE'LL BE ABLE TO AVOID A PROBLEM.
I HOPE SO, FOR EVERYONE'S SAKE.

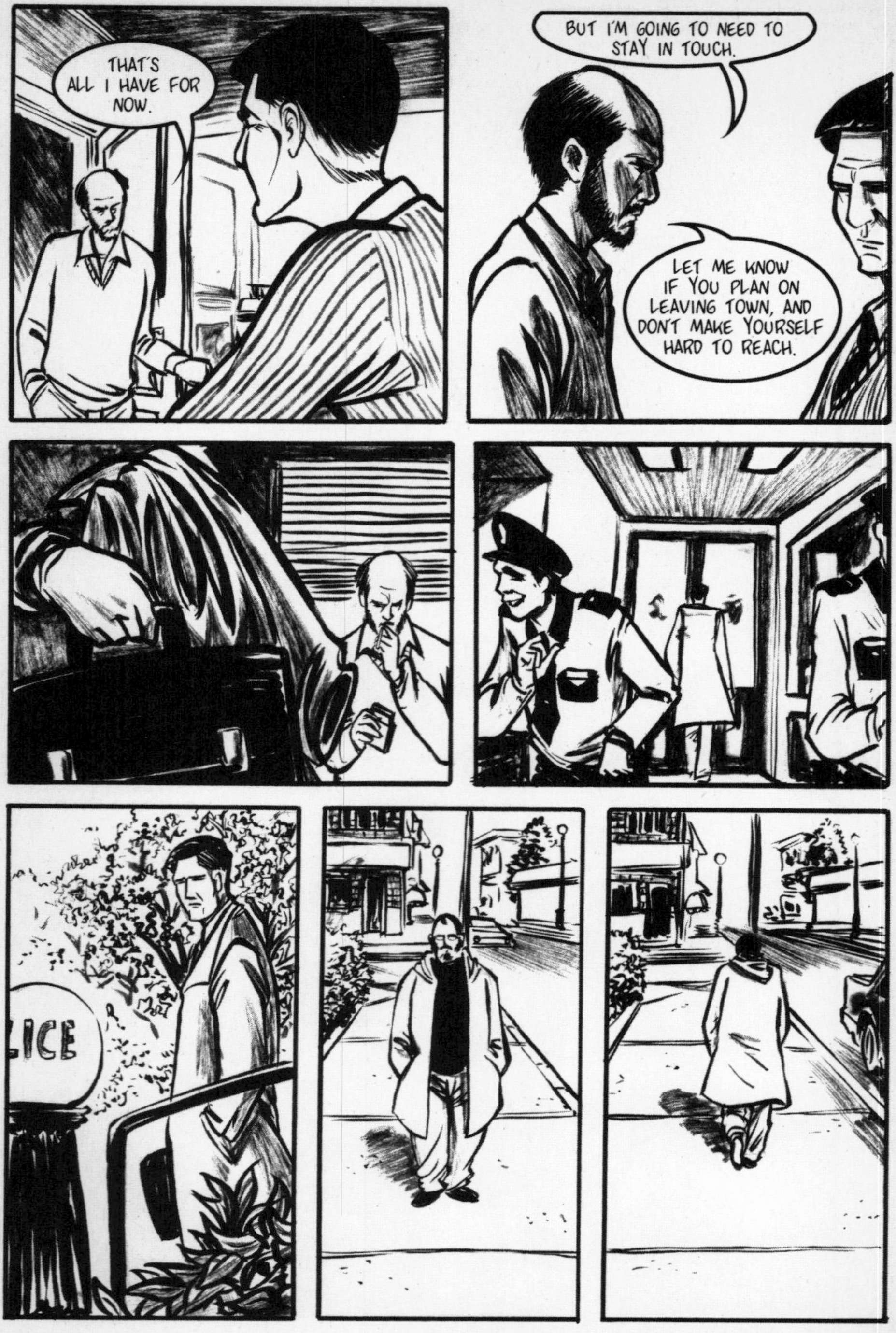
THAT'S ALL I HAVE FOR NOW.
BUT I'M GOING TO NEED TO STAY IN TOUCH.
LET ME KNOW IF YOU PLAN ON LEAVING TOWN, AND DON'T MAKE YOURSELF HARD TO REACH.
LICE

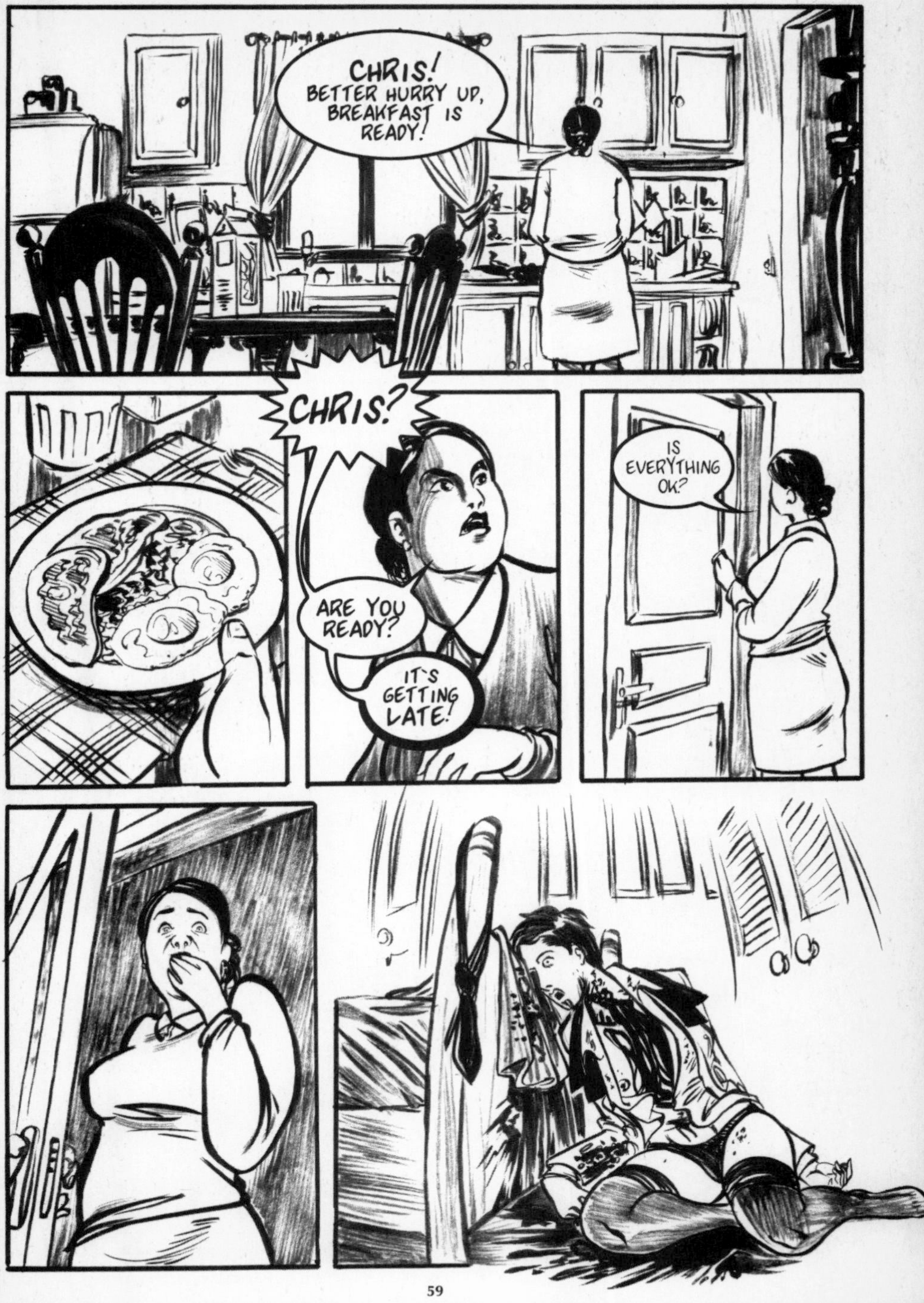
CHRIS! BETTER HURRY UP, BREAKFAST IS READY!
CHRIS?
ARE YOU READY?
IT`S GETTING LATE!
IS EVERYTHING OK?

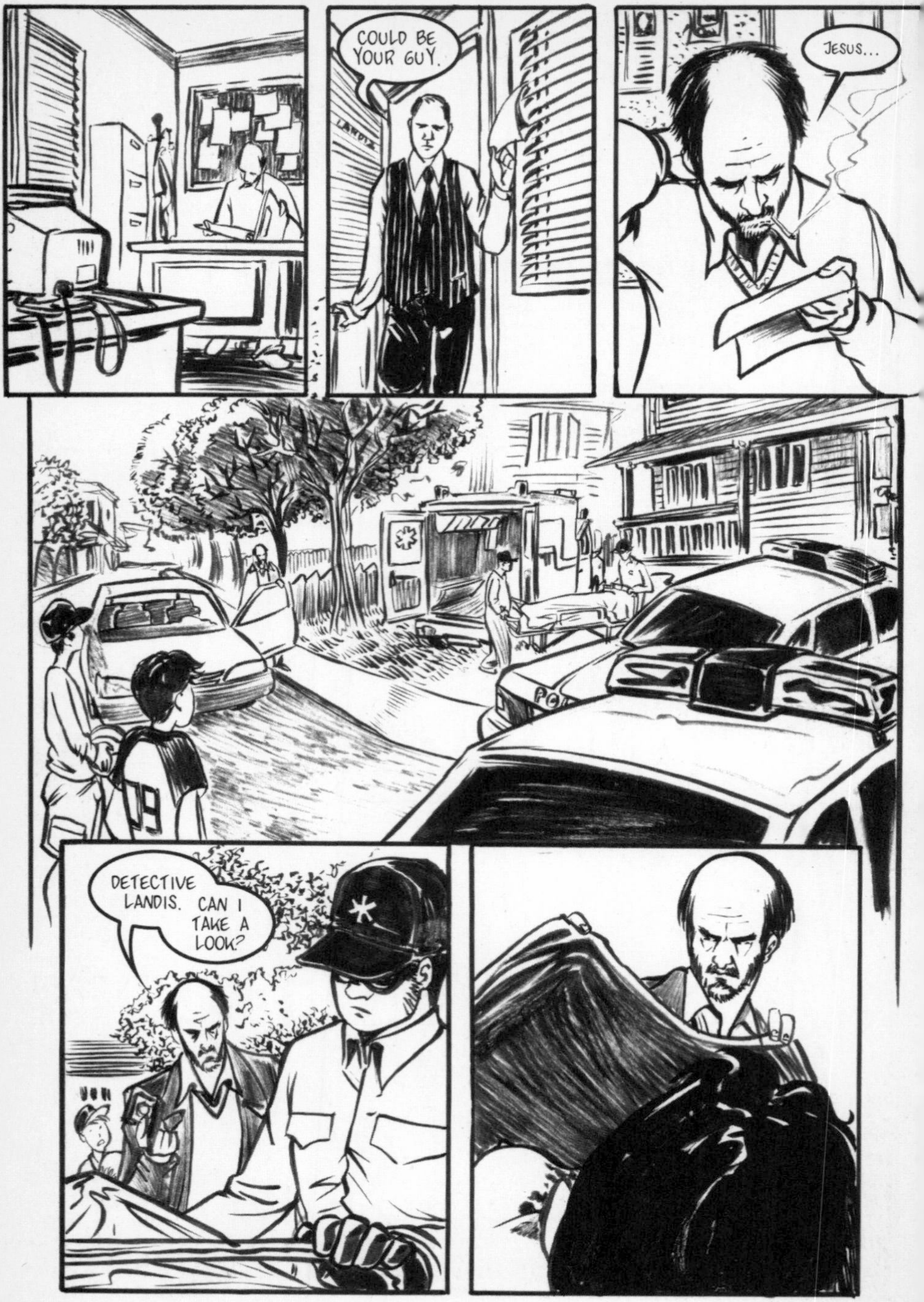
COULD BE YOUR GUY.
JESUS...
DETECTIVE LANDIS. CAN I TAKE A LOOK?

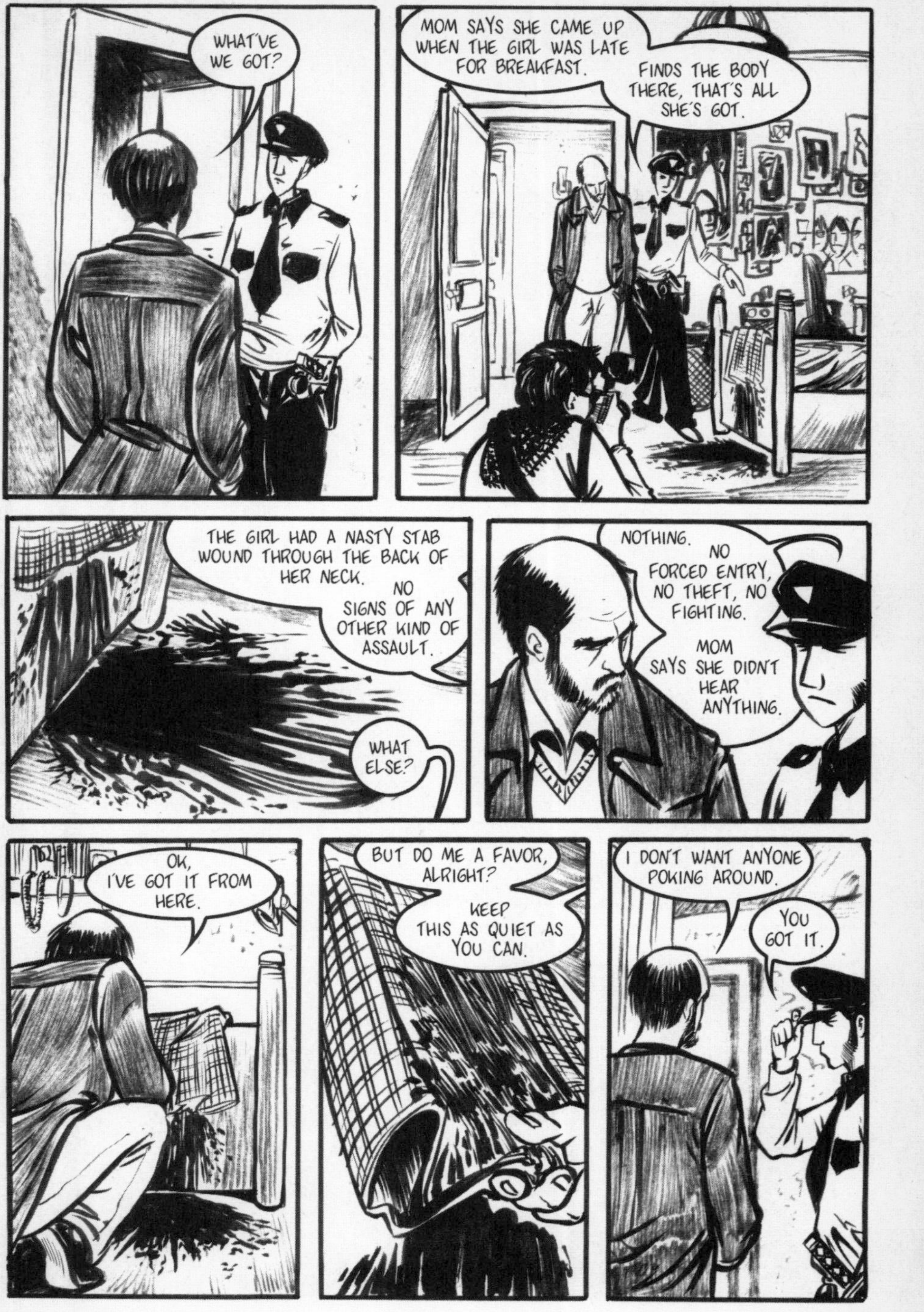
WHAT'VE WE GOT?
MOM SAYS SHE CAME UP WHEN THE GIRL WAS LATE FOR BREAKFAST.
FINDS THE BODY THERE, THAT'S ALL SHE'S GOT.
THE GIRL HAD A NASTY STAB WOUND THROUGH THE BACK OF HER NECK.
NO SIGNS OF ANY OTHER KIND OF ASSAULT.
WHAT ELSE?
NOTHING.
NO FORCED ENTRY, NO THEFT, NO FIGHTING.
MOM SAYS SHE DIDN'T HEAR ANYTHING.
OK, I'VE GOT IT FROM HERE.
BUT DO ME A FAVOR, ALRIGHT?
KEEP THIS AS QUIET AS YOU CAN.
I DON'T WANT ANYONE POKING AROUND.
YOU GOT IT.

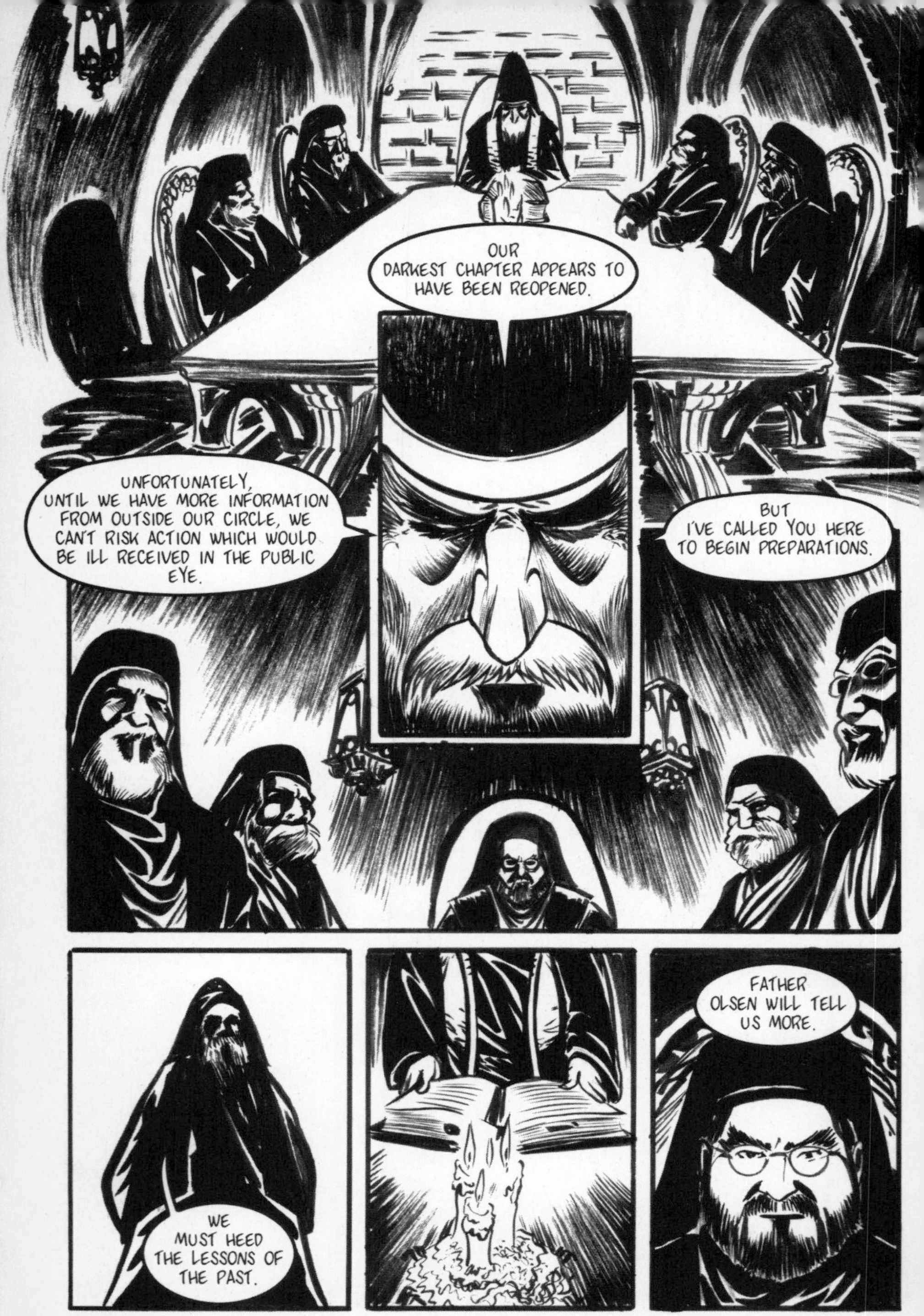
OUR DARKEST CHAPTER APPEARS TO HAVE BEEN REOPENED.
UNFORTUNATELY, UNTIL WE HAVE MORE INFORMATION FROM OUTSIDE OUR CIRCLE, WE CAN'T RISK ACTION WHICH WOULD BE ILL RECEIVED IN THE PUBLIC EYE.
BUT I'VE CALLED YOU HERE TO BEGIN PREPARATIONS.
WE MUST HEED THE LESSONS OF THE PAST.
FATHER OLSEN WILL TELL US MORE.

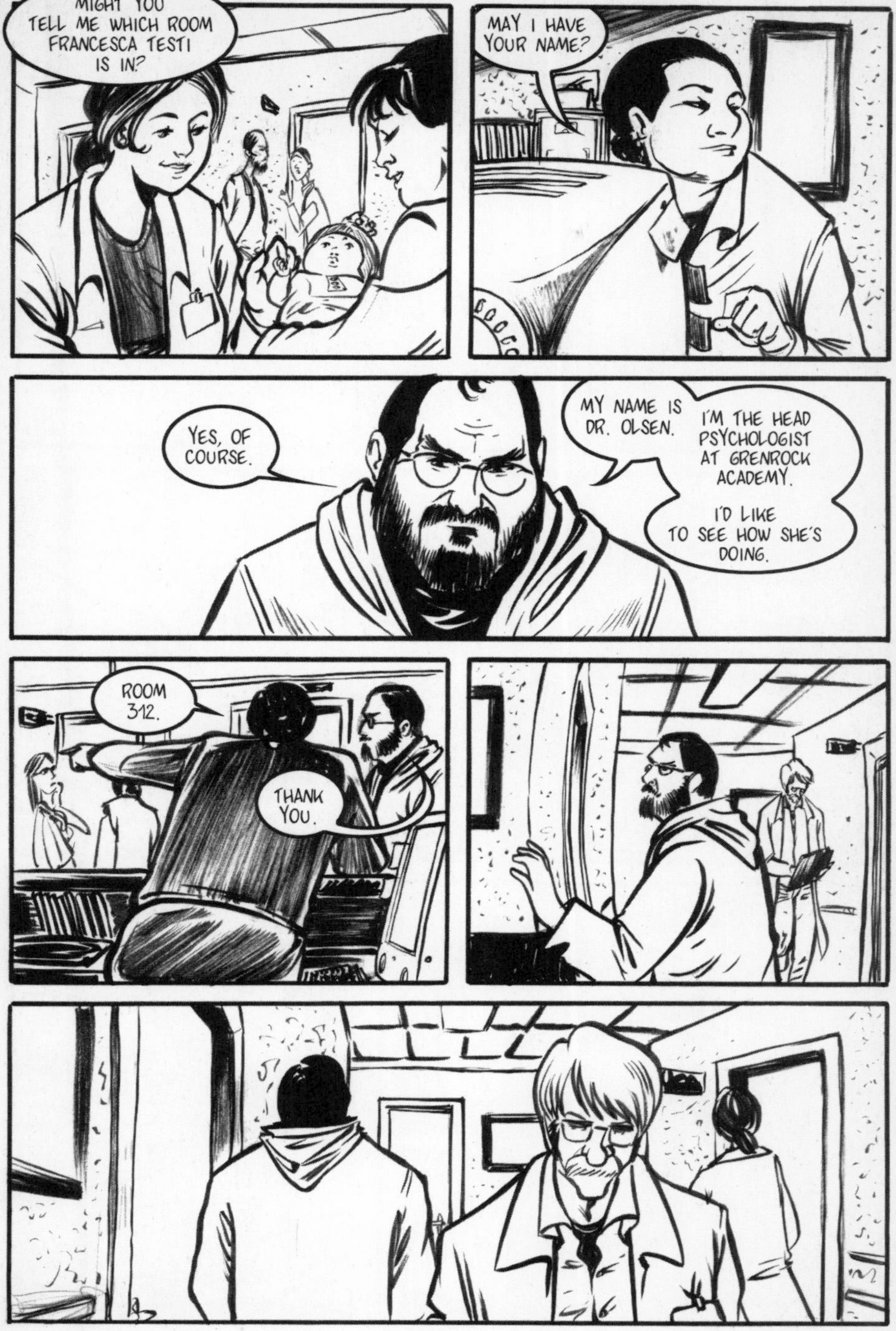
MIGHT YOU TELL ME WHICH ROOM FRANCESCA TESTI IS IN?
MAY I HAVE YOUR NAME?
YES, OF COURSE.
MY NAME IS DR. OLSEN.
I'M THE HEAD PSYCHOLOGIST AT GRENROCK ACADEMY.
I'D LIKE TO SEE HOW SHE'S DOING.
ROOM 312.
THANK YOU.

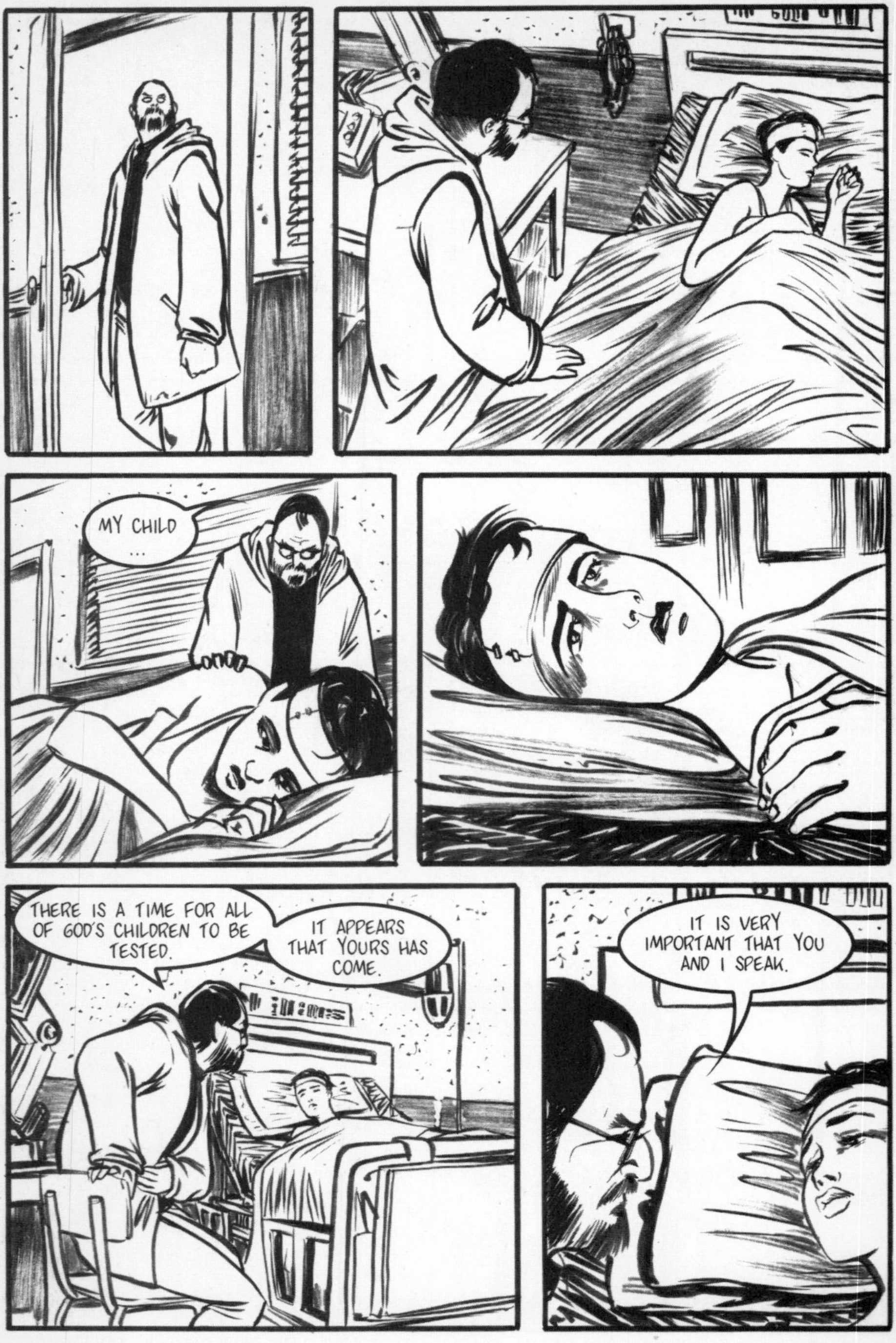
MY CHILD ...
THERE IS A TIME FOR ALL OF GOD'S CHILDREN TO BE TESTED.
IT APPEARS THAT YOURS HAS COME.
IT IS VERY IMPORTANT THAT YOU AND I SPEAK.

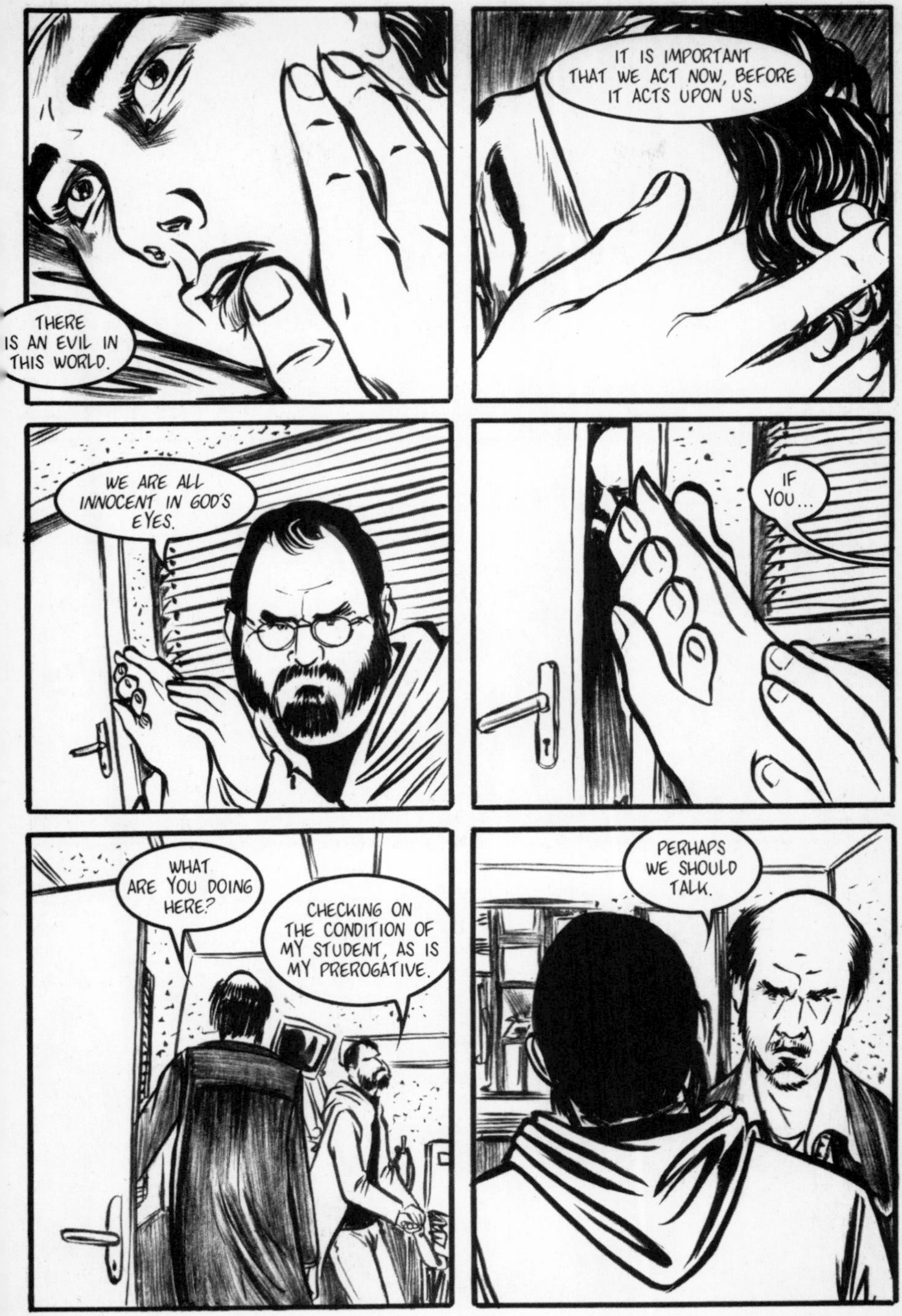
THERE IS AN EVIL IN THIS WORLD.
IT IS IMPORTANT THAT WE ACT NOW, BEFORE IT ACTS UPON US.
WE ARE ALL INNOCENT IN GOD'S EYES.
IF YOU...
WHAT ARE YOU DOING HERE?
CHECKING ON THE CONDITION OF MY STUDENT, AS IS MY PREROGATIVE.
PERHAPS WE SHOULD TALK.

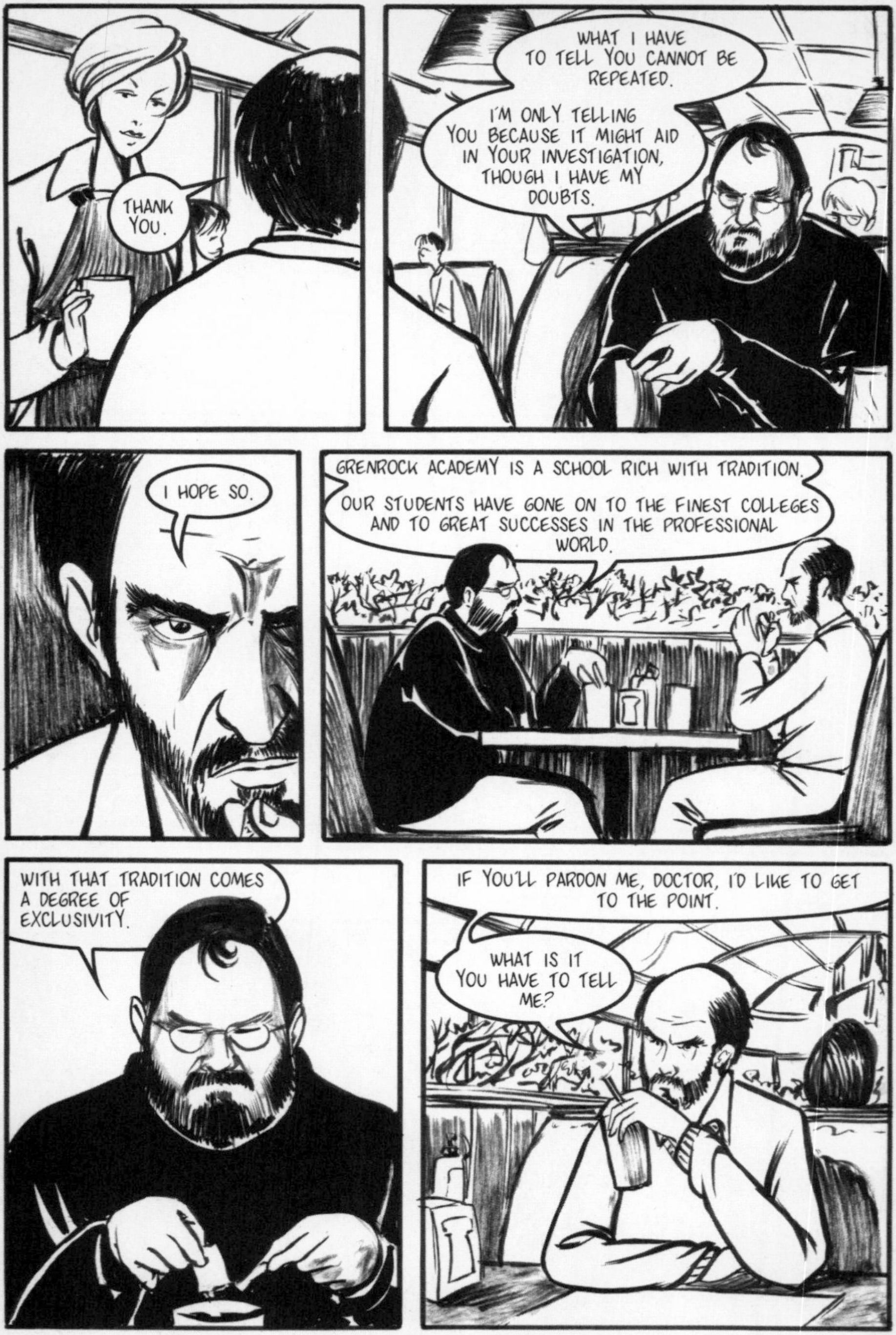
THANK YOU.
WHAT I HAVE TO TELL YOU CANNOT BE REPEATED.
I'M ONLY TELLING YOU BECAUSE IT MIGHT AID IN YOUR INVESTIGATION, THOUGH I HAVE MY DOUBTS.
I HOPE SO.
GRENROCK ACADEMY IS A SCHOOL RICH WITH TRADITION.
OUR STUDENTS HAVE GONE ON TO THE FINEST COLLEGES AND TO GREAT SUCCESSES IN THE PROFESSIONAL WORLD.
WITH THAT TRADITION COMES A DEGREE OF EXCLUSIVITY.
IF YOU'LL PARDON ME, DOCTOR, I'D LIKE TO GET TO THE POINT.
WHAT IS IT YOU HAVE TO TELL ME?

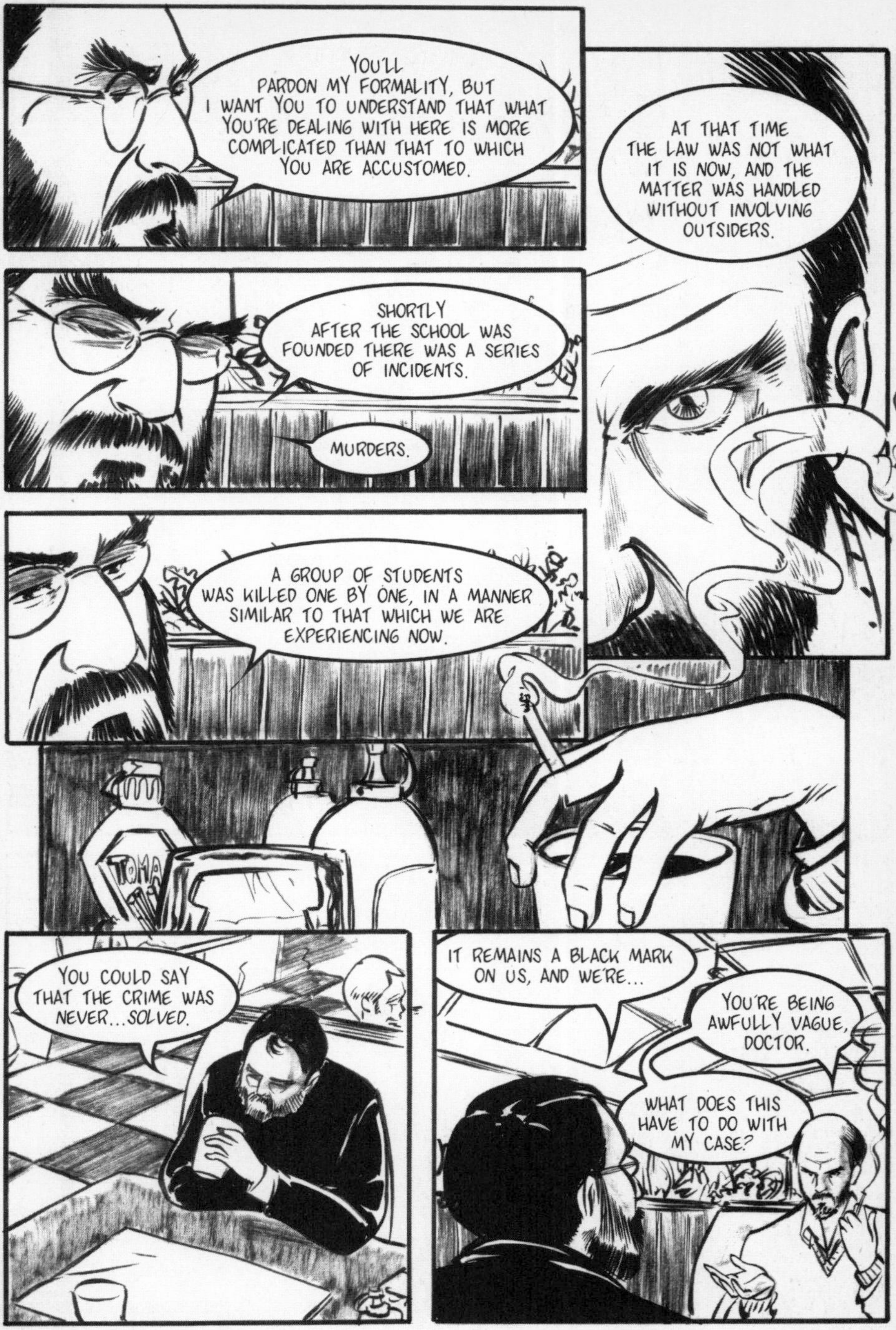
YOU'LL PARDON MY FORMALITY, BUT I WANT YOU TO UNDERSTAND THAT WHAT YOU'RE DEALING WITH HERE IS MORE COMPLICATED THAN THAT TO WHICH YOU ARE ACCUSTOMED.
AT THAT TIME THE LAW WAS NOT WHAT IT IS NOW, AND THE MATTER WAS HANDLED WITHOUT INVOLVING OUTSIDERS.
SHORTLY AFTER THE SCHOOL WAS FOUNDED THERE WAS A SERIES OF INCIDENTS.
MURDERS.
A GROUP OF STUDENTS WAS KILLED ONE BY ONE, IN A MANNER SIMILAR TO THAT WHICH WE ARE EXPERIENCING NOW.
TOMA
YOU COULD SAY THAT THE CRIME WAS NEVER...SOLVED.
IT REMAINS A BLACK MARK ON US, AND WE'RE...
YOU'RE BEING AWFULLY VAGUE, DOCTOR.
WHAT DOES THIS HAVE TO DO WITH MY CASE?

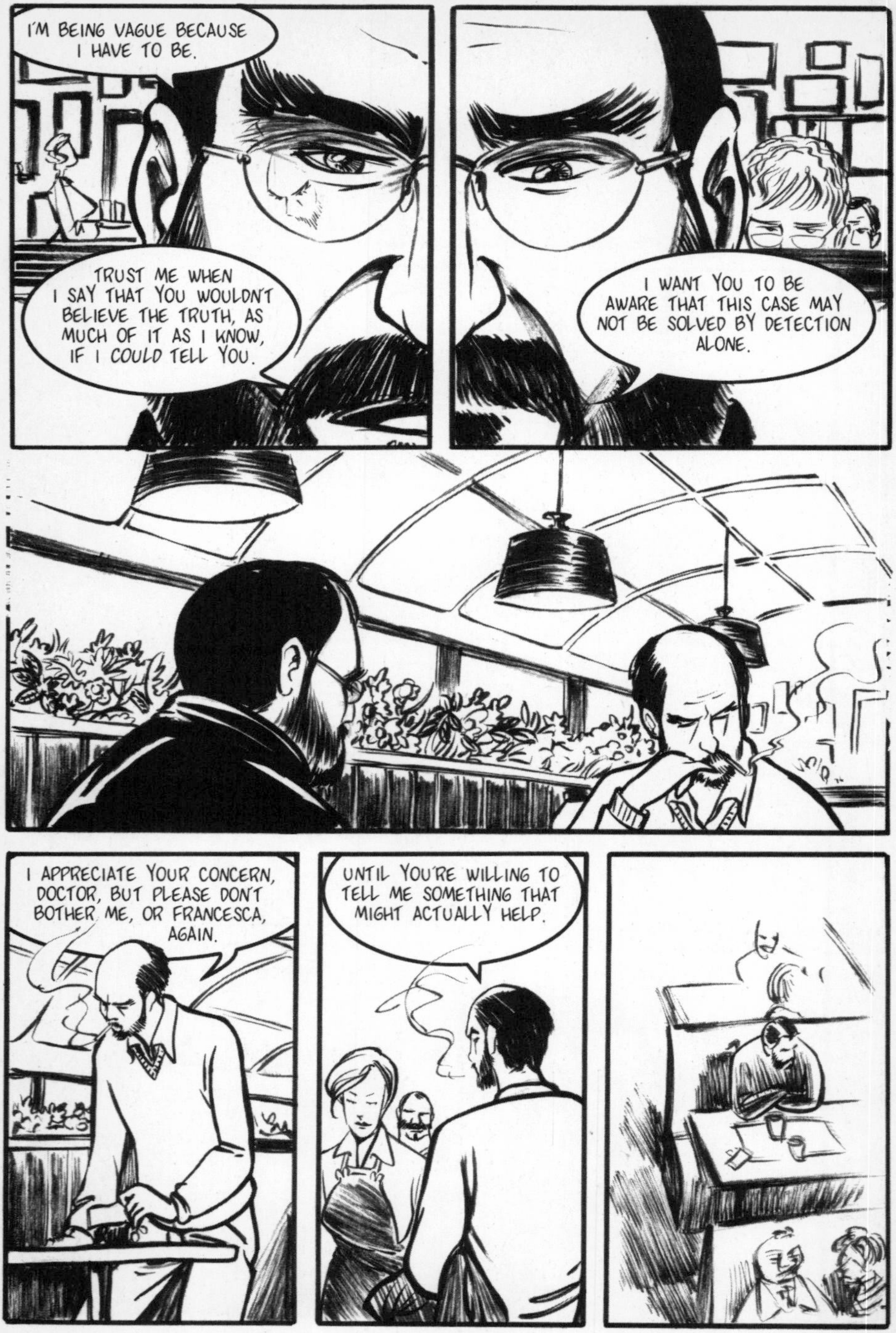
I'M BEING VAGUE BECAUSE I HAVE TO BE.
TRUST ME WHEN I SAY THAT YOU WOULDN'T BELIEVE THE TRUTH, AS MUCH OF IT AS I KNOW, IF I COULD TELL YOU.
I WANT YOU TO BE AWARE THAT THIS CASE MAY NOT BE SOLVED BY DETECTION ALONE.
I APPRECIATE YOUR CONCERN, DOCTOR, BUT PLEASE DON'T BOTHER ME, OR FRANCESCA, AGAIN.
UNTIL YOU'RE WILLING TO TELL ME SOMETHING THAT MIGHT ACTUALLY HELP.

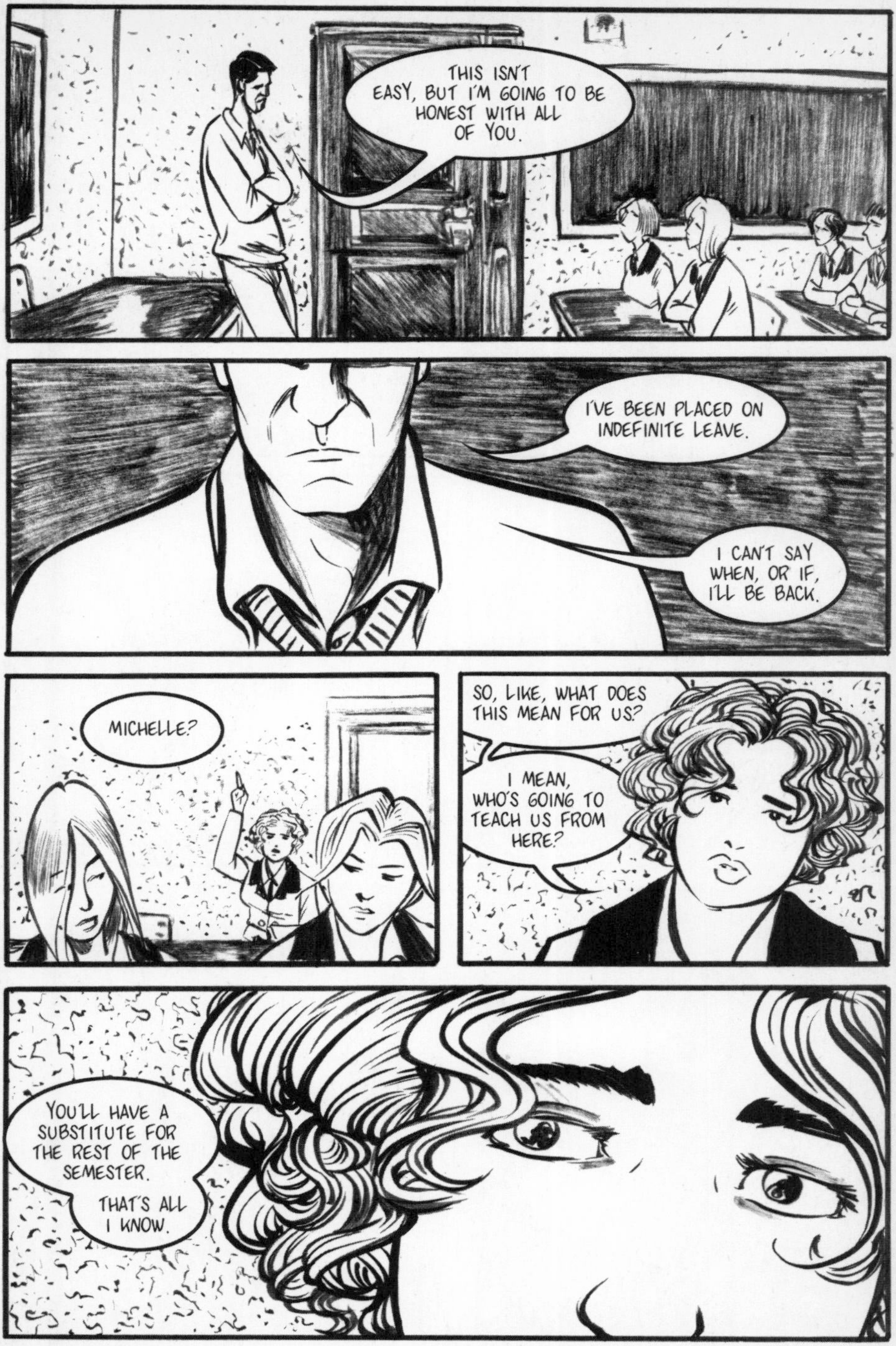
THIS ISN'T EASY, BUT I'M GOING TO BE HONEST WITH ALL OF YOU.
I'VE BEEN PLACED ON INDEFINITE LEAVE.
I CAN'T SAY WHEN, OR IF, I'LL BE BACK.
MICHELLE?
SO, LIKE, WHAT DOES THIS MEAN FOR US?
I MEAN, WHO'S GOING TO TEACH US FROM HERE?
YOU'LL HAVE A SUBSTITUTE FOR THE REST OF THE SEMESTER.
THAT'S ALL I KNOW.

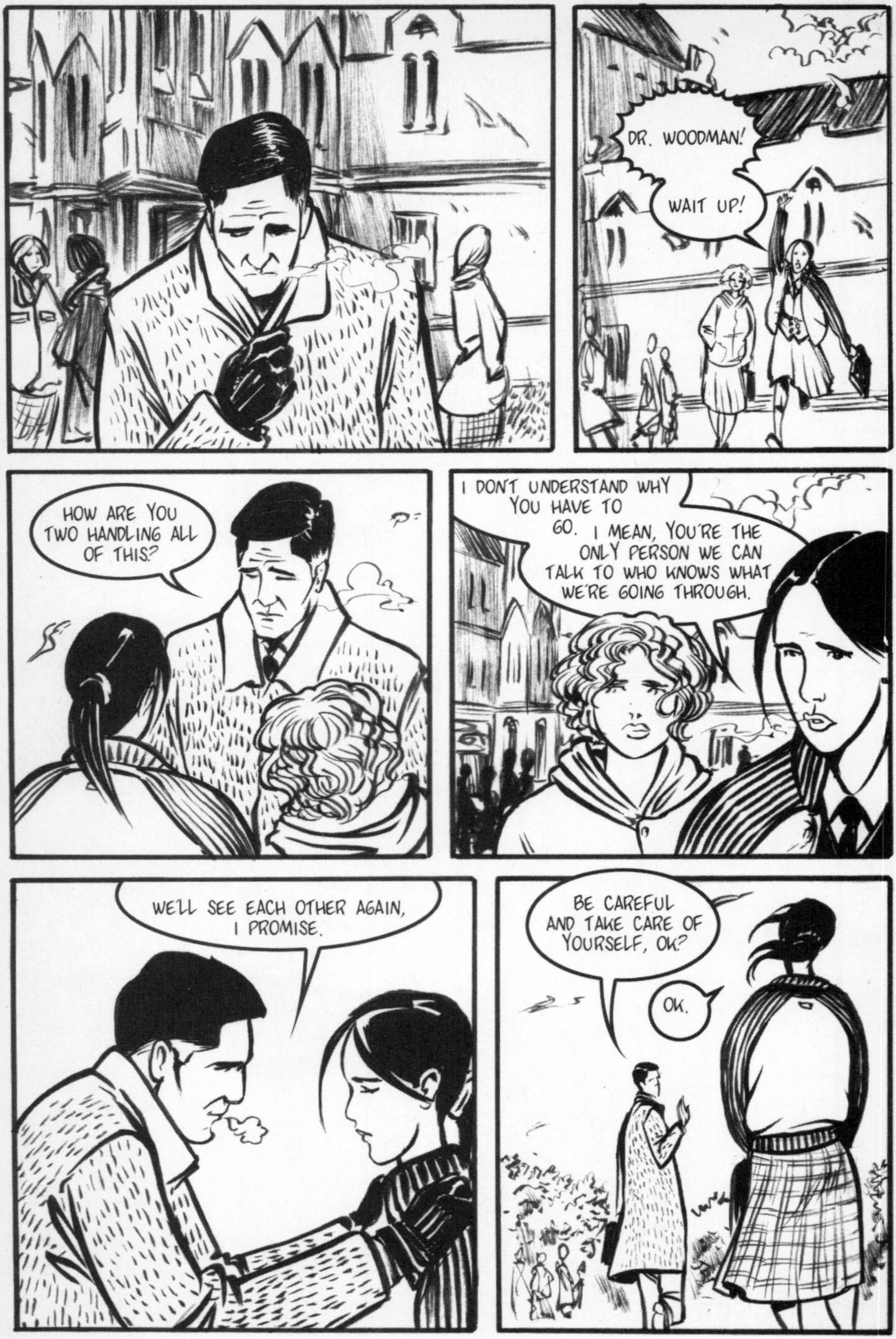
DR. WOODMAN!
WAIT UP!
HOW ARE YOU TWO HANDLING ALL OF THIS?
I DON'T UNDERSTAND WHY YOU HAVE TO GO. I MEAN, YOU'RE THE ONLY PERSON WE CAN TALK TO WHO KNOWS WHAT WE'RE GOING THROUGH.
WE'LL SEE EACH OTHER AGAIN, I PROMISE.
BE CAREFUL AND TAKE CARE OF YOURSELF, OK?
OK.

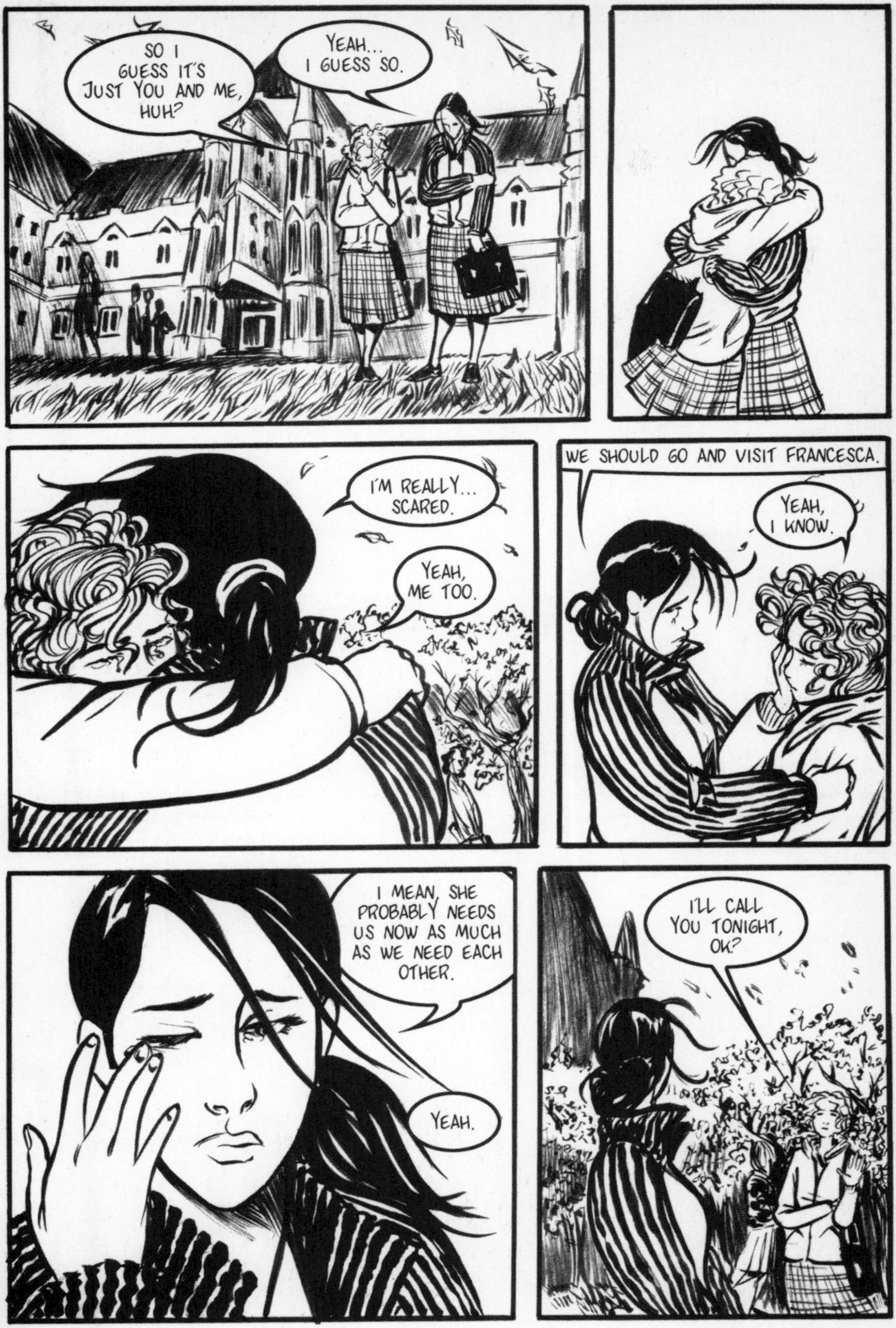

SO I GUESS IT'S JUST YOU AND ME, HUH?
YEAH... I GUESS SO.
I'M REALLY... SCARED.
YEAH, ME TOO.
WE SHOULD GO AND VISIT FRANCESCA.
YEAH, I KNOW.
I MEAN, SHE PROBABLY NEEDS US NOW AS MUCH AS WE NEED EACH OTHER.
YEAH.
I'LL CALL YOU TONIGHT, OK?

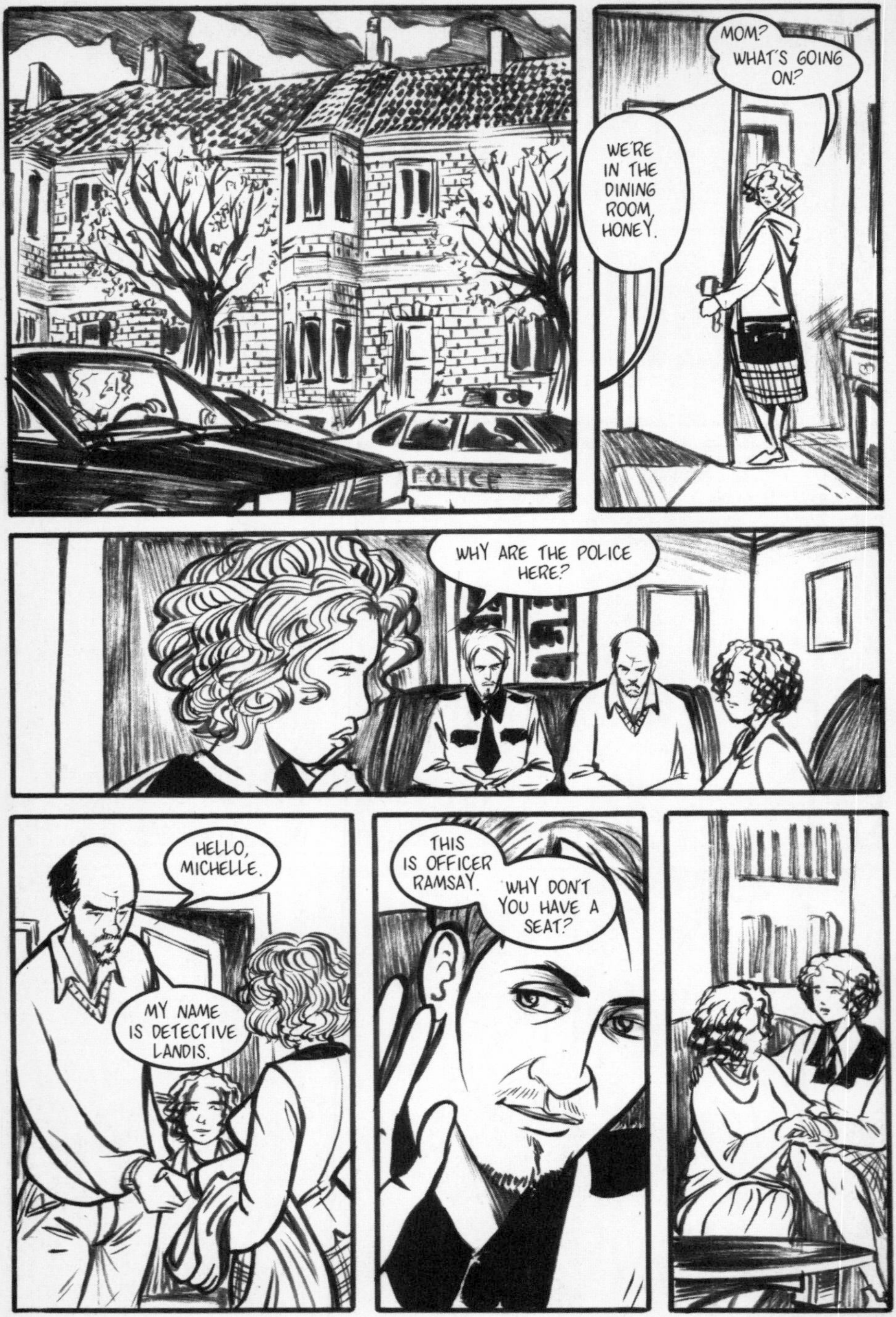
POLICE
MOM? WHAT'S GOING ON?
WE'RE IN THE DINING ROOM, HONEY.
WHY ARE THE POLICE HERE?
HELLO, MICHELLE.
MY NAME IS DETECTIVE LANDIS.
THIS IS OFFICER RAMSAY.
WHY DON'T YOU HAVE A SEAT?

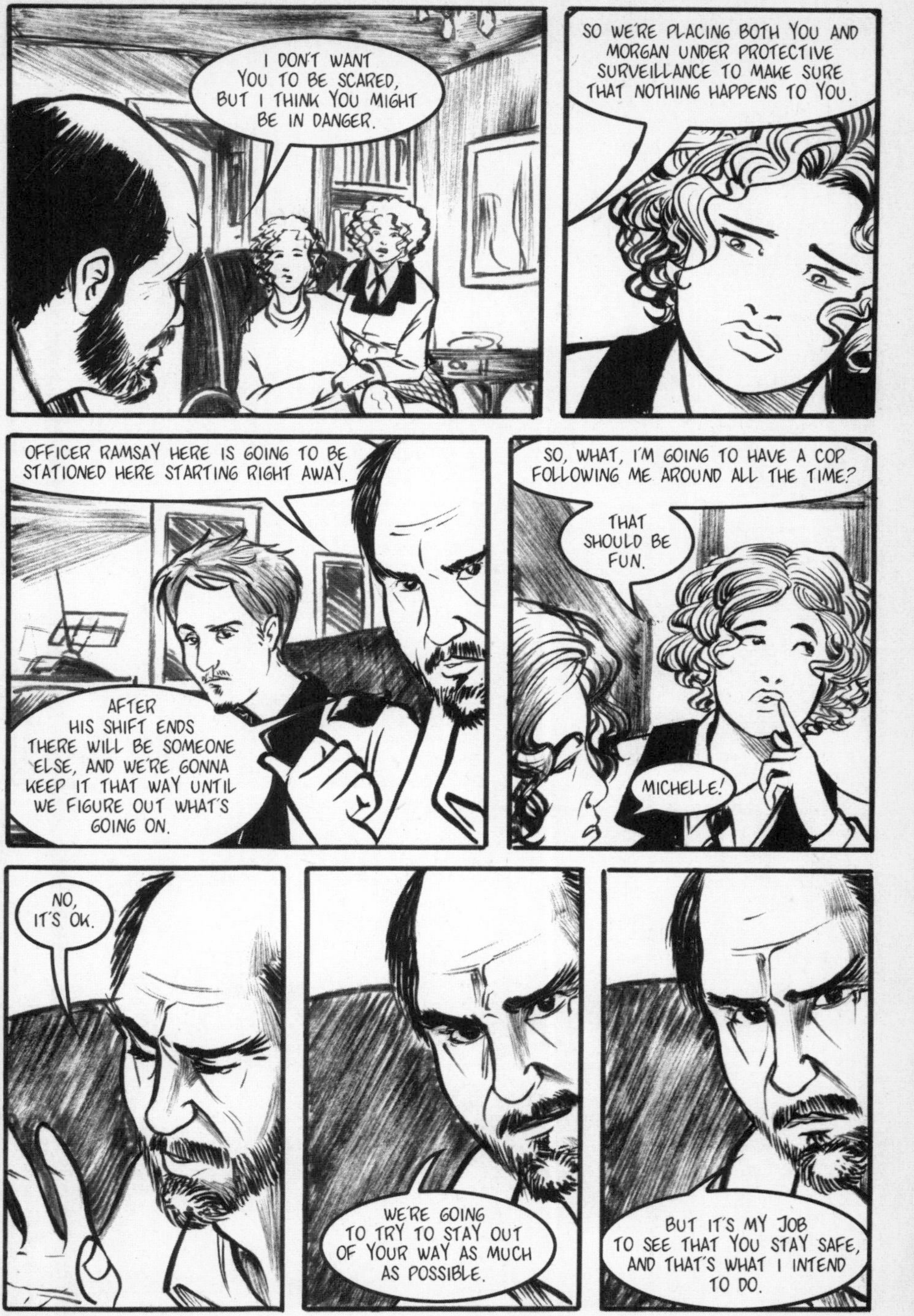
I DON'T WANT YOU TO BE SCARED, BUT I THINK YOU MIGHT BE IN DANGER.
SO WE'RE PLACING BOTH YOU AND MORGAN UNDER PROTECTIVE SURVEILLANCE TO MAKE SURE THAT NOTHING HAPPENS TO YOU.
OFFICER RAMSAY HERE IS GOING TO BE STATIONED HERE STARTING RIGHT AWAY.
AFTER HIS SHIFT ENDS THERE WILL BE SOMEONE ELSE, AND WE'RE GONNA KEEP IT THAT WAY UNTIL WE FIGURE OUT WHAT'S GOING ON.
SO, WHAT, I'M GOING TO HAVE A COP FOLLOWING ME AROUND ALL THE TIME?
THAT SHOULD BE FUN.
MICHELLE!
NO, IT'S OK.
WE'RE GOING TO TRY TO STAY OUT OF YOUR WAY AS MUCH AS POSSIBLE.
BUT IT'S MY JOB TO SEE THAT YOU STAY SAFE, AND THAT'S WHAT I INTEND TO DO.

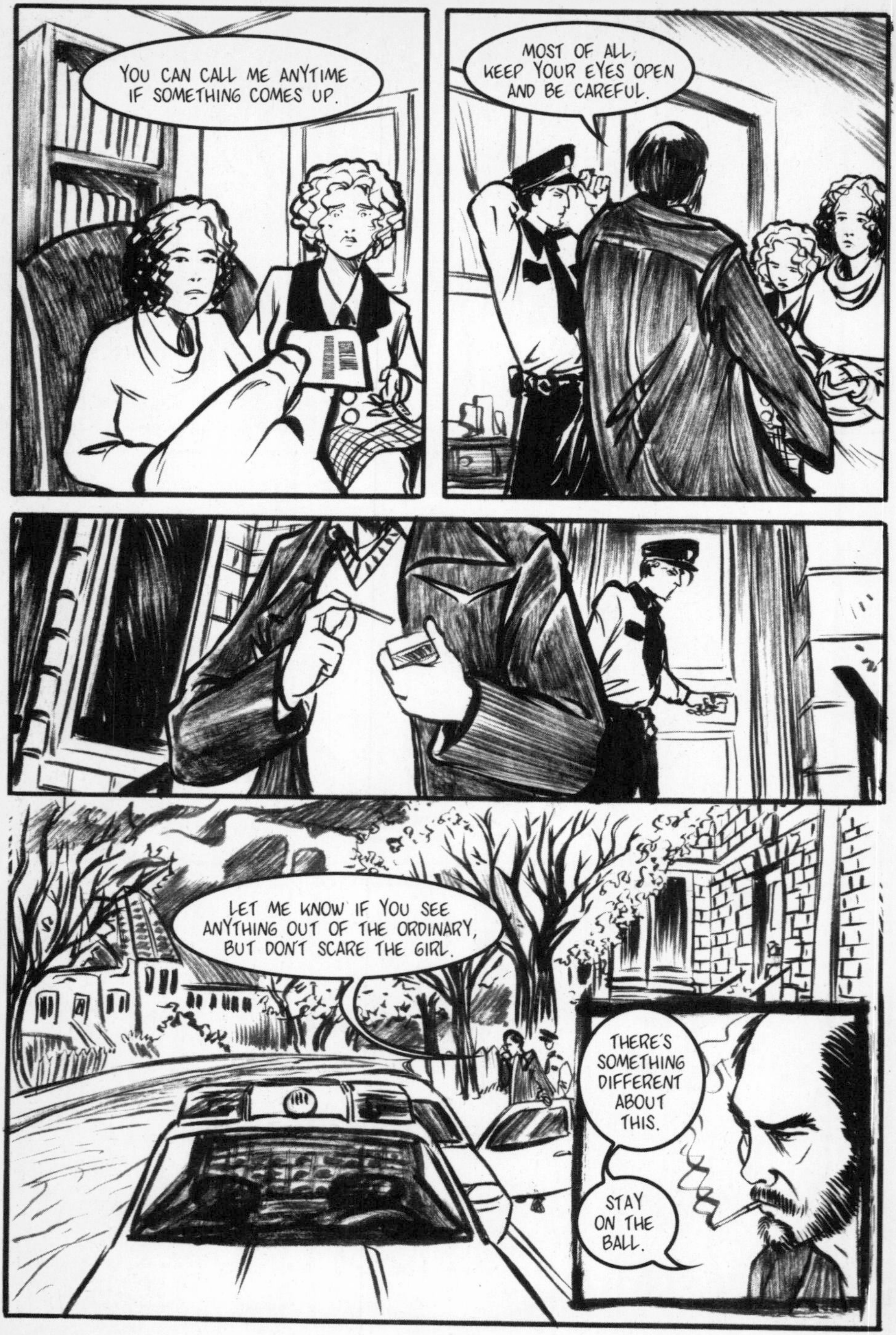

YOU CAN CALL ME ANYTIME IF SOMETHING COMES UP.
MOST OF ALL, KEEP YOUR EYES OPEN AND BE CAREFUL.
LET ME KNOW IF YOU SEE ANYTHING OUT OF THE ORDINARY, BUT DON'T SCARE THE GIRL.
THERE'S SOMETHING DIFFERENT ABOUT THIS.
STAY ON THE BALL.

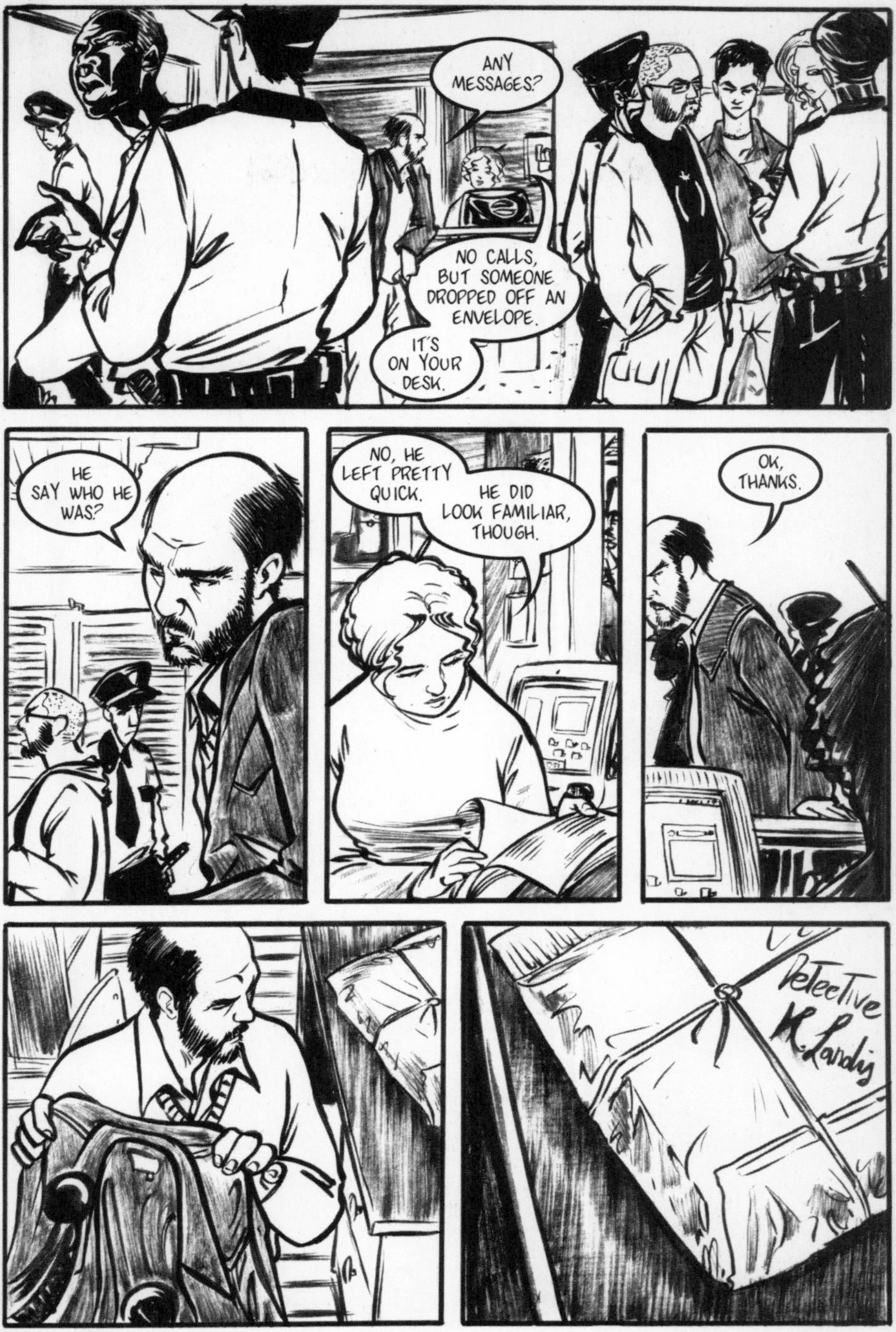
ANY MESSAGES?
NO CALLS, BUT SOMEONE DROPPED OFF AN ENVELOPE.
IT'S ON YOUR DESK.
HE SAY WHO HE WAS?
NO, HE LEFT PRETTY QUICK.
HE DID LOOK FAMILIAR, THOUGH.
OK, THANKS.
Detective M. Landis

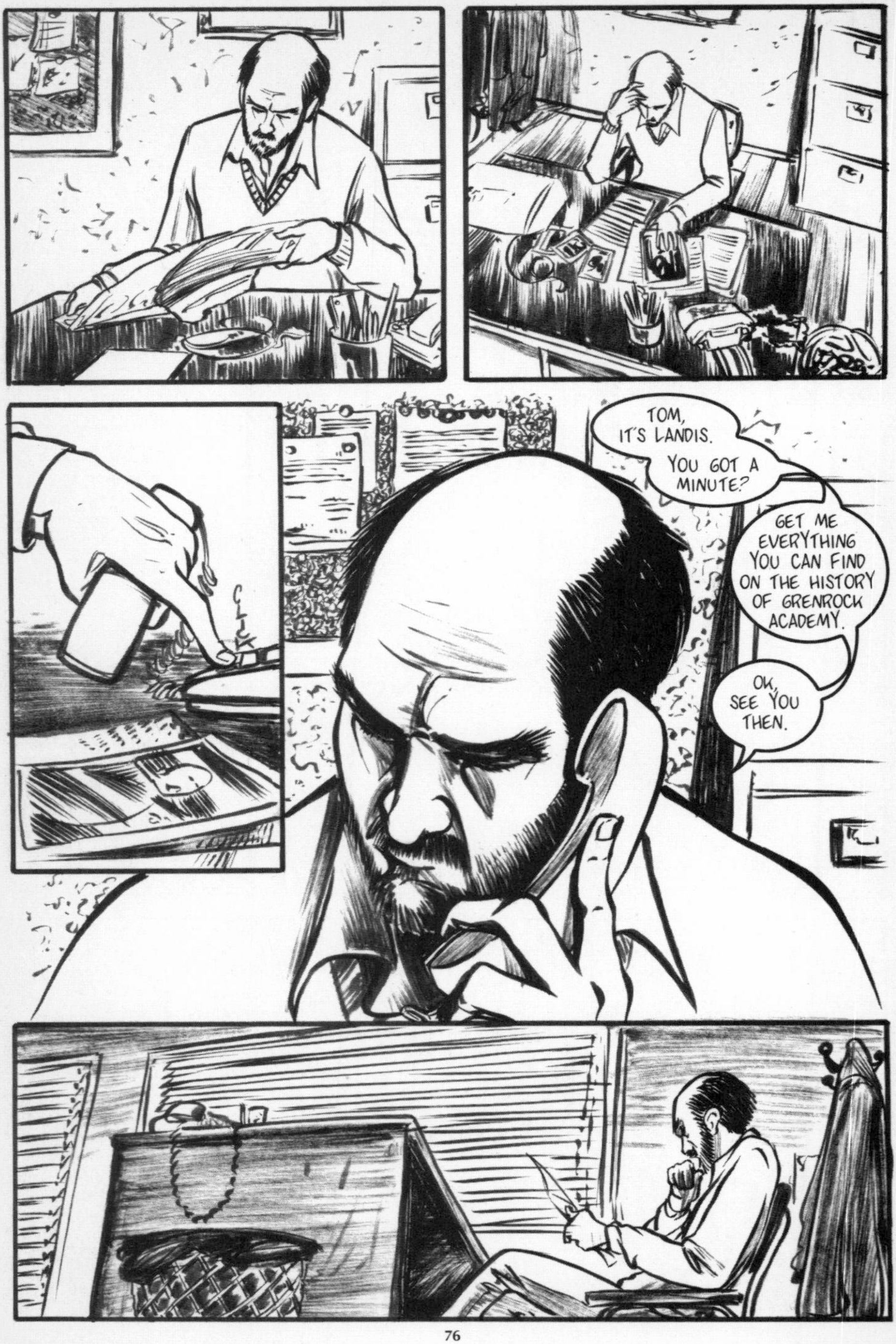
CLICK
TOM, IT'S LANDIS.
YOU GOT A MINUTE?
GET ME EVERYTHING YOU CAN FIND ON THE HISTORY OF GRENROCK ACADEMY.
OK, SEE YOU THEN.

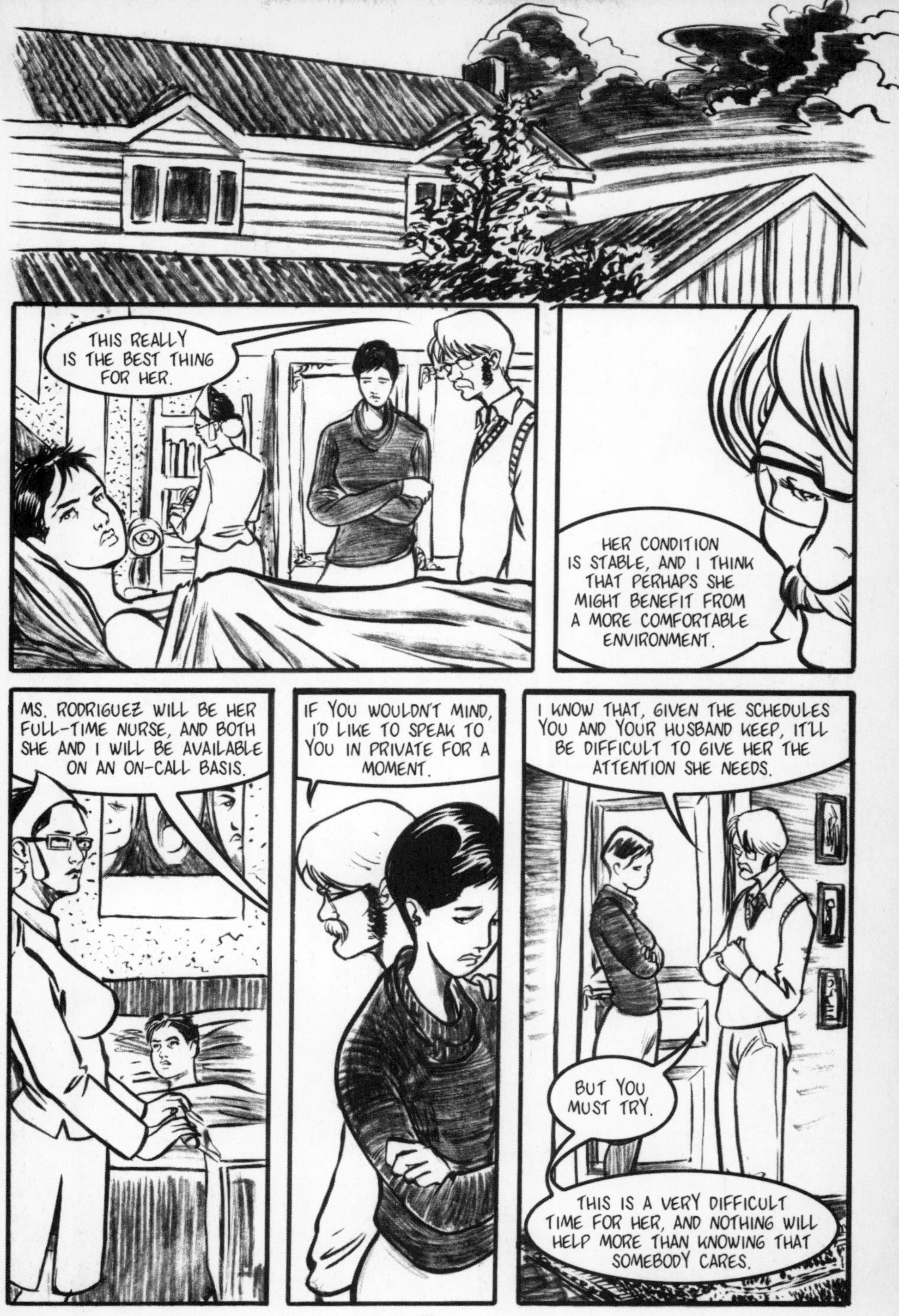
THIS REALLY IS THE BEST THING FOR HER.
HER CONDITION IS STABLE, AND I THINK THAT PERHAPS SHE MIGHT BENEFIT FROM A MORE COMFORTABLE ENVIRONMENT.
MS. RODRIGUEZ WILL BE HER FULL-TIME NURSE, AND BOTH SHE AND I WILL BE AVAILABLE ON AN ON-CALL BASIS.
IF YOU WOULDN'T MIND, I'D LIKE TO SPEAK TO YOU IN PRIVATE FOR A MOMENT.
I KNOW THAT, GIVEN THE SCHEDULES YOU AND YOUR HUSBAND KEEP, IT'LL BE DIFFICULT TO GIVE HER THE ATTENTION SHE NEEDS.
BUT YOU MUST TRY.
THIS IS A VERY DIFFICULT TIME FOR HER, AND NOTHING WILL HELP MORE THAN KNOWING THAT SOMEBODY CARES.

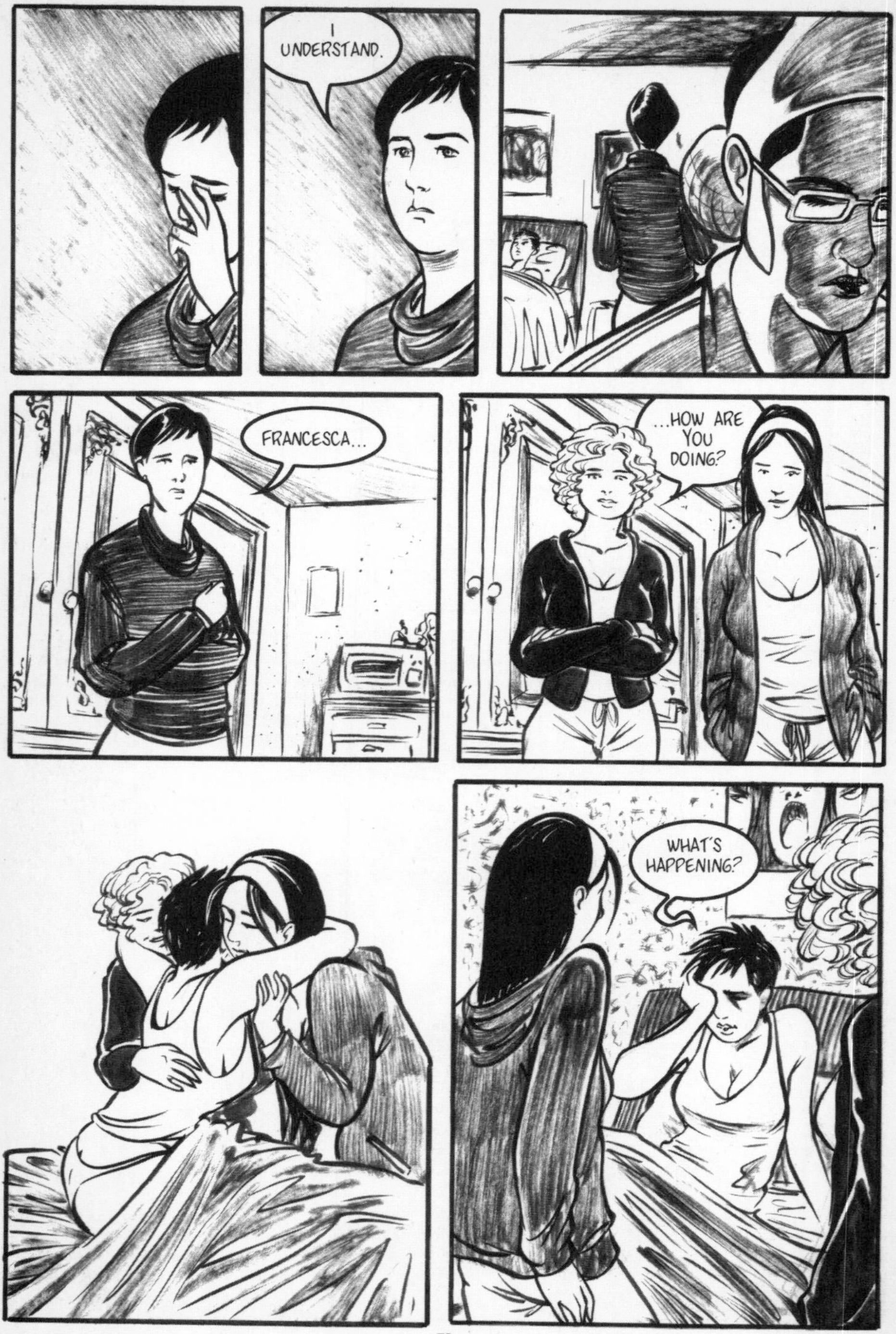
I UNDERSTAND.
FRANCESCA...
...HOW ARE YOU DOING?
WHAT'S HAPPENING?

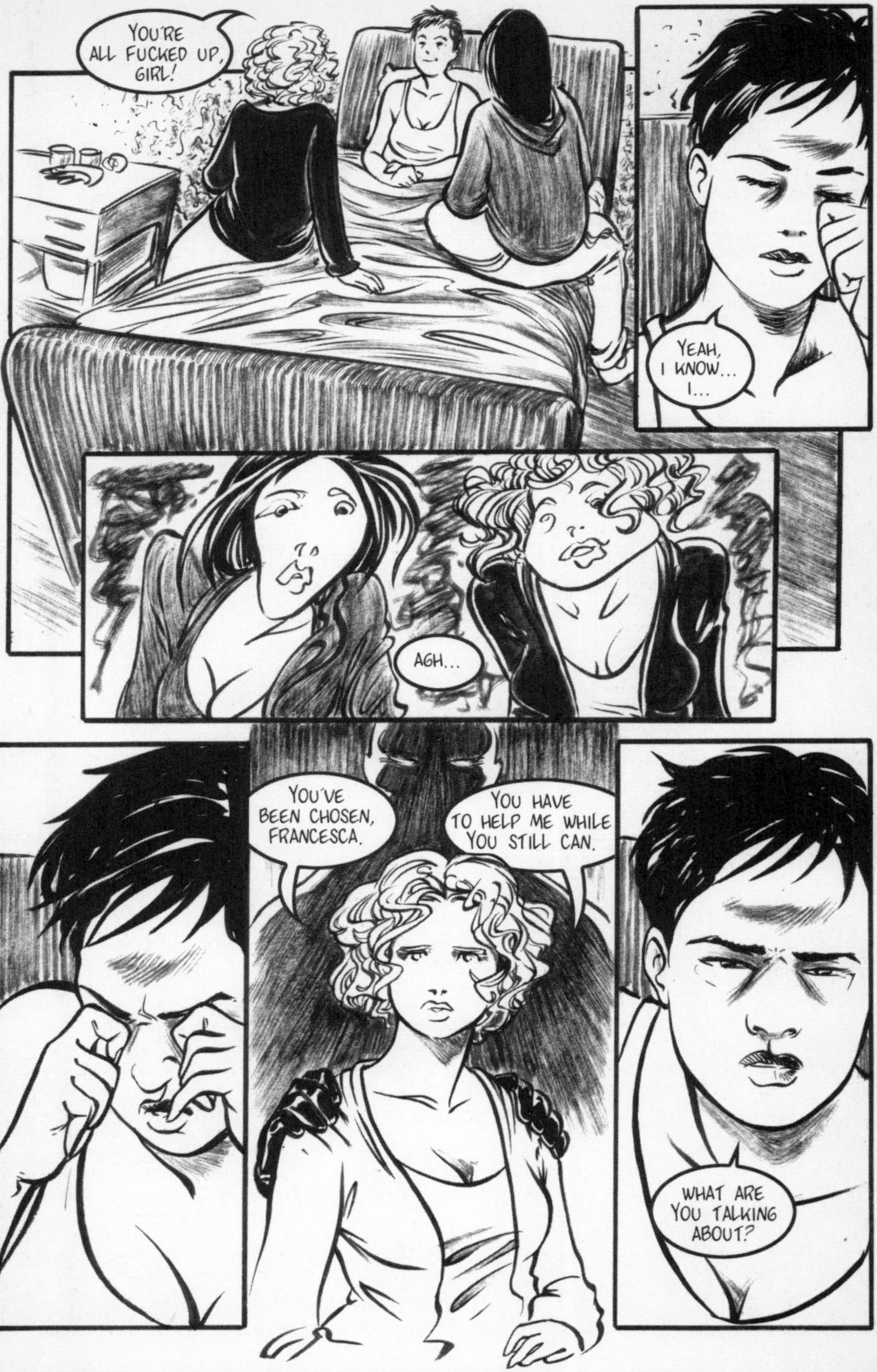
YOU'RE ALL FUCKED UP, GIRL!
YEAH, I KNOW... I...
AGH...
YOU'VE BEEN CHOSEN, FRANCESCA.
YOU HAVE TO HELP ME WHILE YOU STILL CAN.
WHAT ARE YOU TALKING ABOUT?

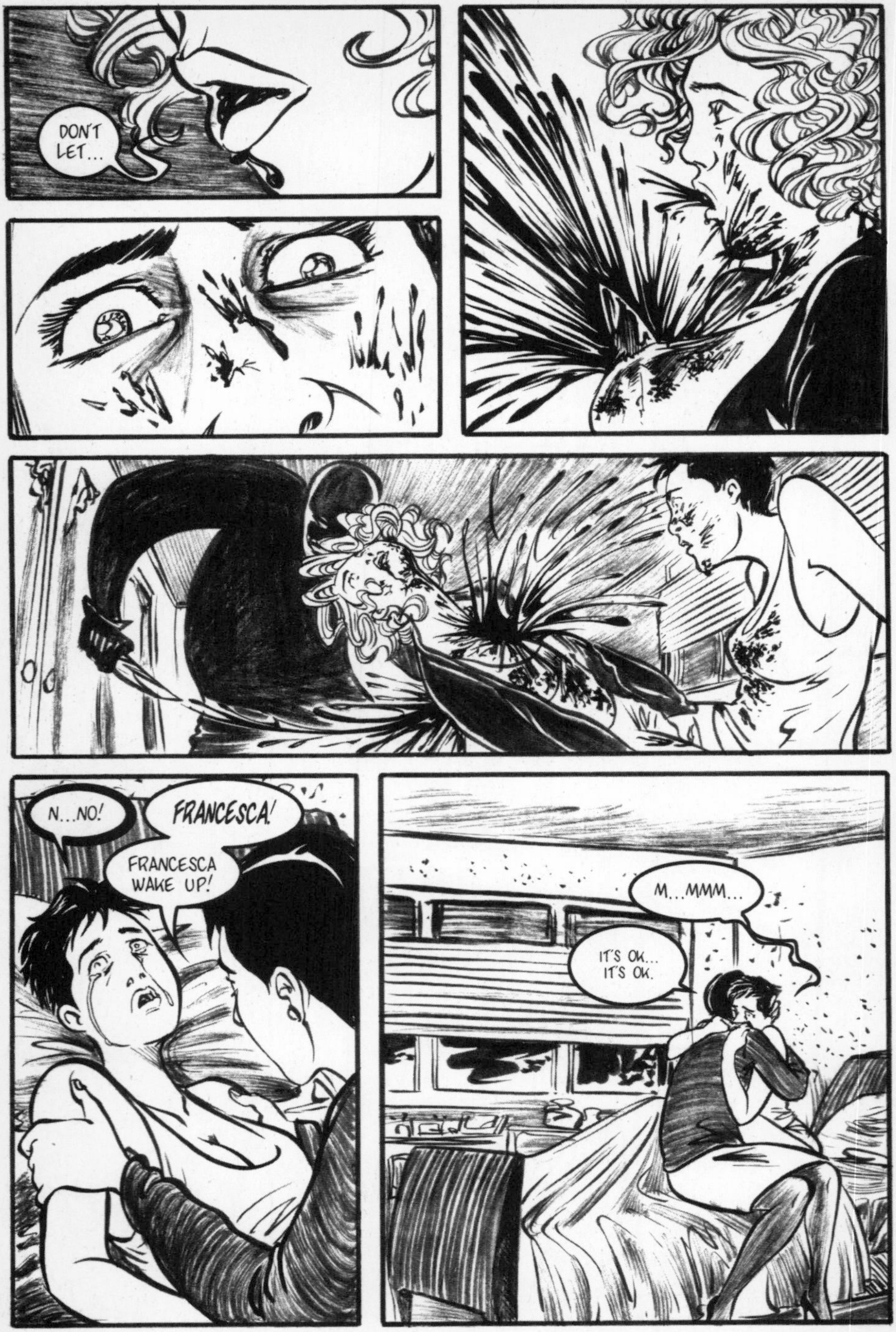
DON'T LET...
N...NO!
FRANCESCA!
FRANCESCA WAKE UP!
M...MMM...
IT'S OK... IT'S OK.

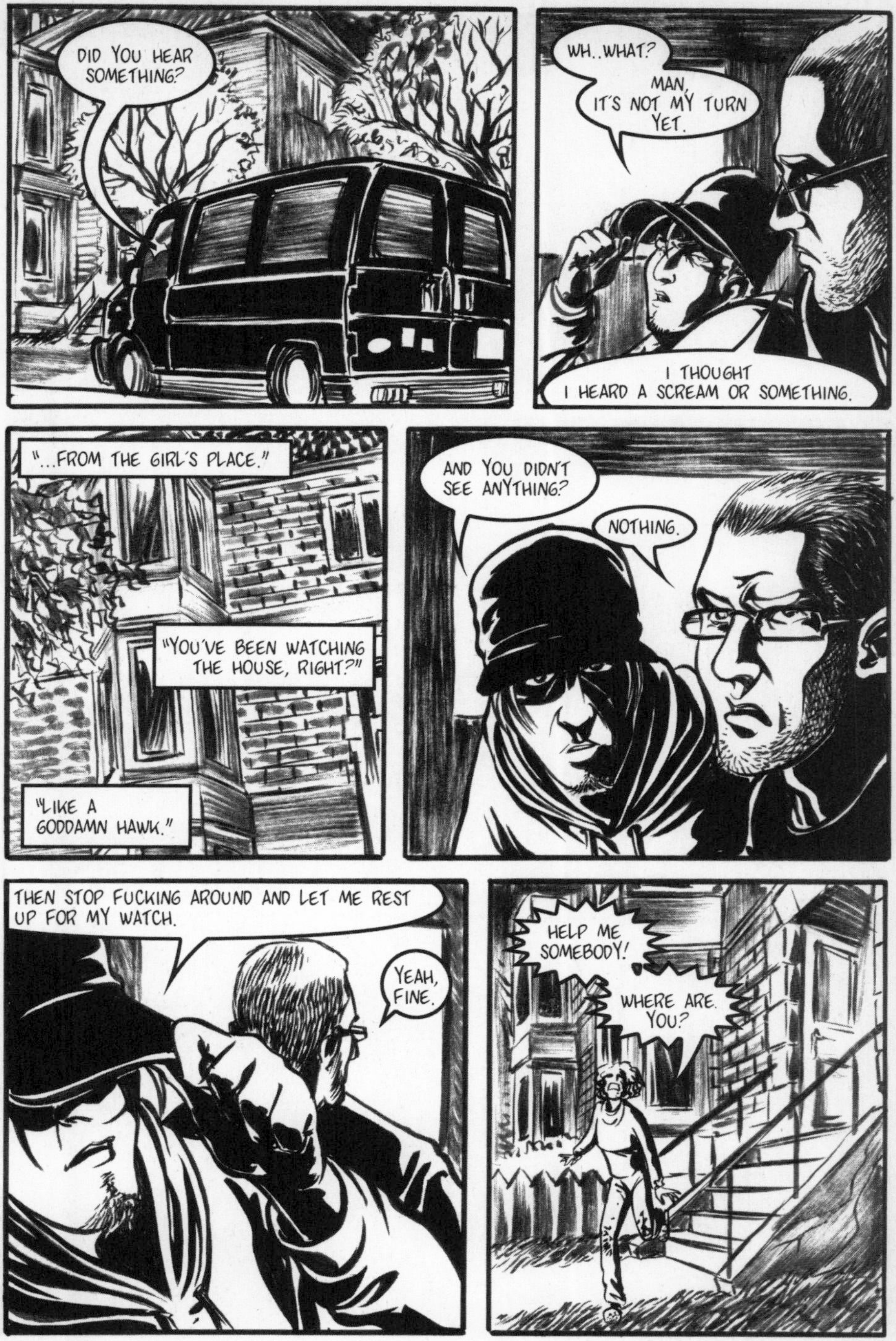
DID YOU HEAR SOMETHING?
WH..WHAT?
MAN, IT'S NOT MY TURN YET.
I THOUGHT I HEARD A SCREAM OR SOMETHING.
"...FROM THE GIRL'S PLACE."
"YOU'VE BEEN WATCHING THE HOUSE, RIGHT?"
"LIKE A GODDAMN HAWK."
AND YOU DIDN'T SEE ANYTHING?
NOTHING.
THEN STOP FUCKING AROUND AND LET ME REST UP FOR MY WATCH.
YEAH, FINE.
HELP ME SOMEBODY!
WHERE ARE YOU?

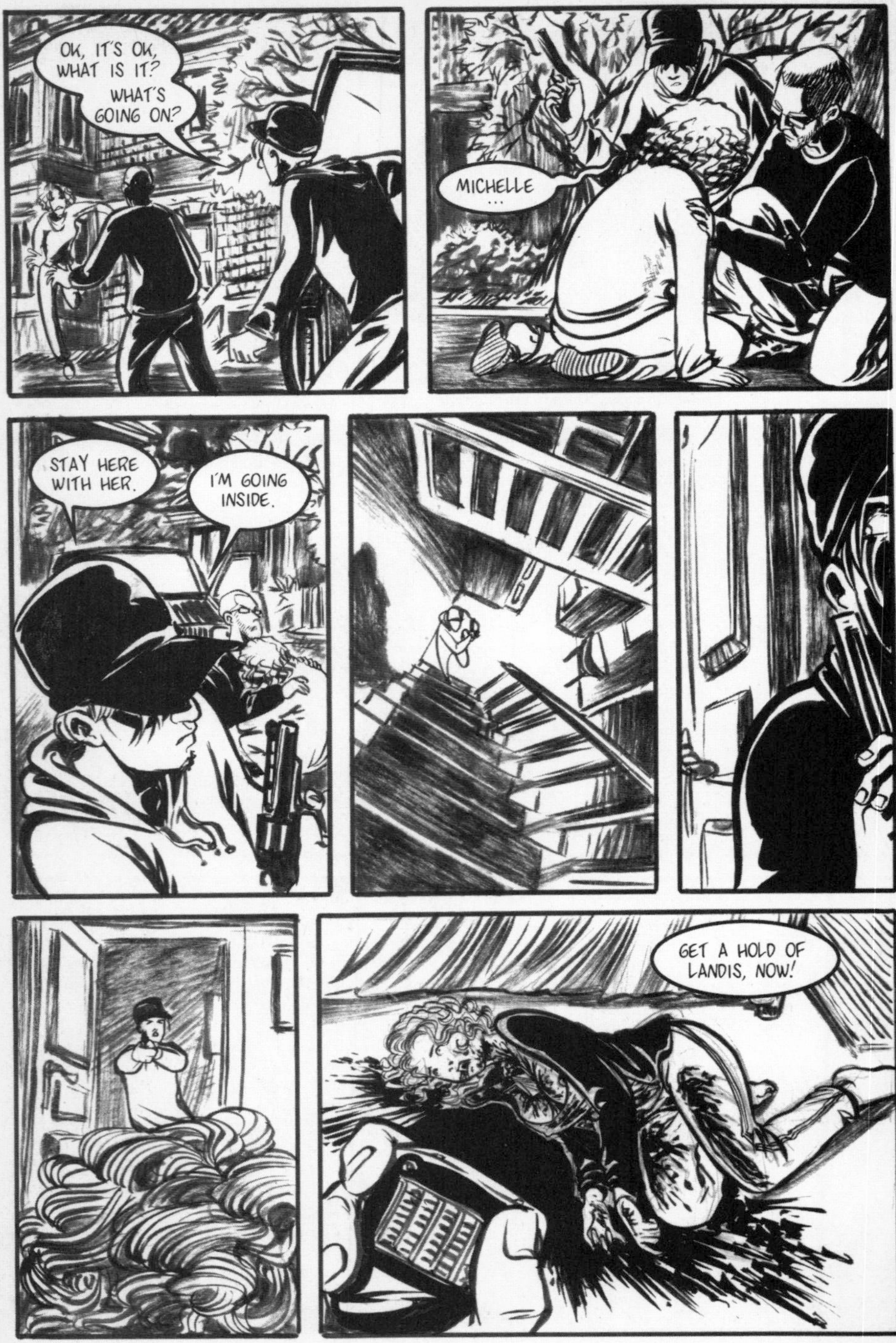
OK, IT'S OK, WHAT IS IT?
WHAT'S GOING ON?
MICHELLE ...
STAY HERE WITH HER.
I'M GOING INSIDE.
GET A HOLD OF LANDIS, NOW!

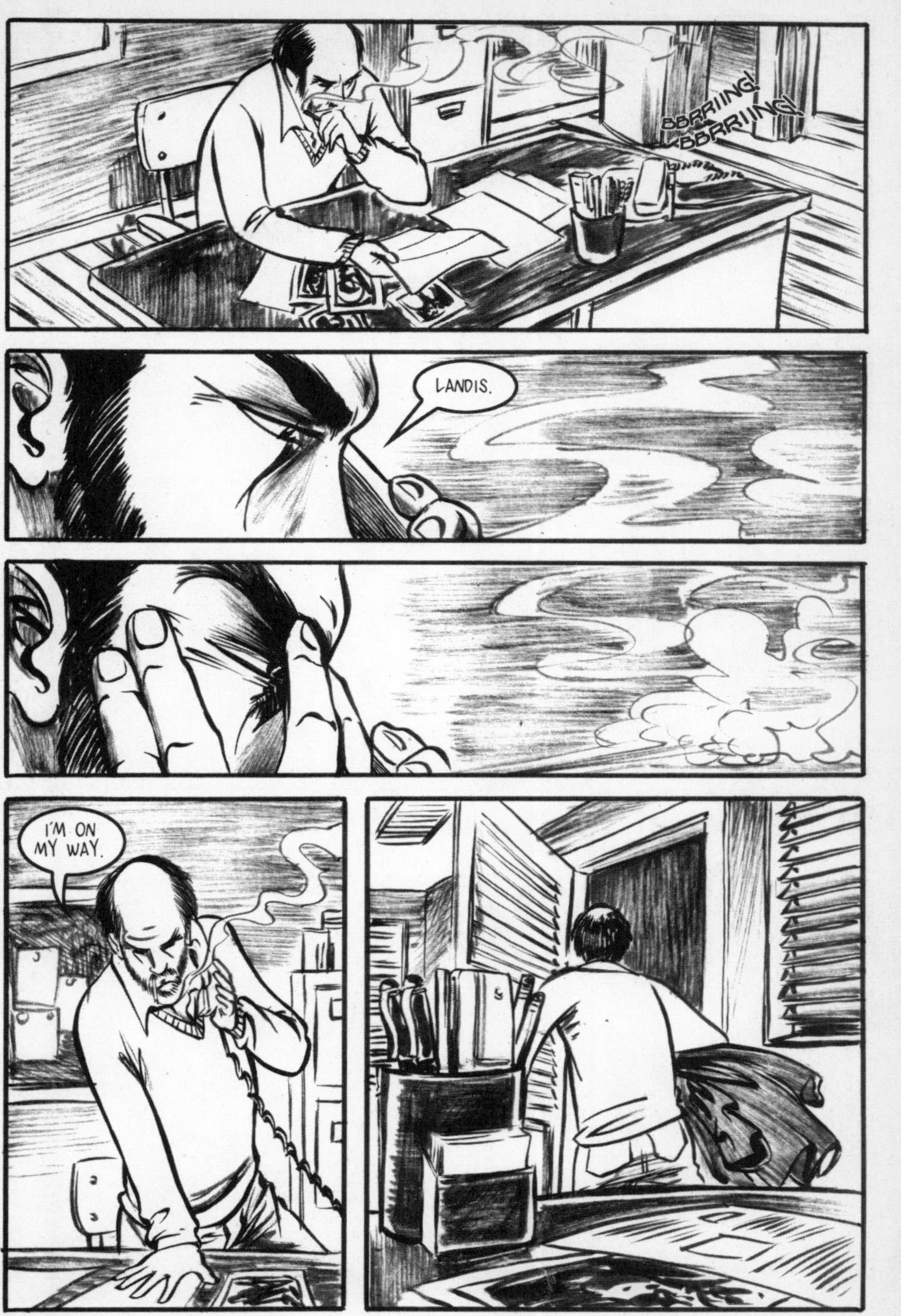
BBRRIING!
BBRRIING!
LANDIS.
I'M ON MY WAY.

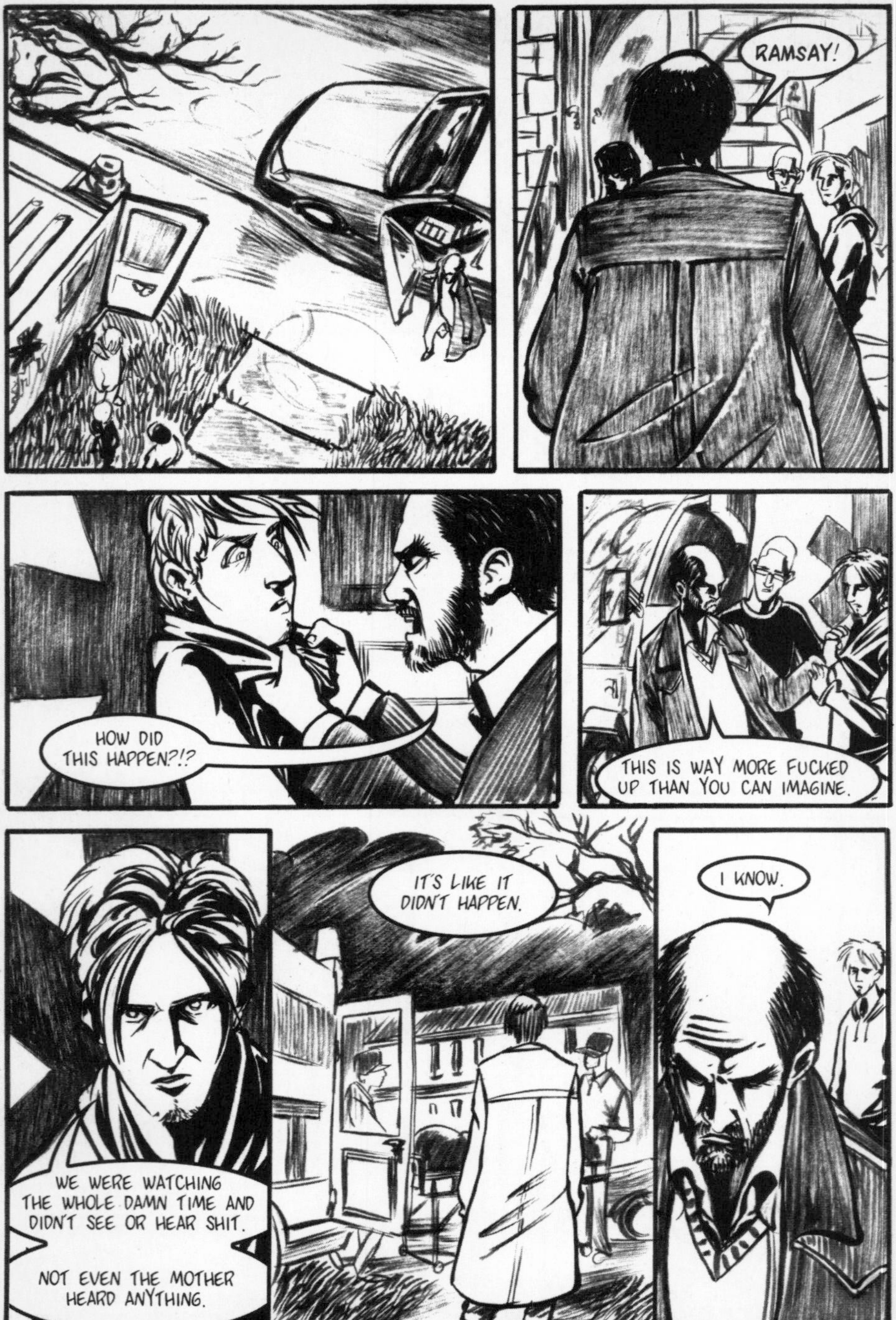
RAMSAY!
HOW DID THIS HAPPEN?!?
THIS IS WAY MORE FUCKED UP THAN YOU CAN IMAGINE.
WE WERE WATCHING THE WHOLE DAMN TIME AND DIDN'T SEE OR HEAR SHIT.
NOT EVEN THE MOTHER HEARD ANYTHING.
IT'S LIKE IT DIDN'T HAPPEN.
I KNOW.

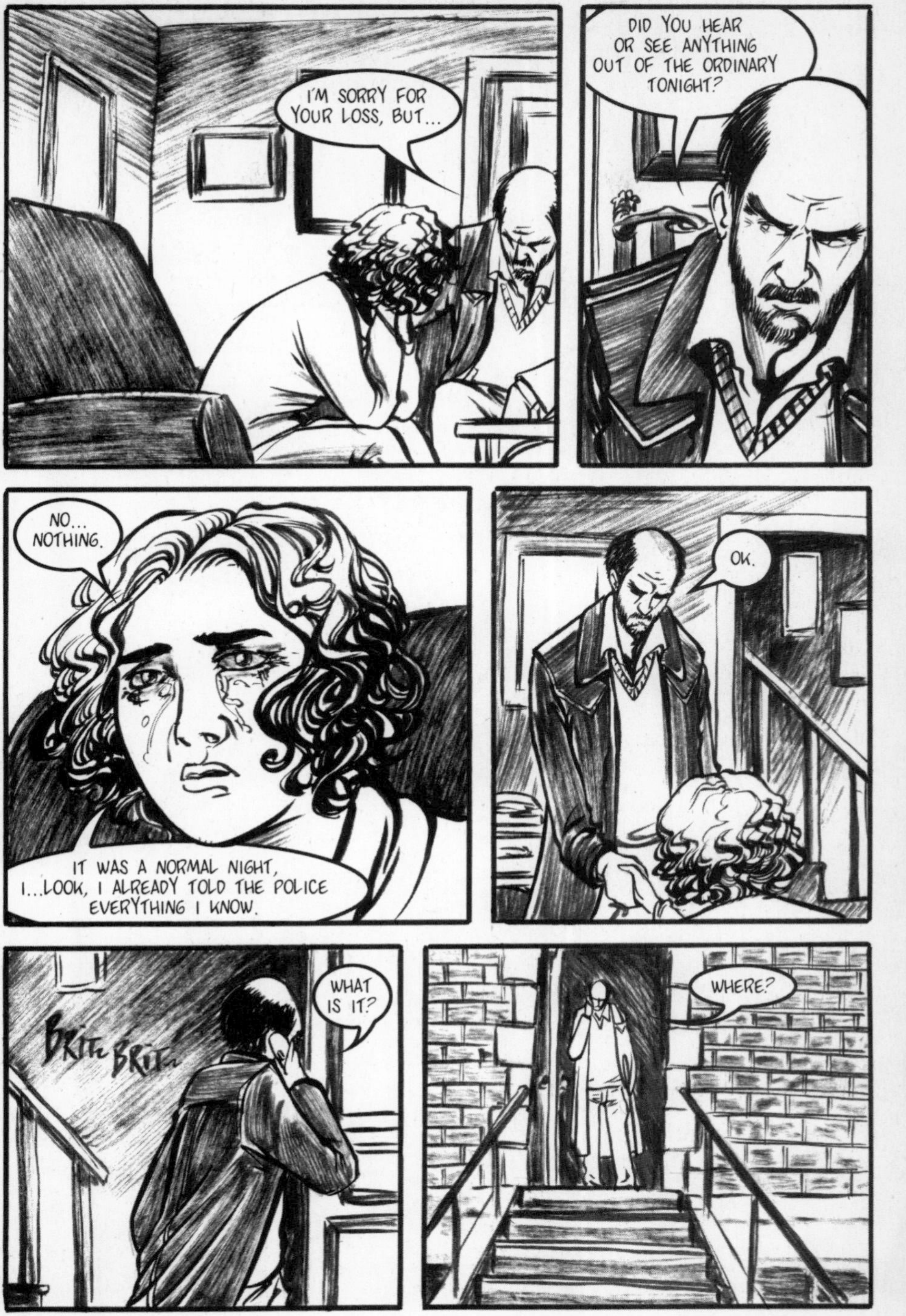
I'M SORRY FOR YOUR LOSS, BUT...
DID YOU HEAR OR SEE ANYTHING OUT OF THE ORDINARY TONIGHT?
NO... NOTHING.
IT WAS A NORMAL NIGHT, I...LOOK, I ALREADY TOLD THE POLICE EVERYTHING I KNOW.
OK.
BRIT BRIT
WHAT IS IT?
WHERE?

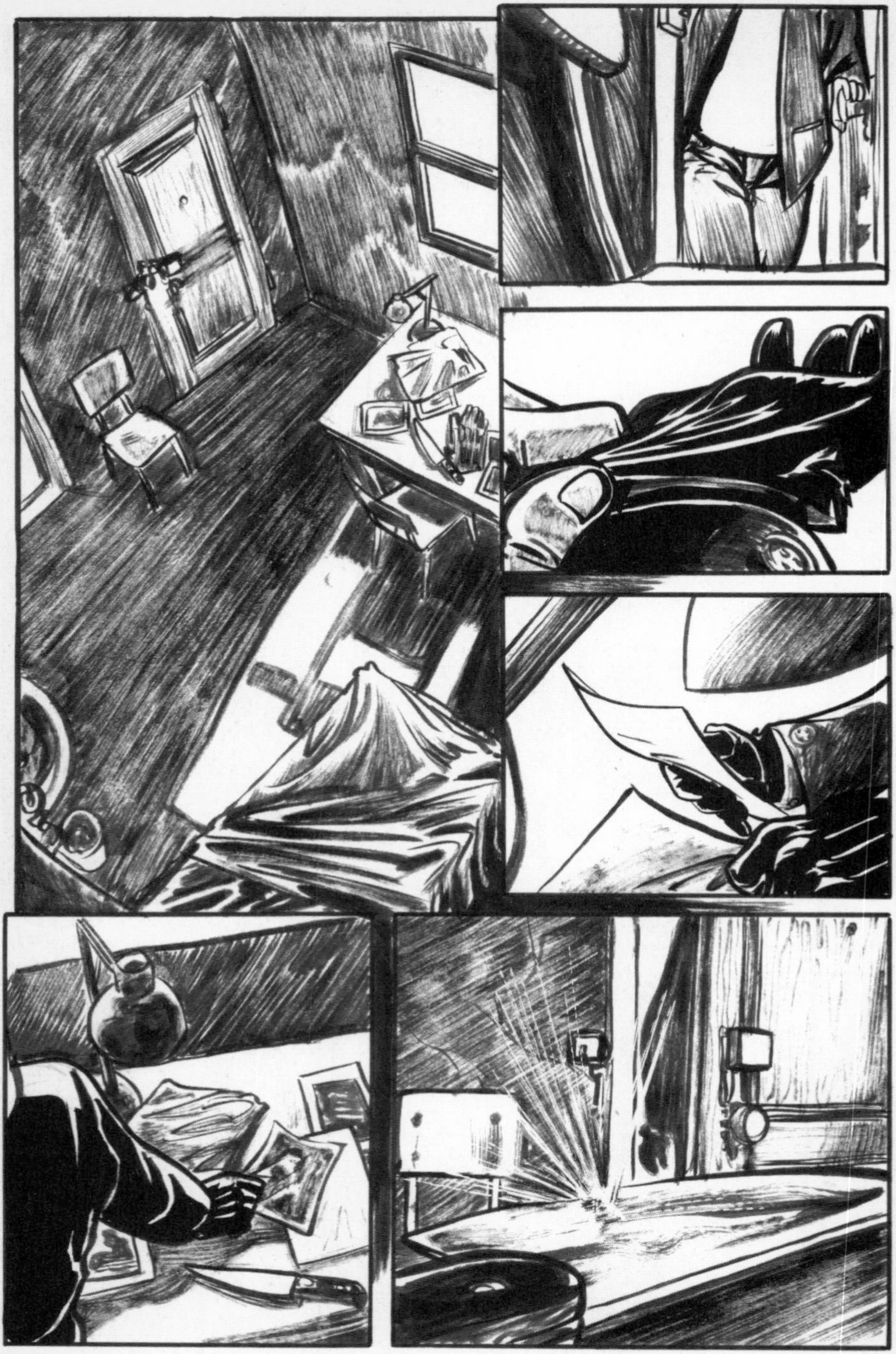

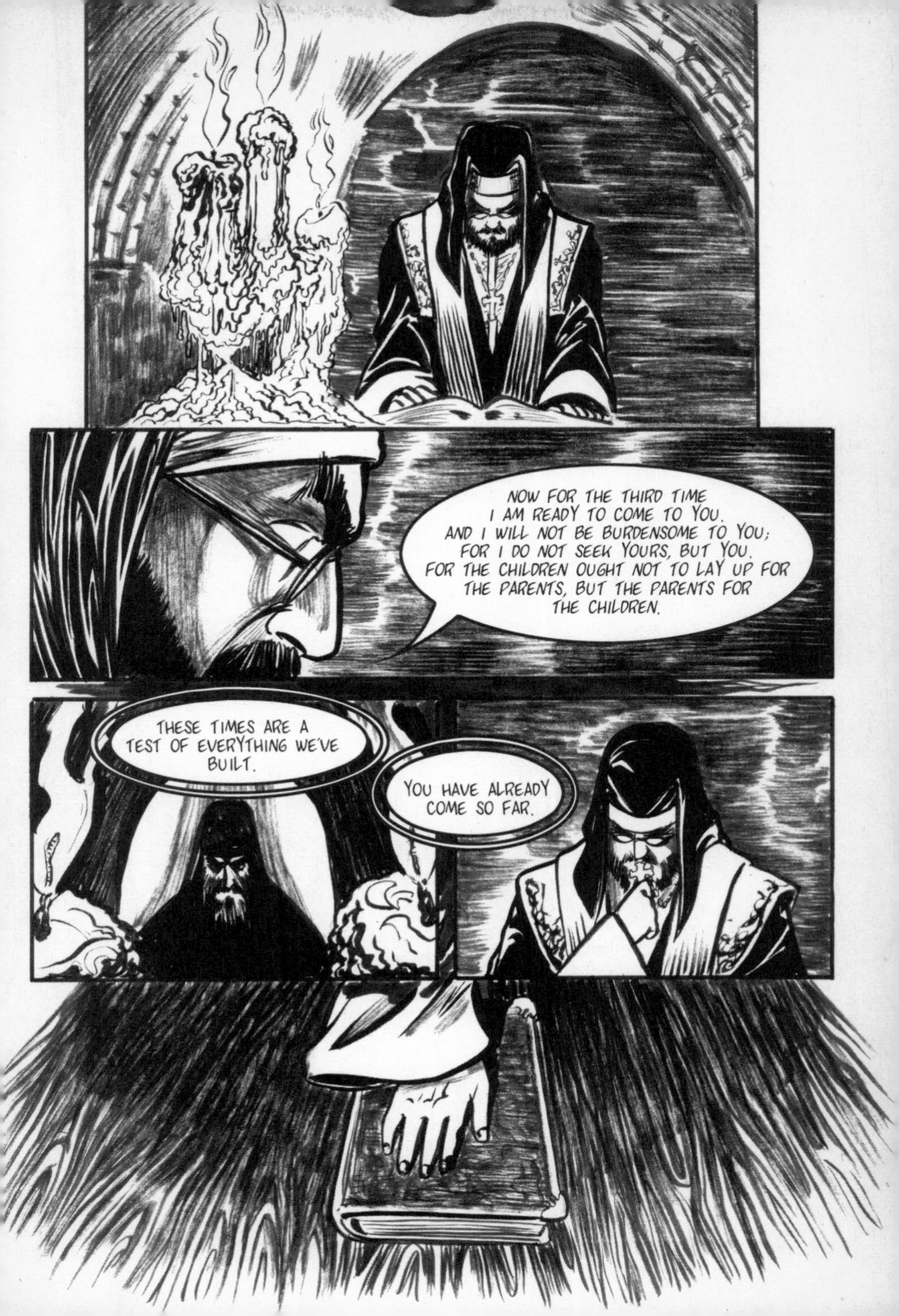
NOW FOR THE THIRD TIME I AM READY TO COME TO YOU. AND I WILL NOT BE BURDENSOME TO YOU; FOR I DO NOT SEEK YOURS, BUT YOU. FOR THE CHILDREN OUGHT NOT TO LAY UP FOR THE PARENTS, BUT THE PARENTS FOR THE CHILDREN.
THESE TIMES ARE A TEST OF EVERYTHING WE'VE BUILT.
YOU HAVE ALREADY COME SO FAR.

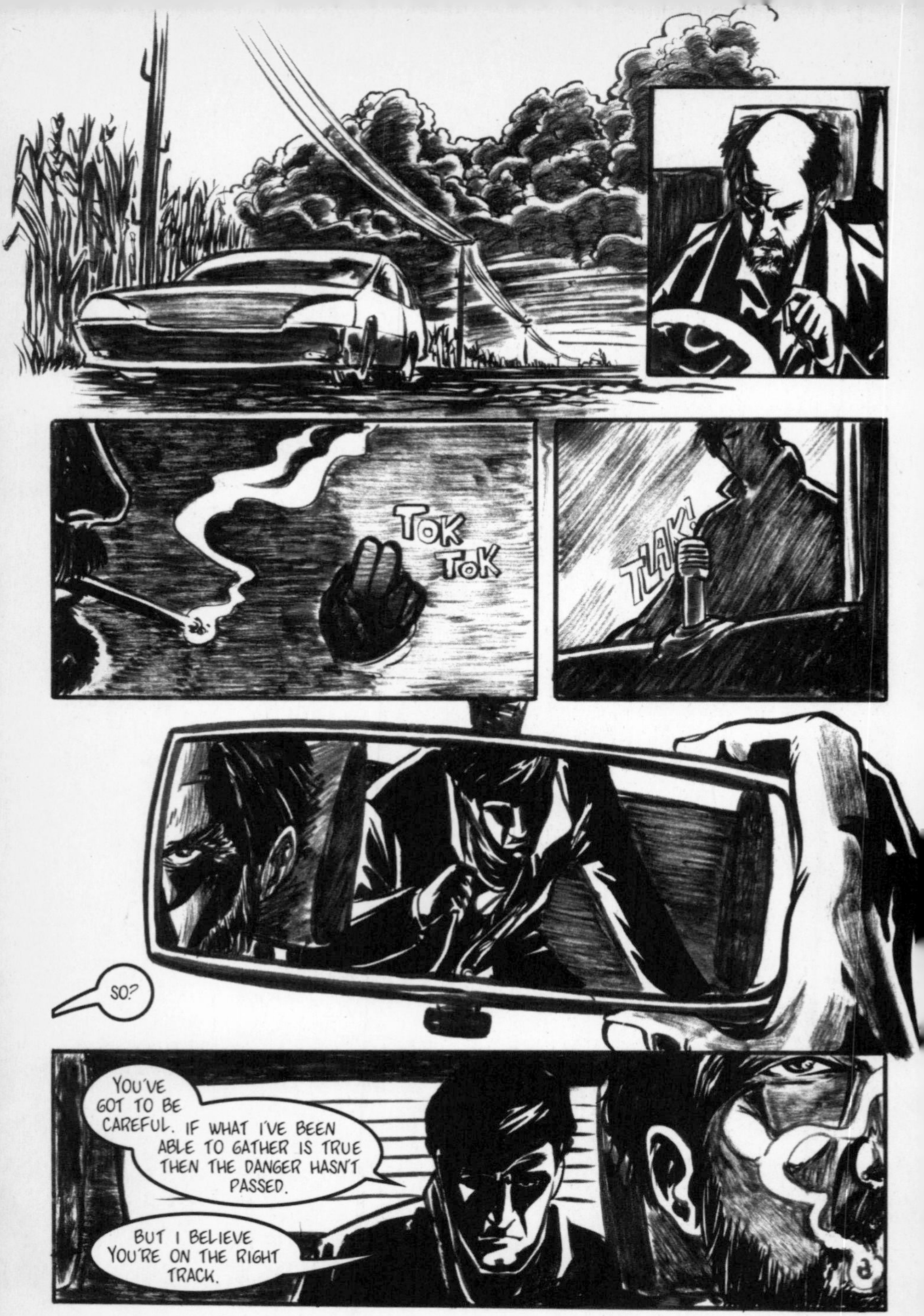
TOK TOK
TLAK!
SO?
YOU'VE GOT TO BE CAREFUL. IF WHAT I'VE BEEN ABLE TO GATHER IS TRUE THEN THE DANGER HASN'T PASSED.
BUT I BELIEVE YOU'RE ON THE RIGHT TRACK.

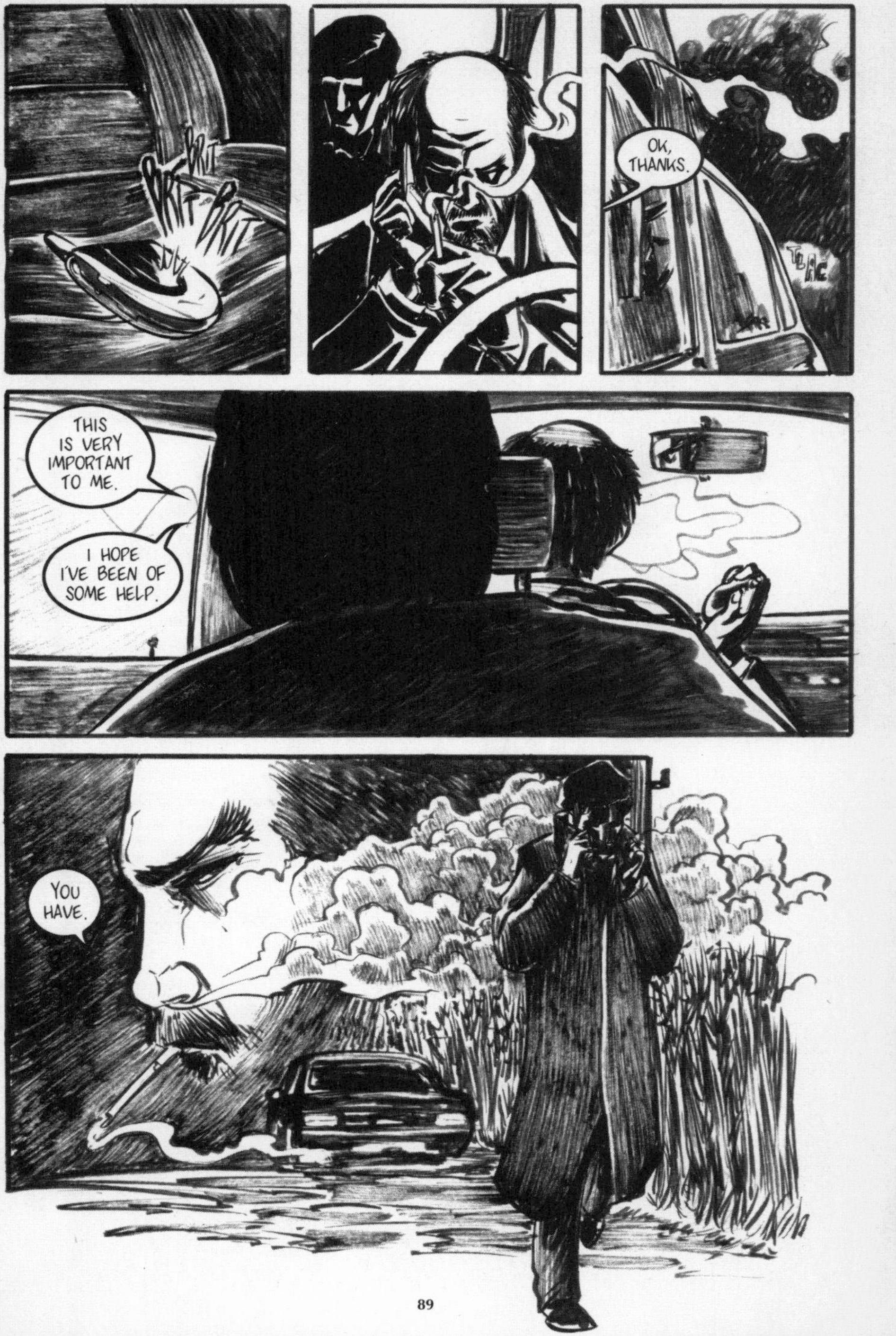
BRIT
BRIT
BRIT
BRIT
OK, THANKS.
TLAC
THIS IS VERY IMPORTANT TO ME.
I HOPE I'VE BEEN OF SOME HELP.
YOU HAVE.

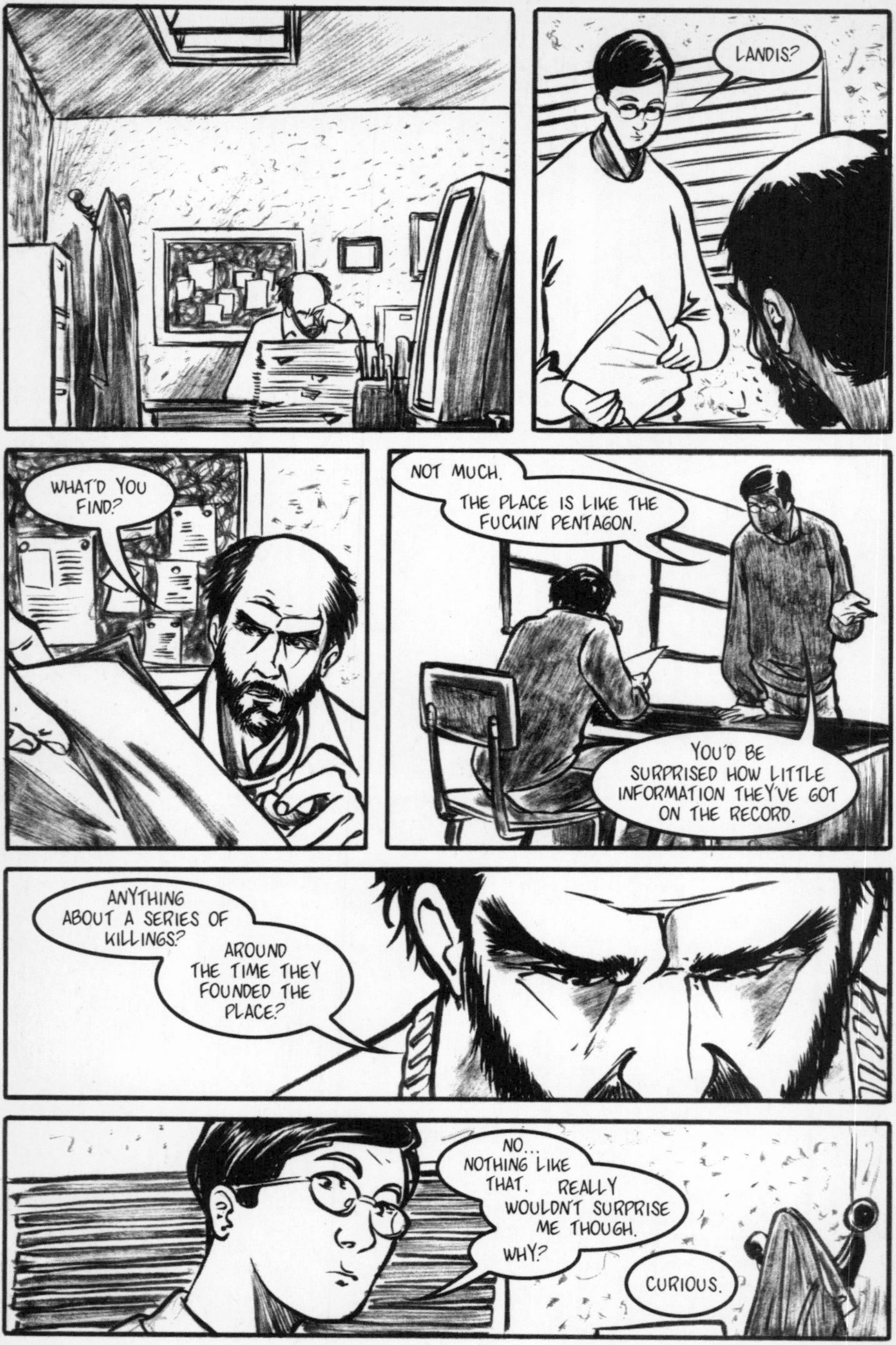
LANDIS?
WHAT'D YOU FIND?
NOT MUCH.
THE PLACE IS LIKE THE FUCKIN' PENTAGON.
YOU'D BE SURPRISED HOW LITTLE INFORMATION THEY'VE GOT ON THE RECORD.
ANYTHING ABOUT A SERIES OF KILLINGS?
AROUND THE TIME THEY FOUNDED THE PLACE?
NO... NOTHING LIKE THAT.
REALLY WOULDN'T SURPRISE ME THOUGH.
WHY?
CURIOUS.

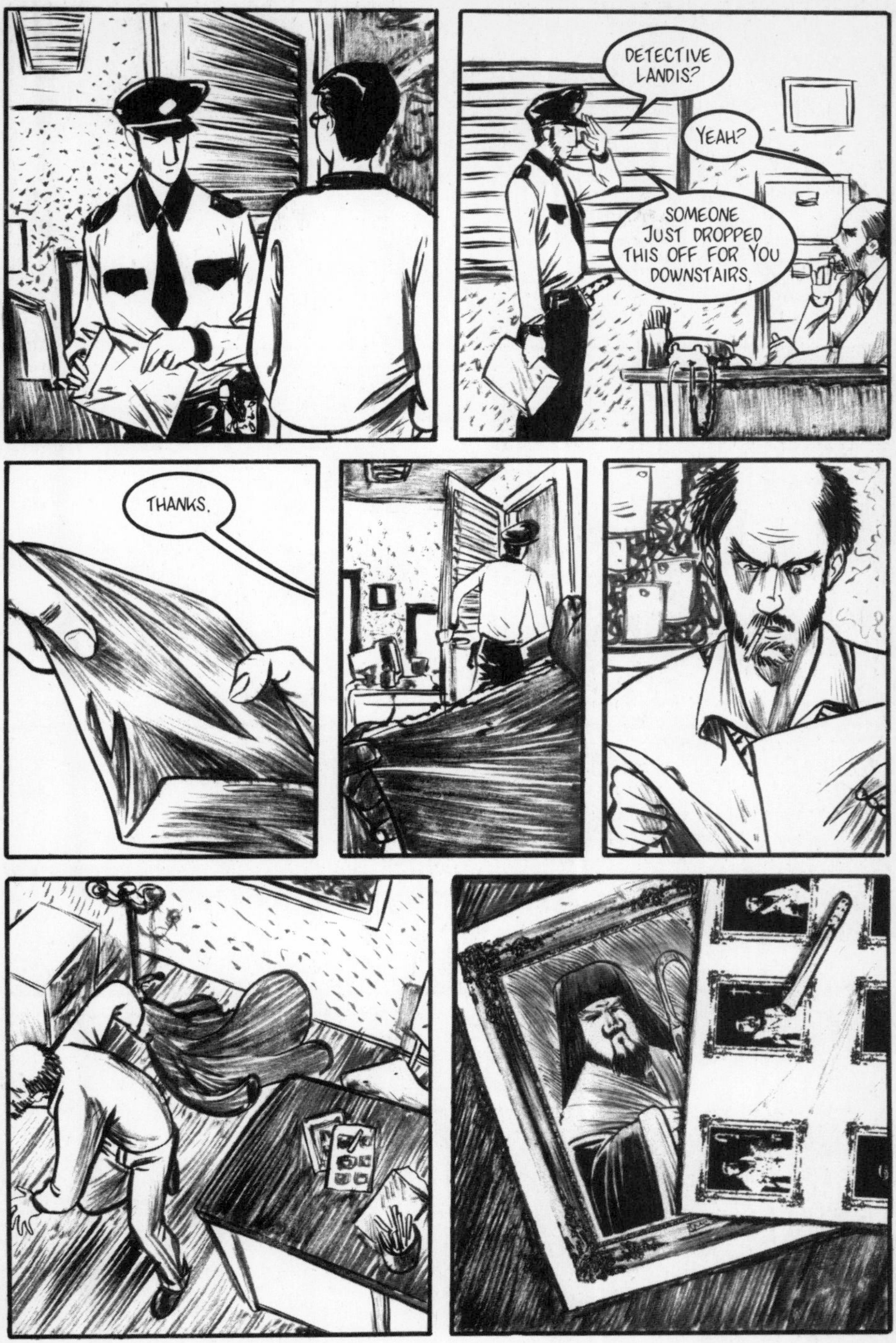

DETECTIVE LANDIS?
YEAH?
SOMEONE JUST DROPPED THIS OFF FOR YOU DOWNSTAIRS.
THANKS.

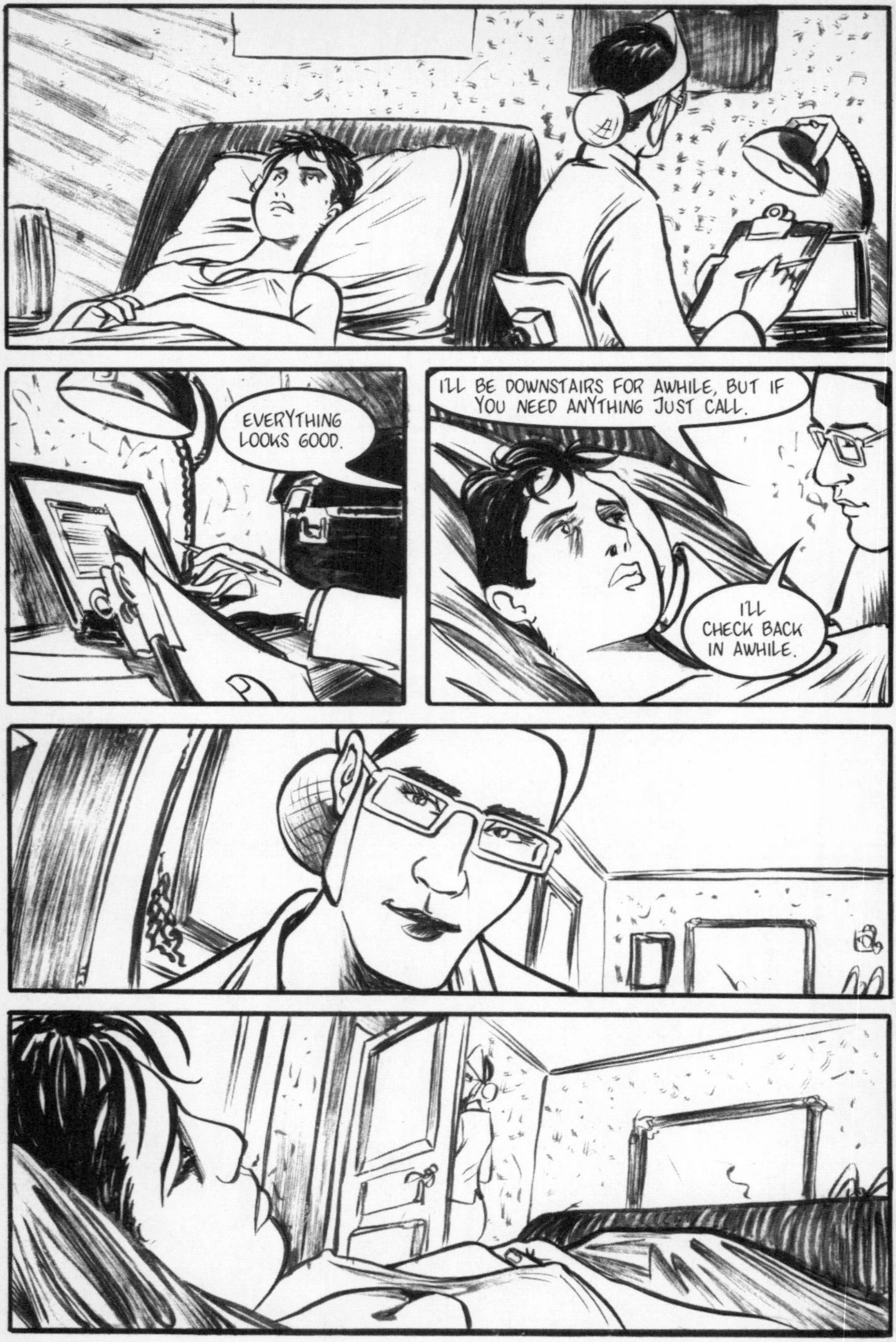
EVERYTHING LOOKS GOOD.
I'LL BE DOWNSTAIRS FOR AWHILE, BUT IF YOU NEED ANYTHING JUST CALL.
I'LL CHECK BACK IN AWHILE.

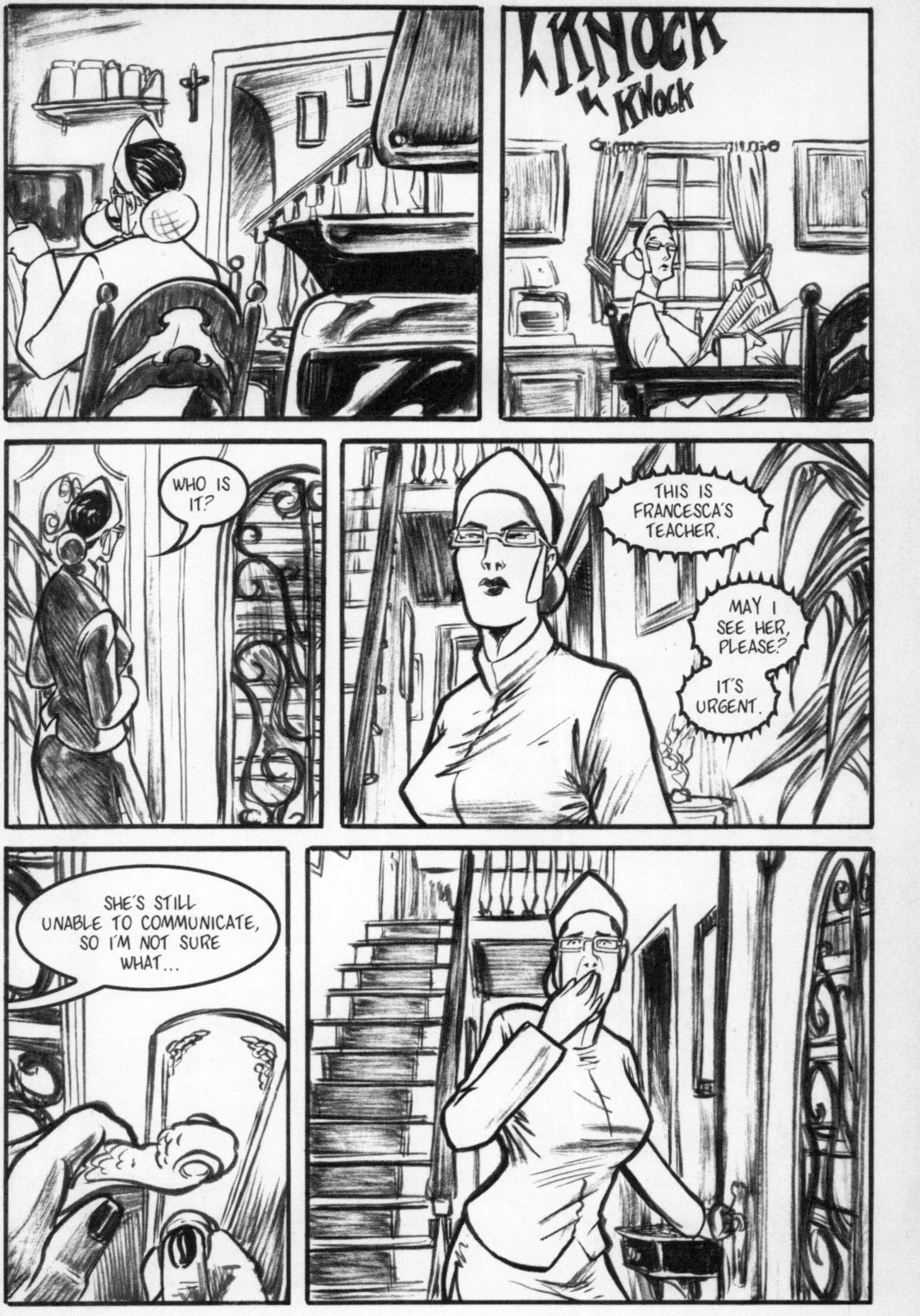
KNOCK
KNOCK
WHO IS IT?
THIS IS FRANCESCA'S TEACHER.
MAY I SEE HER, PLEASE?
IT'S URGENT.
SHE'S STILL UNABLE TO COMMUNICATE, SO I'M NOT SURE WHAT...

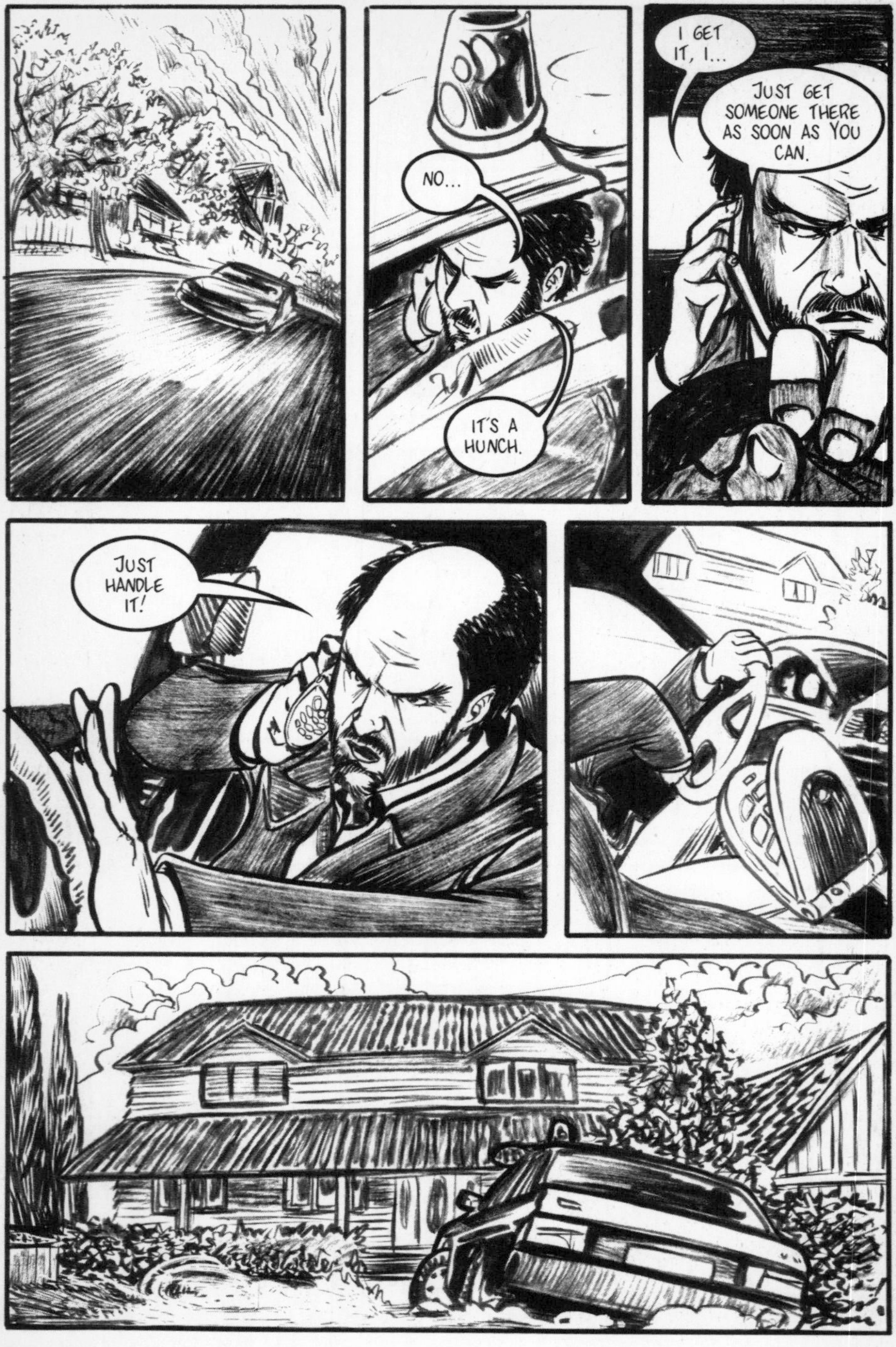
NO...
IT'S A HUNCH.
I GET IT, I...
JUST GET SOMEONE THERE AS SOON AS YOU CAN.
JUST HANDLE IT!

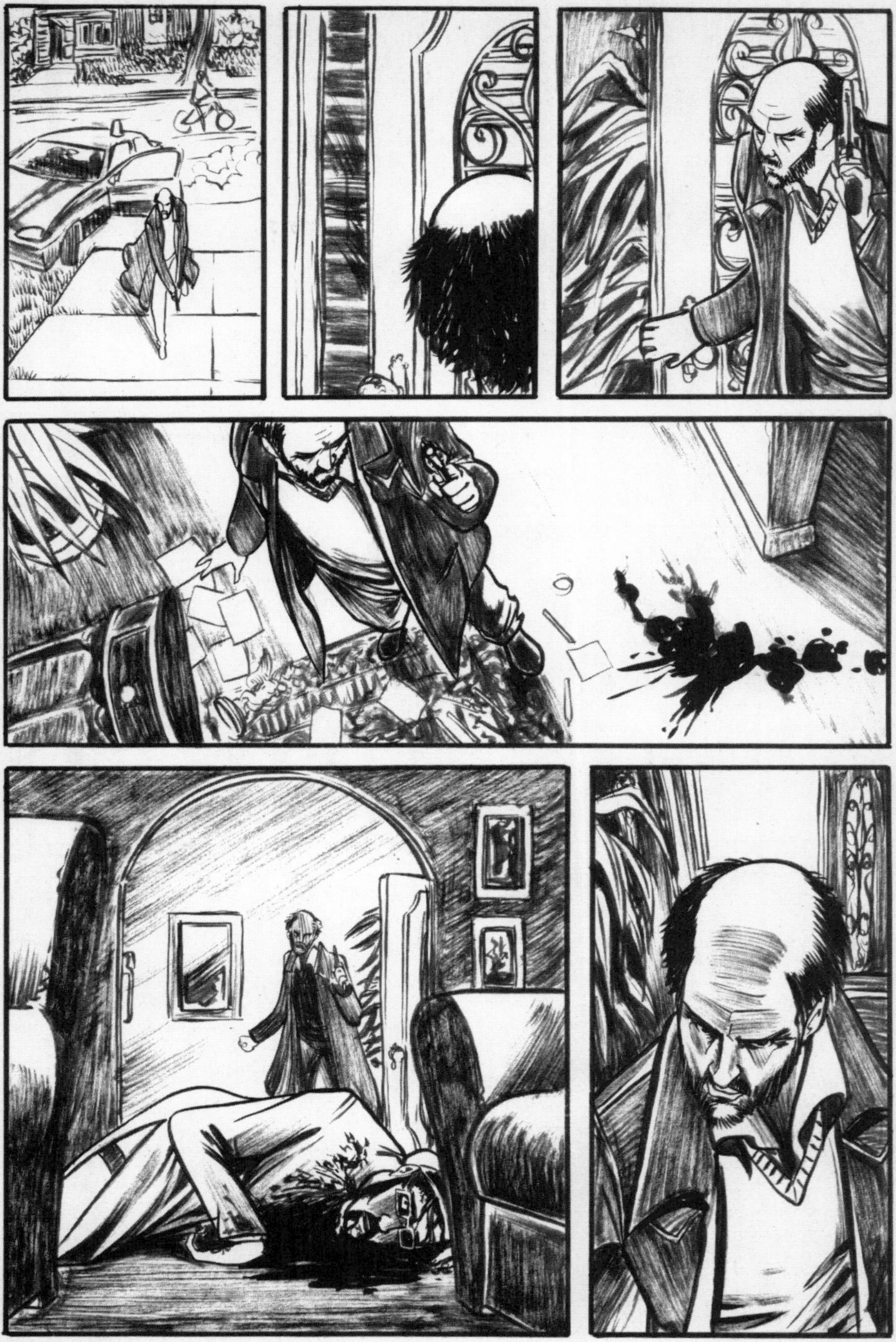

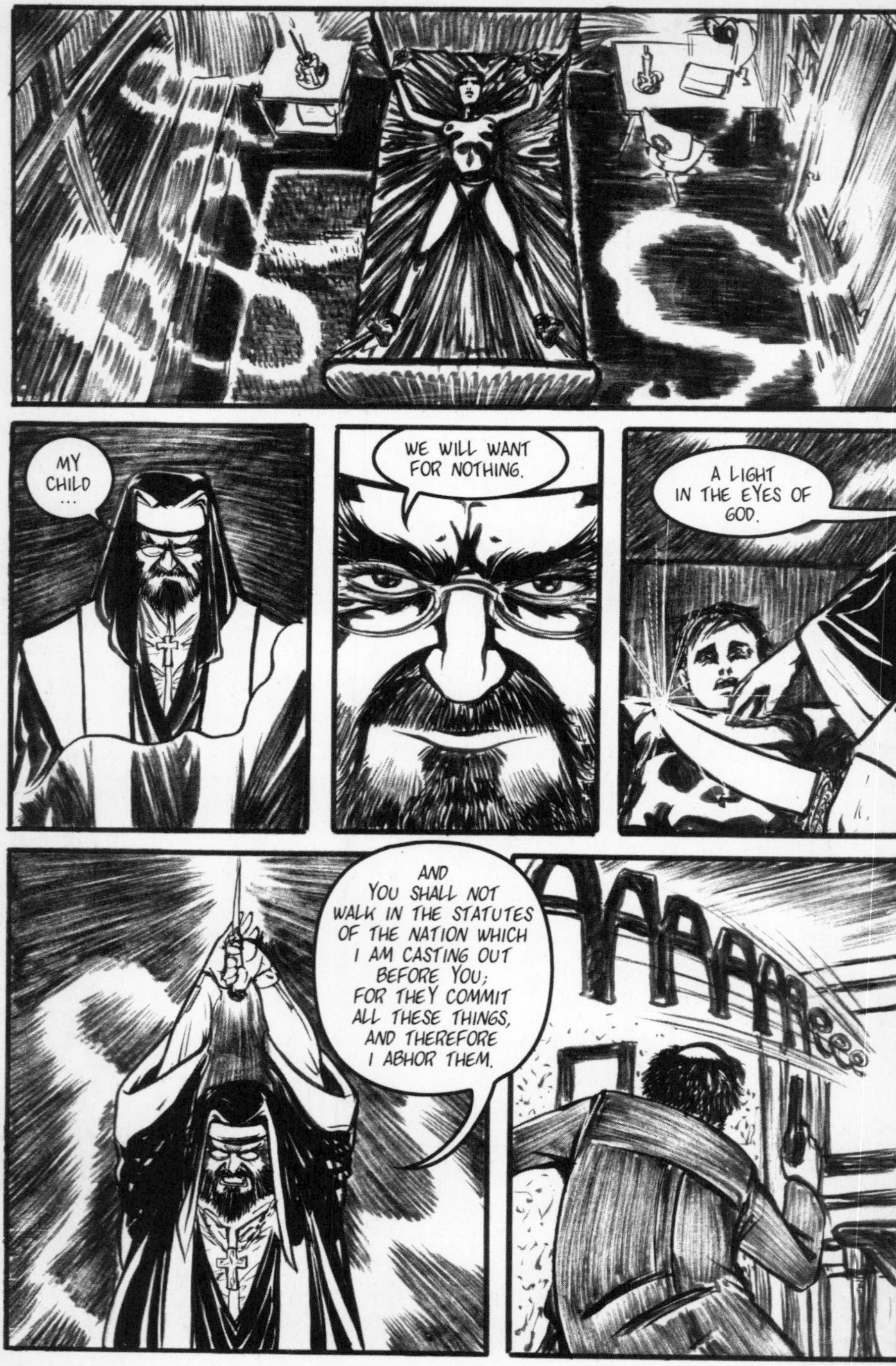
MY CHILD ...
WE WILL WANT FOR NOTHING.
A LIGHT IN THE EYES OF GOD.
AND YOU SHALL NOT WALK IN THE STATUTES OF THE NATION WHICH I AM CASTING OUT BEFORE YOU; FOR THEY COMMIT ALL THESE THINGS, AND THEREFORE I ABHOR THEM.
AAAAAAAAee

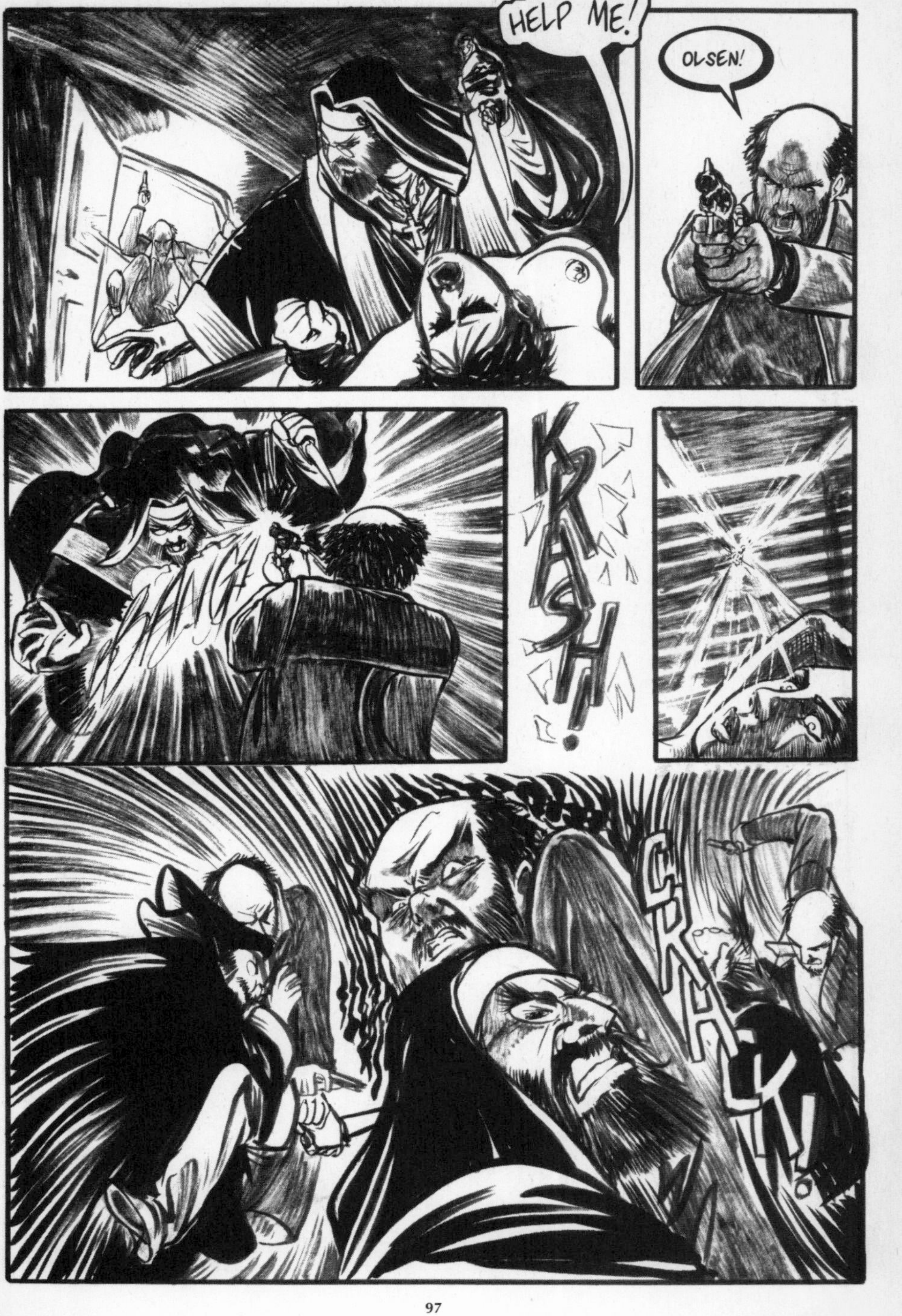
HELP ME!
OLSEN!
KRASH!
CRACK!

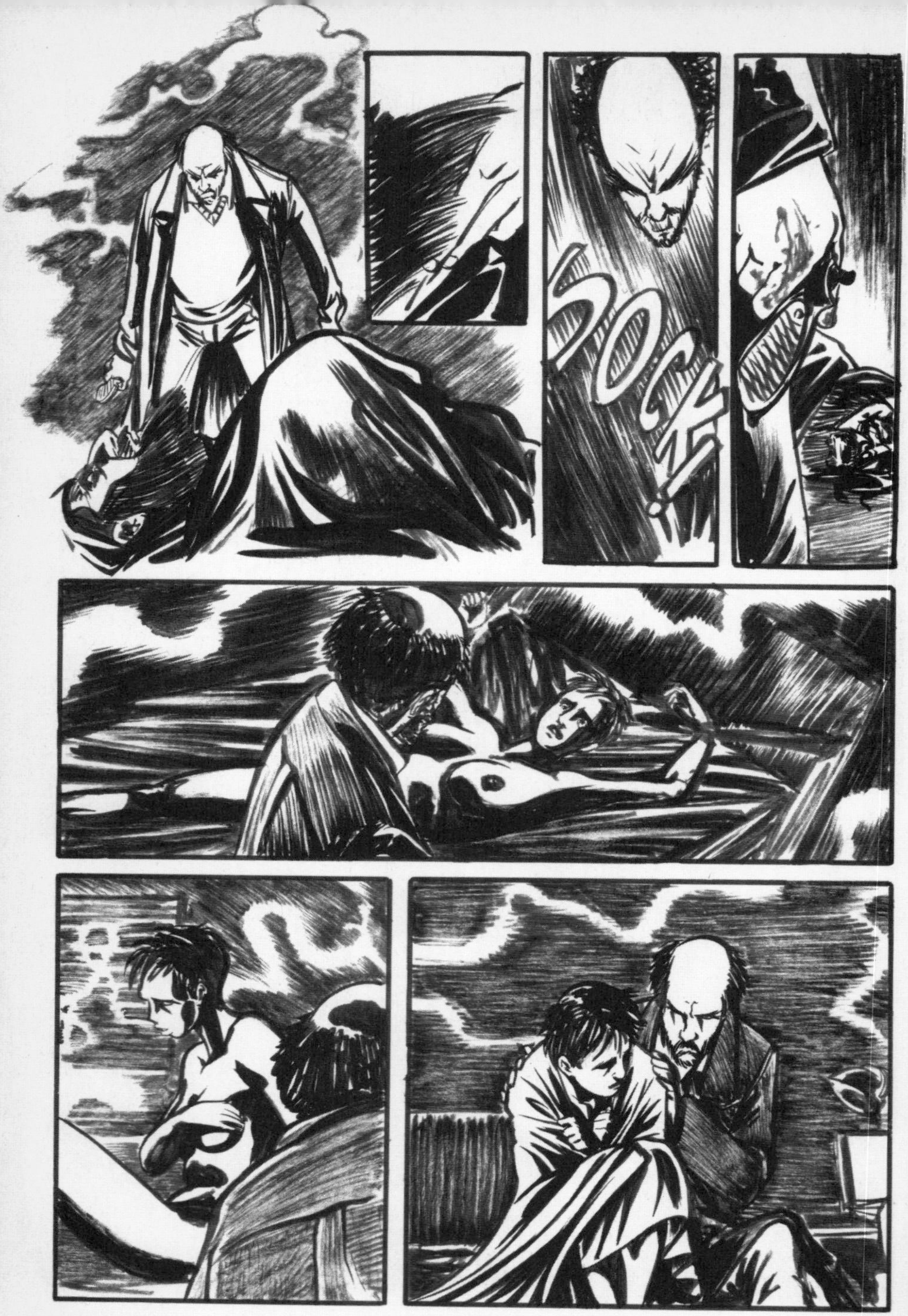
SOCK

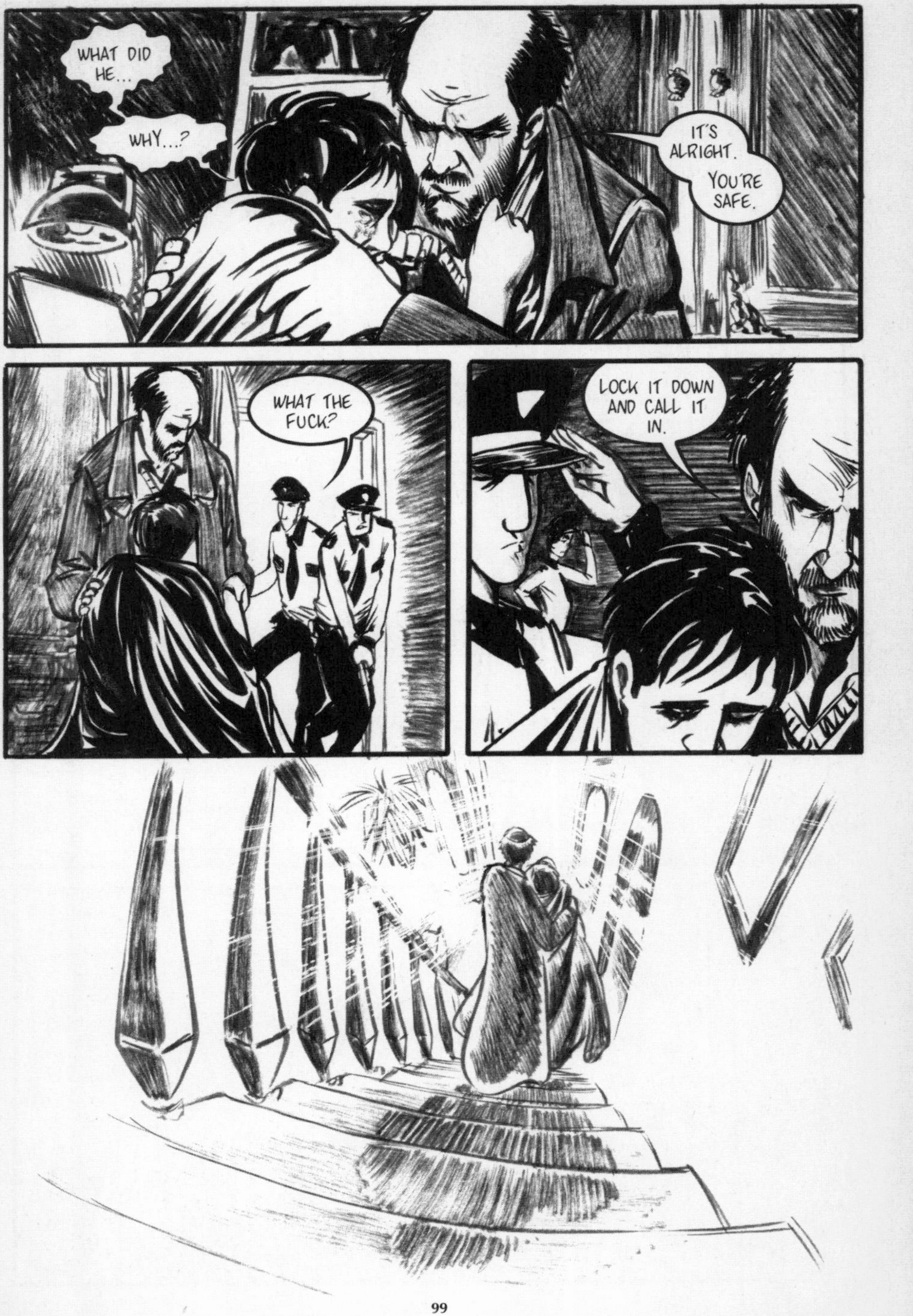
WHAT DID HE...
WHY...?
IT'S ALRIGHT.
YOU'RE SAFE.
WHAT THE FUCK?
LOCK IT DOWN AND CALL IT IN.

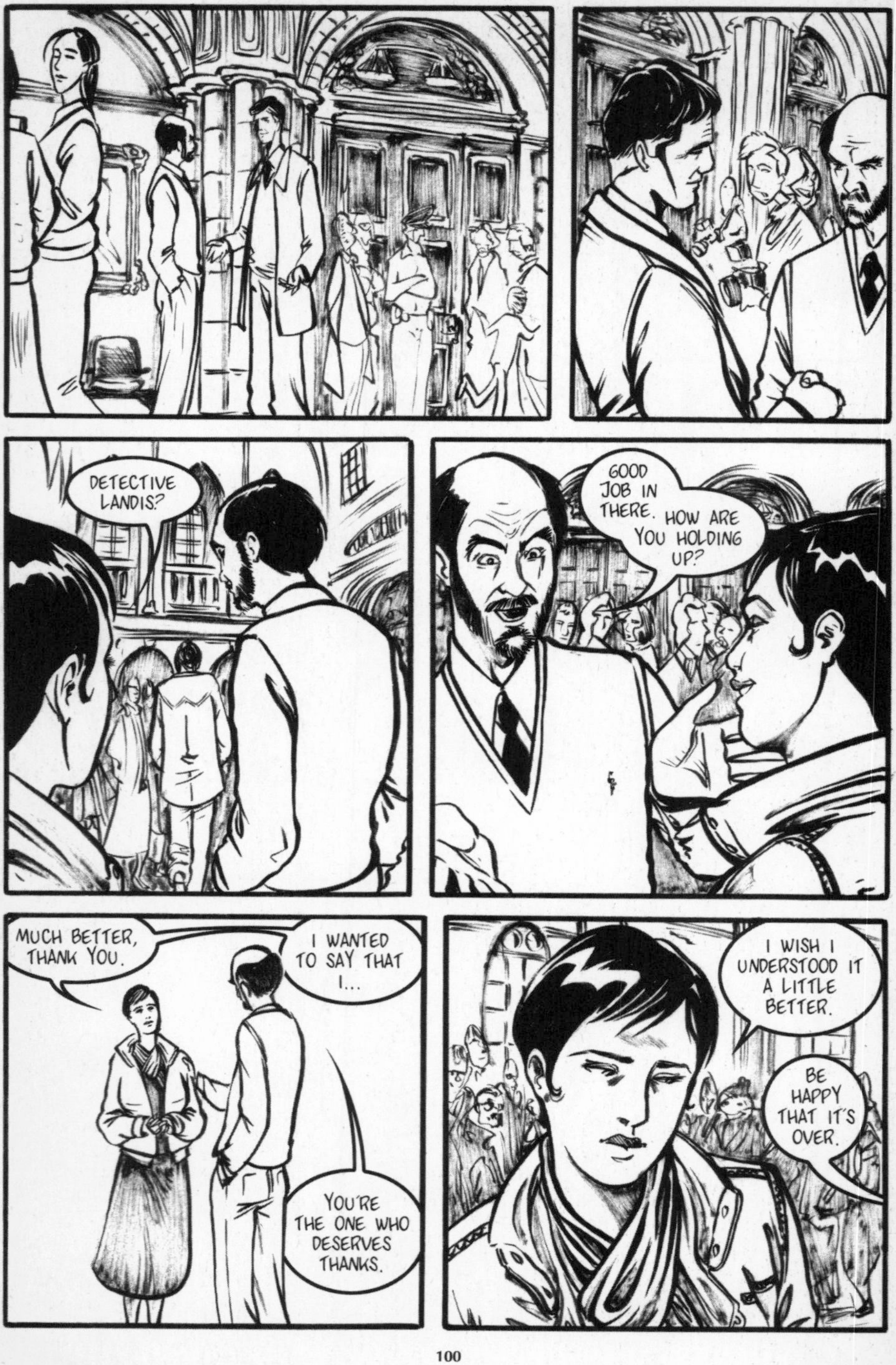
DETECTIVE LANDIS?
GOOD JOB IN THERE.
HOW ARE YOU HOLDING UP?
MUCH BETTER, THANK YOU.
I WANTED TO SAY THAT I...
YOU'RE THE ONE WHO DESERVES THANKS.
I WISH I UNDERSTOOD IT A LITTLE BETTER.
BE HAPPY THAT IT'S OVER.

Olsen was given an indefinite
sentence at Maryland's Patuxent
Institution, a maximum security
facility for the criminally insane.

———— ✦ ————

Throughout the process he didn't
speak a word, not even in his own
defense. He still hasn't.

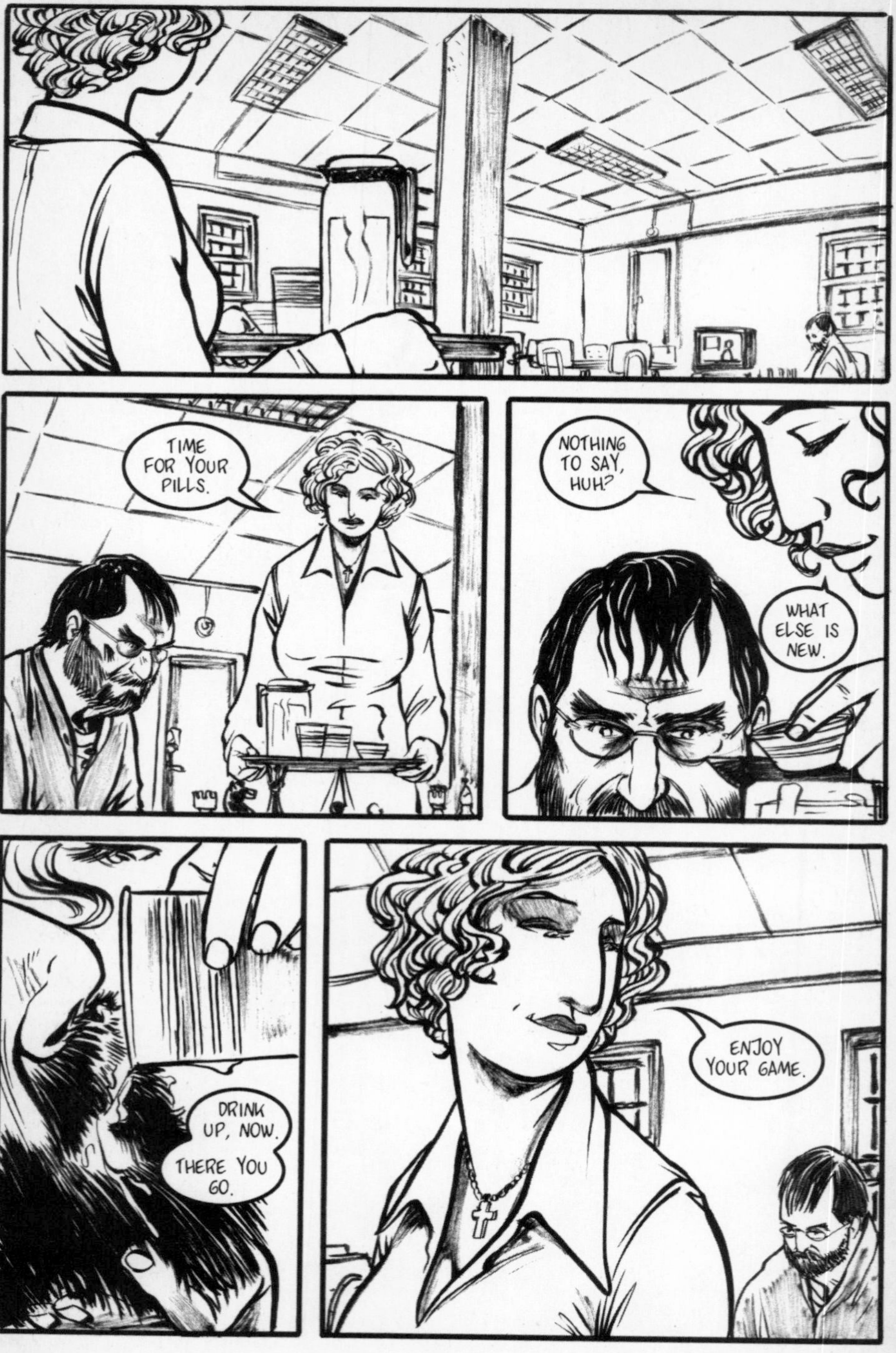
TIME FOR YOUR PILLS.
NOTHING TO SAY, HUH?
WHAT ELSE IS NEW.
DRINK UP, NOW.
THERE YOU GO.
ENJOY YOUR GAME.

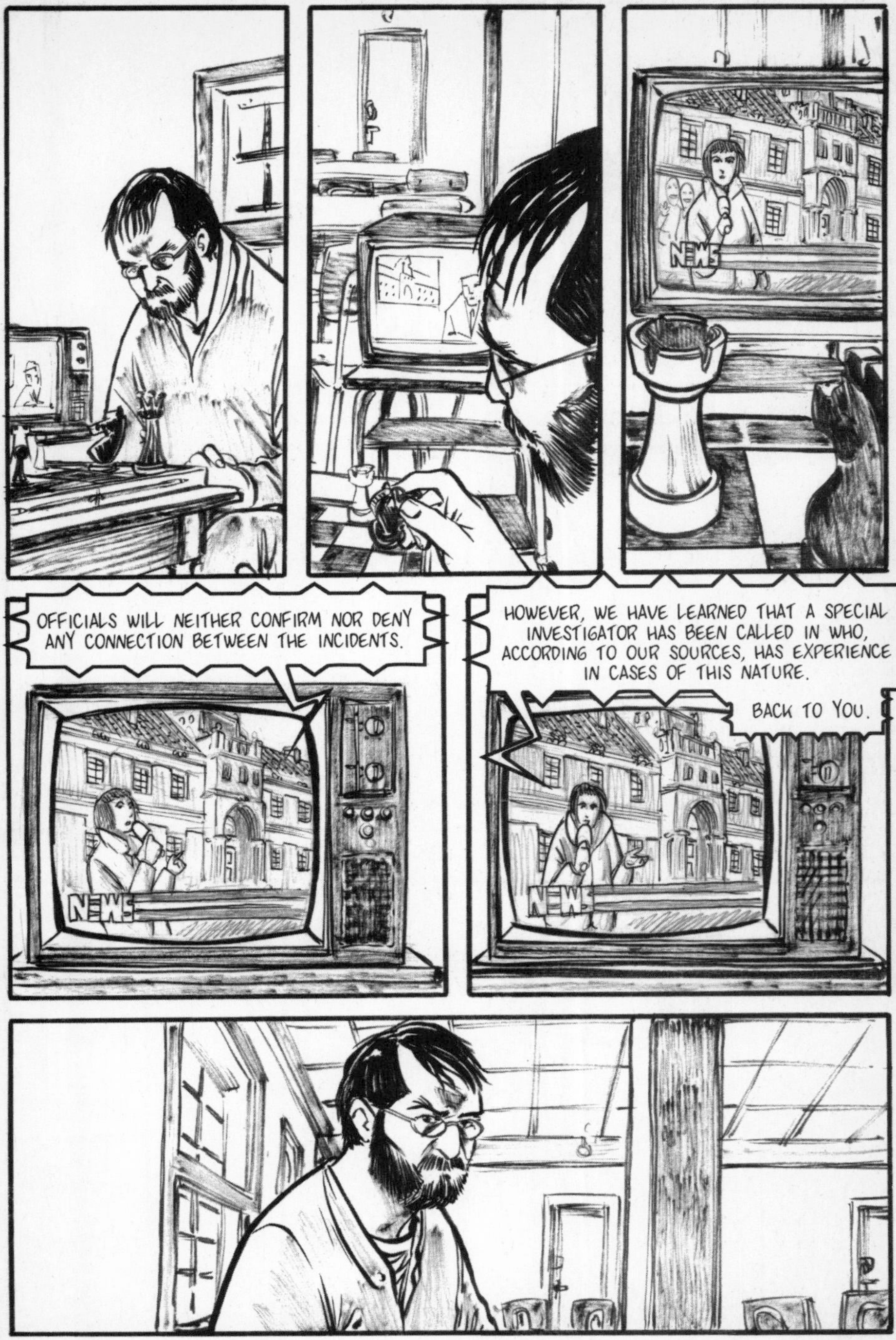
OFFICIALS WILL NEITHER CONFIRM NOR DENY ANY CONNECTION BETWEEN THE INCIDENTS.
HOWEVER, WE HAVE LEARNED THAT A SPECIAL INVESTIGATOR HAS BEEN CALLED IN WHO, ACCORDING TO OUR SOURCES, HAS EXPERIENCE IN CASES OF THIS NATURE.
BACK TO YOU.
NEWS
NEWS
NEWS

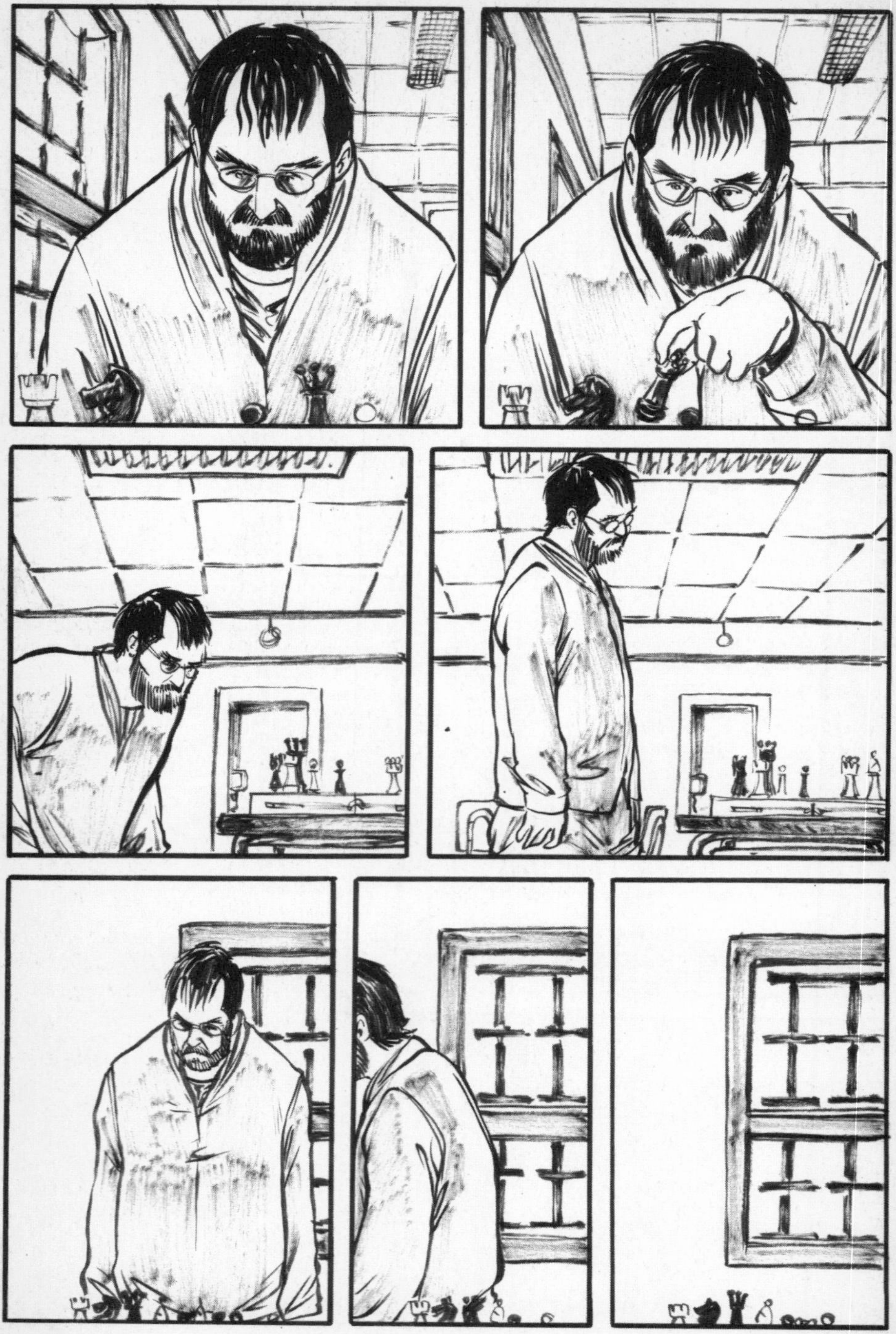

More great books from Neal Shaffer and Oni Press...

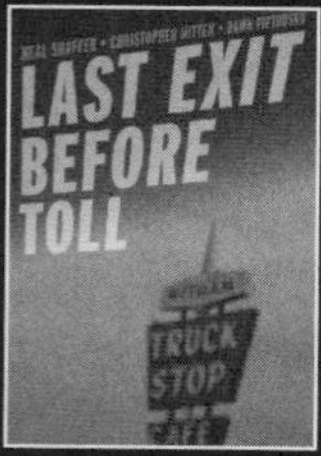
LAST EXIT BEFORE TOLL
TRUCK STOP

LAST EXIT BEFORE TOLL™
By Neal Shaffer, Christopher Mitten, & Dawn Pietrusko
96 pages, b&w interiors
$9.95 US
ISBN 1-929998-70-8

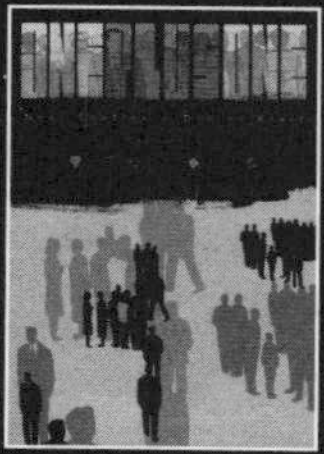

ONE PLUS ONE™
By Neal Shaffer & Daniel Krall
160 pages, b&w interiors
$14.95 US
ISBN 1-929998-65-1

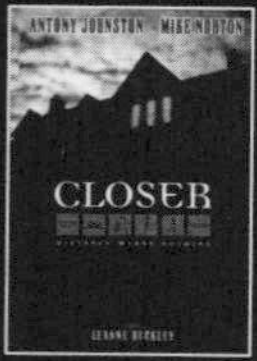
ANTONY JOHNSTON · MIKE NORTON
CLOSER

CLOSER™
By Antony Johnston, Mike Norton, & Leanne Buckley
144 pages, b&w interiors
$14.95 US
ISBN 1-929998-81-3

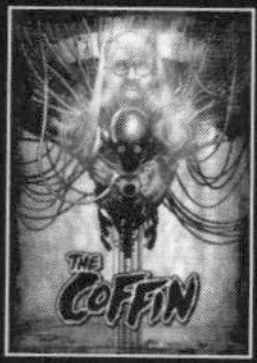
THE COFFIN

THE COFFIN™
By Phil Hester & Mike Huddleston
120 pages, b&w interiors
$11.95 US
ISBN 1-929998-16-3

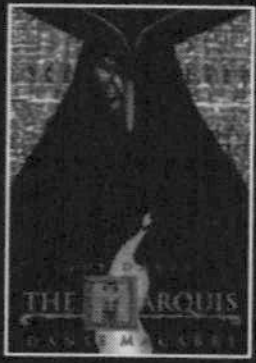
THE MARQUIS

THE MARQUIS: DANSE MACABRE™
By Guy Davis
192 pages, b&w interiors
$18.95 US
ISBN 1-929998-15-5

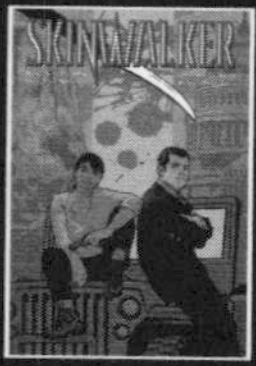
SKINWALKER

SKINWALKER™
By DeFilippis, Weir, Hurtt & Dela Cruz
128 pages, b&w interiors
$11.95 US
ISBN 1-929998-16-3

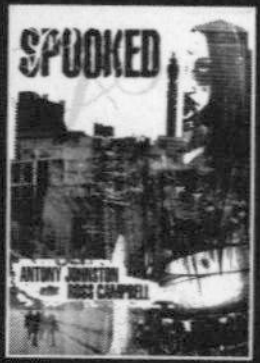
SPOOKED

SPOOKED™
By Antony Johnston & Ross Campbell
168 pages, b&w interiors
$14.95 US
ISBN 1-929998-79-1

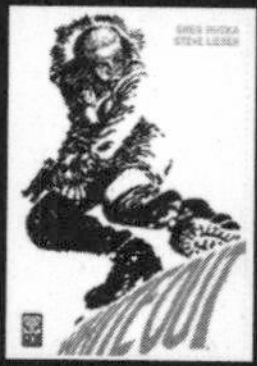
WHITEOUT

WHITEOUT™
By Greg Rucka & Steve Lieber
120 pages, b&w interiors
$11.95 US
ISBN 0-9667127-1-4

Available at finer comics shops everywhere and at www.onipress.com/store. To find a comics store near you, call 1-888-COMIC-BOOK or visit www.the-master-list.com.
For more Oni Press titles and information visit www.onipress.com